T0113970

BOOKS BY LAURENCE GONZALES

One Zero Charlie
The Still Point
Artificial Horizon
El Vago
The Last Deal
Jambeaux

SIMON & SCHUSTER

NEW YORK • LONDON • TORONTO

SYDNEY • TOKYO • SINGAPORE

ONE ZERO CHARLIE

ADVENTURES IN GRASS ROOTS AVIATION

Laurence Gonzales

SIMON & SCHUSTER
Simon & Schuster Building
Rockefeller Center
1230 Avenue of the Americas
New York, New York 10020

Designed by Edith Fowler
Manufactured in the United States of America

10 9 8 7 6 5 4 3 2 1

Library of Congress Cataloging-in-Publication Data

Gonzales, Laurence, date
One Zero Charlie : adventures in grass roots aviation / Laurence Gonzales.
p. cm.
1. Galt Airport. 2. Aeronautics—Illinois—Chicago Region. I. Title.
TL726.4.C45G66 1992 92-31821 CIP
629.13'09773'1—dc20
ISBN 1-4165-7641-X

this book is dedicated to
Elena and Amelia . . .

Alfa
Bravo
Charlie
Delta
Echo
Foxtrot
Golf
Hotel
India
Juliett
Kilo
Lima
Mike
November
Oscar
Papa
Quebec
Romeo
Sierra
Tango
Uniform
Victor
Whiskey
X-ray
Yankee
Zulu

CONTENTS

As I reach a high peak a village appears in the distance.
The old pines are full of poems;
I bend down for a drink of pure spring water.
There is a gentle breeze, and the round moon hangs overhead.
Standing by a deserted building,
I pretend to be a crane softly floating among the clouds.

—Ryōkan

AUTHOR'S NOTE

WHEN I TAKE OFF from Galt Airport on a very clear day, I can see Milwaukee and Chicago at the same time. I can watch big jets landing at O'Hare Airport to the south, and I can see the sharp outline of downtown Milwaukee against the royal blue curtain of Lake Michigan, icy and forbidding, even in the prettiest of weather. Here is this old airstrip, then, wedged between the great shield of the frozen lake on one side and the almost equally frightening threat of O'Hare's airspace to the south or Milwaukee's airspace to the north. To the west is Rockford's radar service area. Galt Airport, like so many small fields, is making its last stand against those giants.

Galt Airport (known in FAA code as 10C), with its two narrow runways, one of mowed grass, one of asphalt, lies right in the middle of a cornfield, right in the middle of America, and nothing special goes on here that doesn't go on at thousands of similar airstrips all over the nation. Every few miles, nearly everywhere in the U.S., there's another airport like Galt and another group of people not too different from the ones in this book. When I began to fly here, a number of forces were about to run together in our culture like tributaries that would form a swift and difficult river. Some of those streams developed out of images that had been indelibly engraved on our minds with the tattoo needle of the cinema: Tom Cruise laughing and flying an F-14 Tomcat in *Top Gun* with his face mask hanging off; Sam Shepard chewing gum and breaking the sound barrier in *The Right Stuff*. On every street corner we began to see ourselves dressed as aviators. We wore bomber jackets now, camouflage, berets. We displayed the accouterments of battle.

Through that process of assimilation, the real world of aviation in which I live my daily life and fly my little airplane became obscured. Even people who are interested in airplanes now have little notion of what the life of the common American aviator is like, who is neither a fighter pilot nor an astronaut.

The reason I wrote about One Zero Charlie, Galt Airport, is to bear witness before it's all gone. American aviation is made up of little airports out in the farm fields where regular people are flying and dying in ordinary airplanes on the ordinary days of their lives. Their recondite, almost invisible, passage is what struck me as important—and as far more American than the mock battles we stage with imagined enemies in faraway places.

Every year more airspace is eaten up by big airports, and more rules are made that prevent small airplanes from flying. More expensive equipment is required. More airplanes are put back in the hangar. It won't be long before there will only be the airlines, the military jets, and the wealthy. One Zero Charlie will be gone. This book is my attempt to leave an honest record of the sounds and smells and the feel of events in the waning days of the last of America's grass roots aviators.

ONE

STARDUSTER

ONE DAY a GM executive called Galt Airport asking if he could be taken to a big meeting in Anderson, Indiana, not far from Muncie. Jim Liss, one of the airplane mechanics and a commercial pilot, asked me if I would mind flying copilot for him that day. I said I'd do it, and that cold and windy Friday morning we met at the field at 5 A.M. in total darkness to prepare the airplane for our executive passenger's trip.

Liss had left the Cessna 210 in the shop the night before to keep it warm. After checking the weather, I found him out there, a short, muscular, balding man in his thirties with a neatly cropped ginger-colored beard, manipulating the control surfaces to make sure they were sound. We were ready to roll out at five forty-five when the executive arrived, looking as if he'd been raised from the dead. I held the door for him, and he climbed up, threw himself on the back seat, snapped his belt, and was sound asleep before we had rolled the airplane out of the shop.

Liss took off and then gave me the controls. As we rose away from the narrow runway, the darkened farmhouses and cornfields withdrew, and the immense and glowing panorama of Chicago and its suburbs opened in a shimmering fabric of orange phosphorescence. Mysterious green and red and white and amber flashes pulsed at us in the distance, as if we read the million-year-old signals of distress from some far galaxy.

As I turned south, we flew into a light snow squall, and the wingtip strobe lights caught and illuminated the million snow crystals traveling backward at 200 miles per hour and produced the effect of an instantaneous photograph of white streaks that seemed caught and frozen in the black ether.

Liss said, "It's amazing the things we do cruising along in this machine." With the throbbing of the engine keeping our GM executive asleep in back, the headphones provided a cloak of secrecy for our conversations.

Now a white cast began to soak through the dark layers of cloud above us as day attempted to break the wintry overcast. By the time we reached the open farmland south of Midway Airport, daylight had illuminated the landscape, but through the clouds it seemed as if we drove beneath a stratum of gray rock. The clouds began spitting out snow and little pellets of ice. With a tail wind of nearly forty knots, it wasn't long before we were in central Indiana. But as we approached the field, the weather turned.

With little warning, we were aswirl in the dirty laundry of clouds, and we blew right past the airport without even seeing the town of Anderson. The air traffic controller cleared us to land, but suddenly we were in solid white. I would rather have been on radar for the avoidance of other aircraft and the steel towers that generally stick up from those flatlands, but Jim took the controls and tried again. The second time we came dripping out of a ragged afterbirth of clouds to find the orange runway lights like a luminous centipede in the hazy distance.

As the executive fled to the bad news of the car business in a white sedan, both Liss and I looked at the clock and then at each other. It was going to be a long day. We had been up since four o'clock, and now the apprehension and tension of anticipation, followed by the excitement of the ride, were beginning to wear off, as if we'd taken some sort of amphetamine medicine and were starting to come down. All those Indiana airfields look the same in winter: lines of dark trees stripped bare by the wind, and the pale yellow-green of faded grass and the ripped-up fabric of clouds in folds and pleats of gray and white with occasional geese and hawks for accent. Now and then the air comes brimming with light and abruptly fills with great creamy flakes, which seem carved in such a way, like chips of soap, that you think for a moment they'll float. But then they come crashing to the black asphalt and shatter to dust like white bone china.

The airport factotum drove us to a place called the Waffle House. I picked up the Indianapolis *Star*. The front page featured a five-column color photograph of the "smoldering wreckage of a C-130B transport plane" which crashed into a motel and restaurant, killing sixteen people. I pushed it in front of Jim, who had ordered lunch, even though it was only nine o'clock.

"I don't want to look at that shit," he said.

"Keep it," I said. "Maybe our passenger would like to read on the way home."

By ten o'clock we were wandering in the local mall, which seemed to stretch from approximately Milwaukee to Texas. I asked Liss what he had done before he became involved in airplanes. He said that his father worked for Redi-Mix, a cement company in McHenry, Illinois, and by the time Liss was eighteen, he and his brother were working there, too. "Man, you wouldn't believe the shit they made us do. The owners were crazy."

Liss was assigned to fix the cement trucks when the chains broke. The chain turned the drum that carried the Redi-Mix cement. If the chain broke, the drum stopped, the cement hardened, and the truck was useless. So he had to drag a pneumatic hammer inside the truck and fracture the solidified cement into blocks that could be tossed out. The job was deafening, but that's not all. Cement trucks have fins inside the drum to keep the Redi-Mix mixed. The slurry of cement acts as an abrasive on the heavy steel fins as the drum turns, and after a few months of lapping, the fins are sharp enough to shave with. So Liss was in there with his jackhammer chipping cement one day, and he had gotten about a thousand pounds of it broken into sixty- or eighty-pound blocks when one of the old employees jumped into the cab of the truck, started it up, and began to drive away. Liss had already fixed the chain, and so the drum began to turn. "There I was," Liss said, "inside the drum, screaming and dancing around, trying to avoid being chopped to pieces by these razor sharp fins or crushed to death by the loose cement. I finally grabbed the jackhammer and drove the bit right through the drum and into the frame of the truck, and the drum stopped and broke the chain again." Liss came boiling out of there set to kill the old man.

After that he quit and started his own auto body business. He worked 6 A.M. until 3 P.M. on the body business, went home and took a shower, and then went to work the second shift at the McHenry Brake Parts factory. He worked until midnight, and sometimes he came back and did body work until dawn. After three years of paint fumes, his nose wouldn't stop bleeding, and he went to see a doctor, who told him to quit. Liss was destined to move on anyway. He was restless and smart. He had a plan. He wanted to do something interesting, to make his own way.

While he was working at the brake factory he met Neva, one of the girls who put together the kits of brake parts, which had to be neatly shrink-wrapped to a card for display.

"It was a nowhere job," Liss said. "I told her to get out." They started dating. Neva told Liss about her life. She had gotten pregnant at seventeen and now had a daughter, Faith. Neva showed Liss the newspaper clippings she kept. The father had abandoned her when she became pregnant. A year later, he was drunk one night and fell asleep on the railroad tracks in Chicago. A train decapitated him. It was all over the news.

"It was the best thing that ever happened to her," Liss said. "He was a loser." Now Faith is just like a daughter to Liss, and people mistake Neva and Faith for sisters.

We wandered among the weight benches in the Sears sporting goods department and then looked at the automobile tools. We bought candy bars at the drugstore and then selected a pizza place and sat in a window drinking Pepsi-Cola and watching the snow move in nervously changing patterns across the half-empty parking lot. Watching the snow, Liss said, "We'll have to file on the way back."

Here's how death comes in. Liss was sitting in the pizza place looking out the window. We were tired and the conversation had flagged. He grew thoughtful, and after a time he said, "I almost quit flying once."

"When was that?" I asked, surprised. He loved flying.

"When I saw Lloyd get killed," he said.

Lloyd Hughes was an American Airlines captain with a military career behind him and 30,000 hours of flight experience. He kept a two-place open-cockpit biplane called a Starduster II in a hangar just behind mine at Galt. One of Lloyd's sons, Scotty, had just gotten his flight instructor's certificate and had brought a friend, Jim Koleno, along to join in the fun. They were taking turns flying with Lloyd. Lloyd's wife, Nancy, was at home doing laundry. A few days earlier I had asked Lloyd to give me a ride, and he had promised that we'd go up together soon. He had shown me what the Starduster could do. I had stood on the ramp and watched his signature takeoff many times, and I wanted to experience it for myself, to see what it felt like. Lloyd would lift off the runway and then allow the plane to race along level, gaining speed. At the last minute, before plunging through the trees, he would pull into a vertical climb, and all that energy he'd gained would carry him up, up, up, as the plane slowed down. Just before reaching the stall, he'd push the nose over and slowly fly away, full power, accelerating once again. Then he would go out over his house in McHenry, where Nancy could step outside and watch, and he'd trace his aerobatics figures against the sky with his lime green plane. He did it for fun, to blow off steam after a week of riding straight and level in those big American Airlines jets.

One afternoon at Galt Airport, Lloyd had stopped by the shop to say hello to Liss. "Got a student?" he asked.

"Yeah," Liss said. "We're going up in a minute."

"Don't hit me up there," Lloyd said and crossed the parking lot, stopping by his gold Corvette for a moment, and then walking back out to the pumps where his plane was being fueled. Lloyd's son Scotty stepped up on the wing and climbed into the open cockpit. Jimmy Koleno had just taken his ride and was now standing on the ramp saluting Lloyd and Scotty.

In the office, Otto Schuster, a police officer from Arlington Heights who parked his Cessna 150 Aerobat in the hangar spot next to my airplane, was standing at the flight desk at Galt Airport idly watching the action on the ramp. Next to him was David Skinner, a flight instructor who would soon join Simmons Airlines, and his instrument student, Phil Proznitz, an assistant state's attorney for McHenry County. Art Galt, the owner of the airport, was in his house at the west end of the runway with his wife, Vera. Carla Nusbaum, the office manager, was upstairs in the office, doing her paperwork.

By the time Lloyd was ready to go, Liss had come out of

the shop, and his student, Sue, had prepared the Cessna 150 for flight. Watching Lloyd and Scotty in the lime-green biplane, Liss strapped into the right seat of the trainer. In the office, all heads turned toward the ramp. "I wanted to see him do it," Otto said later. "He always took off that way, straight up, that's why I was watching. I wanted to see what he'd do." Dave Skinner, Phil Proznitz—everyone turned to watch. It was undoubtedly part of the reason Lloyd did it: We want people to watch us.

But there were problems. In order to perform that maneuver fewer than 1,500 feet from ground, a pilot must have a letter of competency and a low-level waiver saying that he is qualified to fly aerobatics close to the ground. The FAA designates certain aerobatics instructors to sign those letters. Lloyd had not qualified. Even if he had been qualified, it would have been illegal to do it at Galt Airport without yet another waiver. If Lloyd had lived through it and if anyone on the field had reported it to the FAA, Lloyd could have lost his license and his job of twenty-five years at American Airlines. But never mind the job. What overpowering impulse could have caused him to risk even his son, like Abraham leading Isaac into the mountains?

Liss's student, Sue, began to taxi, and Liss, in the right seat, glanced up to see Lloyd begin his usual spectacular daredevil display of flying mastery.

Later Art Galt told me, "His engine had quit before while he was doing that, but he had half-full fuel tanks and no passenger."

A number of people had watched Lloyd five weeks earlier as he pulled into a vertical ascent at the apex of which his propeller simply stopped turning. Because Lloyd was a skillful pilot, he was able to kick the airplane into a hammerhead turn and fly straight back down the vertical line he'd drawn, pulling out just in time to land on the runway in the opposite direction. "I'd done that with him," Liss said. "He'd done that same thing with me in the plane, flew straight up and did a hammerhead and landed back the other way, just to show he could do it."

Here's something that every student pilot is taught: If the engine fails on takeoff, land straight ahead. Never try to turn back to the runway. It will kill you. A lot of Lloyd's friends had read him the riot act about turning back to the runway.

Liss watched Lloyd pull to the vertical. It's strange what we can get used to seeing. We had all seen Lloyd do that so many times that it simply hadn't occurred to us that we were watching him rehearse his own death. We like to think that it hadn't occurred to Lloyd either, or that such knowledge would have moved him to ground his airplane and fix the problem that had caused his engine to quit. Liss looked down into his lap for something, because it simply wasn't interesting enough to keep on watching Lloyd that day. He'd seen him do it a hundred times.

Nancy, Lloyd's wife and Scotty's mother, literally had her head in the dryer when the phone rang. It was Jimmy Koleno, and he sounded strange, but Nancy just said, "Oh, are you back already?" She had been fixing a big dinner, and everyone was supposed to come back there after flying. Todd, her second-oldest son, was already at home.

"There's been an accident, Mrs. Hughes," Jimmy said.

"Oh, but they're all right," she said.

There was a silence on the line. Nancy thought she might have heard Jimmy crying. She had dropped her laundry and stood up straight. Something was wrong with Jimmy's voice. "No, Mrs. Hughes," Jimmy said. "They're dead." Nancy handed the phone to Todd, and a part of her mind went away. She didn't even hear what Todd said.

They had an argument about who would drive to the airport. "Well, you certainly can't drive," Todd told her.

"Well, *you* can't drive," Nancy said.

Todd drove. "That was the longest trip I've ever taken,"

Nancy told me one winter day when I visited her in the Hughes family home in McHenry. "First we were going really fast, and then as we got closer, we started going really slowly. I was scanning the sky looking for smoke, and I looked over and saw that Todd was doing the same. I don't know what we said on the ride. I don't know if we talked at all. And when we got there we drove right down the runway without even thinking. I mean, there might have been an airplane landing or something, we didn't know. But before we got to the end, Marlene, the coroner, stopped us. She wouldn't allow me to go."

"You don't want to remember them that way," Marlene told Nancy.

Nancy was going into shock. She was saying to someone, "Lloyd said he'd stop at the bank on the way to the airport. God, I hope he deposited that check."

Nancy and I sat in the house where she and Lloyd had raised their three boys, Steven, Todd, and the youngest, Scotty, who would have been twenty-four the day before I saw Nancy. I had visited her before, but she had been unable to talk about the crash, and I thought it cruel to insist, so I waited until she was ready. It took nearly three years.

The house was an enormous ranch-style palace of contemporary 1970s Americana with hints of A-frame design and lots of mementos, from guns hanging over the fireplace to ceramic bunnies. It had a kind of *House Beautiful* quality to it, like a photograph out of a sample book in a wallpaper store, where all the draperies have been pleated just so and the green leather furniture shines and smells new. I've known a lot of airline pilots, and this was very much the captain's wife's house. Nothing was out of place. Not a speck of dirt could be found.

Every fighter pilot I know has an Ego Bar in the basement, what my aerobatics instructor, John Morrissey, called "The I Love Me Room," with bottles of liquor to propel the war stories and many photos and plaques behind the bar to strike sparks from the flinty old memory. Lloyd's was extensive, and above the bar on one side were the shirttails of his sons from their first solo flights. It was an old airfield tradition to clip the shirttail off the back of a student after his first solo and pin it on the wall, scrawled with the name and date. Scotty's T-shirt was up there with 12-18-84 on it. Lloyd had one, too, from his first Starduster solo, 6-16-87. On a high shelf was his Navy helmet with oxygen mask still attached.

Lloyd's basement bar opened onto an immense playroom with a pool table, Ping-Pong table, pinball machine, and carpeted conversation pit before a natural stone fireplace. It was now all Nancy's, and she seemed dwarfed in it. She was diminutive anyway, about five feet two inches, well dressed in stylish clothes with short curly brown hair, sparkling, lively blue eyes, and a quick and easy smile. "I must have had seventy-five people in here the night Lloyd died," she said. She had been a Navy wife, and she knew how to put on a good front. She served the food that people brought and kept the coffee maker going, and everyone commented later how well she took it all. "I did my head-beating in the shower stall," she told me.

Lloyd seems to have been born to aviation. His mother had letters from when he was in elementary school saying that he wanted to be a pilot. Nancy and Lloyd were high school sweethearts. They were sixteen when they were thrown into a school play together and had to kiss. They did a fashion spread in the local newspaper showing the teen style of 1954, the year they graduated. The photographs caught Nancy in saddle shoes and pedal pushers and Lloyd in jeans and a flat-top. They were married when Nancy was twenty-two, Lloyd was twenty-one.

Nancy did not go to college, but Lloyd graduated from Ohio State University in 1959 and went straight to Whiting Field, Pensacola, Florida, for preflight training in the Navy. They were assigned to Beeville, Texas, for advanced flight training.

"I had never been away from home," Nancy said. "It was an adventure for me." Despite the fact that there was nothing and no one in Beeville, Texas, except the military base, "We had a wonderful time." Nancy described those early years as "some of the happiest times." They had no money. They couldn't afford twenty cents for the base movie some weekends. "But we made it."

Lloyd was assigned to three years in Puerto Rico. Their first son, Steven, was born there. But by 1963, Lloyd realized that he didn't want the military to be his life. He began to send resumes around to the airlines. Lloyd qualified for them all and had a tough time deciding on American. "We went from making fifteen hundred a month, with cheap groceries from the commissary and all our housing and medical bills paid, to making five hundred a month with nothing paid for." But, Nancy said, "he was so happy." She had never seen him so happy. Lloyd was so happy that for the next twenty years he did nothing but devote himself to that airline. He loved the flying, loved the people, became active in the pilots' union, and never looked back.

It was when Steven grew old enough to express an interest in learning to fly that things began to change. The boys began taking lessons, and somehow, just sitting in those small planes began to bring back to Lloyd the cellular memory in his nerves of flying upside down, pulling G's. It was a tremendous and tragic thing, like a great love he had known and lost and then saw on the street one day, walking back into his life out of the blue. And then somehow it was stuck in his heart, and when he walked away from the little airfield, he was changed.

It started as an offhanded thing, a casual mention of the idea: Maybe I ought to get an airplane. Nancy said there was no way they could spend $20,000 on an airplane while the boys were still in school. But Lloyd kept coming around with it, kind of shy, like a kid who wanted to go to a ball game and couldn't get the idea out of his head.

"He worked out a deal," Nancy said. "Not with me. I don't know how he found that plane. After twenty years of not doing aerobatics, you'd think he'd be over it, but he loved it. He absolutely loved it." And in her face I could see the resigned melancholy of the years piled upon one another: She thought she might have escaped this thing—this Demon Impulse—which had pursued her husband; she thought that they had outdistanced it, only to discover at the last moment that he was more bewitched than ever before, now after decades of peace, as if the true love of her husband's past had shown up at the door carrying luggage.

Lloyd and a friend had gone to look at the Starduster, which was lime green with navy blue and white trim. "It was his baby," Nancy said. Tears rose and cast a glittering net of reflections all across the surface of her eyes. "I lost him after that. I never saw him again. He loved it. It was his nine-to-five job. I'd say, 'What do you do all day? What *can* you do?' "

I said to her, "In other words, once Lloyd got the Starduster he was . . ."

But she didn't let me finish. She filled in the word: "obsessed." And she went on. "He was obsessed, that's the only word for it. I knew that plane would kill him. I knew it from the moment he bought it." She was weeping inside now, but only the play of light around her big blue eyes betrayed it, because like the good Navy wife she was, she knew the drill and she kept up her smile. "He never would have done anything dangerous," as if to reassure herself. "It was something mechanical, I'm sure of it. He had just had the annual. Russell had just done the annual inspection. Lloyd wouldn't have flown it if it hadn't been right." It was part of the family mythology, the way the story would be handed down, the way my mother used to tell us when my brothers and I were children and asked about Dad and his B-17 over Germany: "Your father didn't bomb people. He bombed factories."

Otto, standing at the flight desk with Dave Skinner, watched the whole thing. "Lloyd did a good hammerhead and came straight down. I remember I said to Dave, 'Isn't he a little low to be doing that?' I thought he was going to make it. It looked like he was going to make it. Then he disappeared behind the trees and there was smoke." What Otto saw was particularly eerie, because there was no noise or explosion. "You can't believe you're seeing it," he said.

When Liss looked up from his lap, Lloyd was nowhere in sight, but a big fantail of oily smoke was crawling across the treetops at the departure end of Runway 9. It was about 5 P.M.

Dave Skinner yelled up the stairs to Carla, the office manager, "Lloyd's going down!" and then he and Phil Proznitz grabbed a couple of the big fire extinguishers and put them in Dave's car and raced down the runway. Tony Burrafatl, a former Galt instructor who happened to be at the field, was actually the first one to the scene. "He raced down there on his crotch rocket," Carla told me. Then she smiled her midwestern farm-girl smile and looked embarrassed. "Isn't that what they call those Japanese motorcycles?"

In the landing pattern, Lloyd's friend Howard Stock was just coming back from aerobatics practice in his red Pitts biplane. He, too, had looked, then looked away. "I saw Lloyd take off, but I didn't see him crash," Howard said. "He didn't go *straight* up, like some people said. But he was too steep. Way too steep. I went downwind, and when I turned base, I saw that he'd gone down." Howard flew straight over the field to see what had happened. "I could see him down there." Then he came around again and landed, unstrapping himself from the cockpit as he taxied toward the end, and leaping out practically while his airplane was still rolling. But when he got out and asked Tony if there was anything they could do, Tony just shook his head. "I didn't even look," Howard said. "I didn't look."

The fire lifted up like a huge black-tailed carrion-eater and wrapped its orange wings jealously around the Starduster. Dave and Phil drove down with fire extinguishers and could see Lloyd and Scotty inside the flames. They were so close, and yet there was no way to reach them. They immediately began spraying foam into the flames, but it was no use. The newspapers reported that Dave was treated for smoke inhalation while trying to rescue Lloyd and Scotty, but actually Phil got so excited that he sprayed Dave in the face with a fire extinguisher.

Liss grabbed the controls of the Cessna 150 from Sue and literally flew down the runway, keeping the airplane a few inches off the ground not far behind Dave Skinner's car. "It was like there was a wall of heat. I couldn't even get near the plane," Liss said.

"Did you still think you might be able to save Lloyd?" I asked Liss as we sat in the pizza place in the mall in Anderson, Indiana, watching snow gather in pleated patterns on the asphalt parking lot outside.

Liss shook his head slowly. "He didn't even look human."

Lloyd had his elbows up, hands planted on the canopy rail, as if at any moment he would push himself out and step onto the wing of the biplane and grin at everybody as he always had, pleased with his skill, pleased with his lime-green machine—Lloyd would step out of the hot-air balloon of smoke that was lifting off of the field and into the metal-flake blue sky and he would walk calmly away, and somebody would chuck him on the arm and say, "Hey, cheated the devil again, eh, Lloyd?"

Only Lloyd was black. He was as black as the Bible. His head was thrown back in an attitude of ecstasy or epiphany, and his mouth was open. The skin was burned off his forehead so that Liss could see his skull. His eyelids were gone and his eyeballs stared up through the flames at the beautiful sky. And as the fire whirled around him, the wings of prey enfolding, he gently rocked back and forth, as if he were in some sort of slow, ecstatic dream.

“What about his son?” I asked.

“Worse. I almost quit flying after that. It really shook me,” Liss said, sipping his Pepsi and pursing his lips and staring fixedly out the window at the snow.

Within a few minutes of the crash, everyone except Carla had gathered at the end of the runway, and the fire trucks were on their way. Carla stood at the entrance to the parking lot and tried to keep people out. Some of the instructors brought fire extinguishers and sprayed them into the flames, but the bird of fire simply wrapped its wings more firmly around Lloyd and Scotty, and the black beak of smoke turned disdainfully away toward the west.

Art Galt drove down from his house on the edge of the property as soon as he realized that there had been a crash, but there was nothing he could do except watch, fascinated, as the two bodies moved in the flames and wonder what it was that made them keep on moving when they were obviously dead.

When the fire fighters arrived and had their big hoses going, the fire went out quickly. It might have been better to let the fire complete the job of cremation, but that would have suggested something unthinkable about our sovereign right to control the forces of physics, nature, and the world.

The FAA investigators came out and asked questions and checked that the control cables were working. They stepped around in the mud and dug right into the ashes where the airplane lay. They moved the controls. The throttle was retarded, but so many people had had so many hands in the cockpit since the crash that the investigators were unable to draw any inference from that. Someone could have bumped it while trying to get Lloyd or Scotty out. The investigators could find nothing wrong with the airplane and classified it as a stall-spin accident, just another pilot who tried to turn back to the runway when he should have gone straight. It was hard to believe anything that spectacular could be that prosaic.

When the airplane hit the ground, it buried the engine, so the wet peat bog protected the carburetor from the huge fire; and Galt's chief mechanic Bob Russell, along with FAA investigators, was able to check the continuity: There was fuel in all parts of the carburetor, indicating that it had not stopped working. Even so, the pattern of the propeller hitting the ground indicated that the engine was producing little or no power. They could tell by the number of prop strikes and their distance apart in the mud. In other words, Lloyd's death, or at least the mechanical cause of it, if any, remains a complete mystery. Many people, though not all, think that the engine stopped.

Howard Stock said, "That PS-five pressure carburetor killed him."

"He could have pulled it back to idle," Russell said later, "once he saw that he was heading for mother earth."

The FAA found that it was a survivable accident. That means that the crunch of hitting the ground was not, by itself, enough to kill Lloyd and Scotty. The killing thing was that cheap, flimsy fuel tank, which is a standard feature on acrobatics airplanes. It ruptured and splashed gasoline all over the inside of the cockpit. Better tanks are available, ones that can't be punctured, ones through which machine-gun tracer bullets can be shot without causing an explosion, but we don't insist on them, and so people continue to die in accidents that the FAA classifies as survivable.

"They were flying when they hit the ground," Russell said. "This man, if he had had twenty feet more room, would have lived."

Lloyd used to say that he'd never get killed in an airplane crash. "He said he'd probably be killed on Route Twelve by somebody coming out of the parking lot of the adult bookstore," Nancy said. Nancy seemed truly to understand what Lloyd had gone through, that he had suffered for his obsession, just as surely as if an ancient enemy pursued him with purpose and tenacity and diligence and finally found him in a vulnerable moment and cut him down. Her eyes filled with tears again. "He just loved that airplane more than anything in the world, and I was jealous." Her voice grew hard, but I never saw her bitter. "Yes, there's anger there."

Even though Nancy had lived for years with the hope that one day he would belong to her and not to aviation, in the end she said, "You just can't help but feel it when someone is that happy."

The night of the crash, Marlene Lanz, the McHenry County coroner, called to say she was beginning Lloyd's autopsy. It was a courtesy of her profession. And when she finished, she called and told Nancy, "I'm going to do Scotty now."

The next day Marlene came to visit and brought Scotty's watch and a gold chain he had worn. She said Lloyd and Scotty had died instantly.

"That's what I wanted to hear," Nancy said. "I just wanted to know that they didn't suffer." Marlene said she had found some smoke in Lloyd's lungs, but that Scotty's were clear and pink. "And he was such a heavy smoker," Nancy said. "When Lloyd used to smoke, Scotty was just a little boy, maybe eight years old, and he'd come home from school crying, saying Lloyd would die and begging him to quit." It was as if Lloyd and Scotty could almost see the burnt offering that bound them in their future. "Later, after Lloyd quit," Nancy continued, "we used to say the same thing to Scotty, trying to get him to quit. And after all that smoke, he still had those nice healthy lungs."

Marlene said, "I take it they liked salsa and chips."

Nancy had to laugh. Before they went flying, Nancy was cooking that big dinner, and the boys were all eating chips and salsa, and she warned them not to spoil their appetites. She told Marlene, "You probably found about two bottles of *picante* sauce, didn't you?" Nancy smiled sadly to herself and said, "Marlene is such a caring person."

Then that is how death comes in: without fanfare, in the

middle of an ordinary day, inappropriate, disorderly, at an inconvenient place, shoving everything else out of the way to establish that, no, it's not our control of nature and its forces that is sovereign in this world. This is death's domain.

It was five-thirty when we took off from Anderson, and it didn't take very long before we were in the soup. I kept gently suggesting that we file and get on radar and talk to somebody before a 737 came lumbering out of the murk and stuck its wingtip through our baggage compartment. Liss took the controls and said, "Here, let me climb. We're just gonna come out on top here. I can see light . . ."

And I thought, That sounds like a good epitaph: *I can see light*.

We roared upward through the dim and swirling vapors but to no avail. We were solidly in the clouds, talking to no one, an unseen reef of aluminum on which any passing ship could founder.

"Want me to call Grissom?" I asked.

"Nah, let's see here. We're almost out now." And we roared and climbed, and roared and climbed, but nothing happened. We were already at 6,000 feet. Our passenger was deeply engrossed in his paperwork in the back, oblivious of his plight.

"I think I'm going to call Grissom now," I said.

"Ah, I'll call 'em," Liss said and hit the button on his yoke. He called for a clearance and soon we were on a legal IFR flight plan. The controller instructed us to climb to 8,000, and we burst out into brilliant sunlight over a deck of tumbling white clouds. The daylight moon had spilled its milk to the far horizon. We hurried along close to the clouds, which only through occasional holes revealed our true height by giving us faint glimpses of the dun world of haze and fallow farm fields below.

As we approached Chicago, the air traffic controller directed us to descend from 8,000 to 6,000, and ice began to collect on the airplane as we entered the clouds. I kept track of its accumulation, while Liss flew. I could see its thickness by the little plug of it on the end of the steel temperature probe. They use the word *probe,* but it looked like an oven thermometer stuck through the windshield. The tip had a quarter inch of white ice on it. We had discussed ice while waiting at Anderson, and Liss confessed that he'd never encountered any. I had encountered plenty of it, and I told him what my experience had led me to believe: Get out of it fast or your airplane's going to turn into a $60,000 boat anchor.

"Better ask for three," I said.

They gave him 4,000, and as we descended, the ice stopped accumulating.

We were in the clouds for another fifteen minutes. Then over Joliet, all at once the mist seemed to recede, and we could see all across the Chicago area. The sun was getting low, imparting a strange cast to the light that filtered through the overcast. I could see snow showers falling from luminous clouds in the distance, purple Portuguese men-of-war dangling poisonous tentacles down into the industrial landscape, which sent its tendrils of dark smoke reaching upward into the gloom like feelers from some fragile nautilus. The melancholy coral reef of oil refineries, the snail shells of buildings, the silver fish of aircraft glinting as they schooled around O'Hare Airport, the slimy trails of smoky rivers, now flickering with the red sunlight, which had crept beneath the distant waves of clouds—all contributed to the impression that we were descending in a bathyscaphe to the bottom of the sea. Below us I could see the cars on the freeway turn their headlights on, and I heard Liss say, more to himself than to me, "Left in the dark. Come home in the dark."

TWO

WONDER LAKE

I FIRST CAME to know Galt Airport as an inconspicuous magenta circle on a Chicago sectional chart, a Lambert Conformal Conic Projection of the earth and all its prominent visible features from Muncie, Indiana, to Rochester, Minnesota. I was surprised to find Galt Airport where it was, because I'd been flying in the Chicago area for years and had never noticed it, even though I'd flown over it dozens of times. I had gotten my private pilot's license near Chicago in 1980 and then quit flying for several years. When I returned to flying in May of 1988, the instructor who released me for solo flight again told me I ought to go up to Galt Airport to practice my takeoffs and landings.

"Where's Galt?" I asked.

"Right on the edge of the TCA," he said, unfolding a chart and pointing it out to me, on the rim of the blue circle that represented the airspace for Chicago's O'Hare International Airport. There it was, sure enough, at 42 degrees 24.2 minutes north, 88 degrees 22.5 minutes west, to be precise. Just as LaGuardia is designated as LGA and O'Hare is designated as ORD, so Galt is designated by the FAA as 10C, or One Zero Charlie.

The instructor sent me there because it was a quiet place to practice, away from all the traffic. "It's a really friendly airport," he told me. "You'll like it."

I thought, What could be friendly about an airport? It was a strip of asphalt planted on the earth like a black leech.

I parked the rented Cessna two-seater on the grass and went into the office to see what was so friendly about the place. I found Carla sitting behind the flight desk smiling, and a big sign above her head advertising the lowest gas and airplane rental prices I had seen in the Chicago area since I first dreamed of taking lessons back in the early '70s.

Then in walked Art Galt himself, thin and smiling and baldheaded. He gestured at the helicopter just outside, saying, "Well, it may be fun, but if you take your hand off one of those levers to wipe your nose, why, over you go." He had a piece of mail in his hand and he showed it to Carla. "Look here," he said. "I have officially been declared a winner."

"Great," she said, as if she'd heard it before. "What now?"

"Well," Art went on, "all I have to do is answer this question: 'Who invented the telephone, Alexander Graham Bell or Benjamin Franklin?' " And Art tossed the card into the wastebasket near the flight desk. "I think it's Benjamin Franklin," he said. "God, they must really think I'm stupid. Don't they teach you that in about the third grade?"

Art turned to me and asked, "What can we do for you, young man?"

I said I'd like to get checked out in a Cessna 172.

"Get this man an airplane, Carla," he said. "And make sure it has a lot of gas."

The next thing I knew I was out on the line with a young instructor, taxiing down runway 27* for takeoff. My logbook shows that after my introduction to Galt Airport, I rented an airplane only one more time at Pal-Waukee. By summer's end I had been converted completely; I was a Galt pilot.

Now, years later, I have come to think of Art Galt as I once thought of my own grandfather: a man with many stories to tell, a man with hidden wisdom, hidden humor, a man to learn from, a man who was a little bit crazy. It was probably a year and a half after I'd met Art Galt that I asked him how he first became interested in flying. He didn't hesitate at all. He invited me up to his house to discuss it.

Entering the airport from Greenwood Road, I always passed Art Galt's house. He and his wife, Vera, had lived there since leaving the city in 1949. They bought the land from Mama Schranz, the last surviving matriarch of an old German farming family that had come to northern Illinois in the 1800s.

Today Art's yellow frame house on Greenwood Road is at the very end of Runway 27, and every airplane that departs when the wind is from the west takes off right over his house and pool and tennis courts. As we sat down at the round table in his kitchen, I asked him if he wasn't nervous about having his house at the end of the runway like that, and he laughed. "Now you're a pilot," he said. "If you lost an engine on takeoff, what would you do? Would you fly into my living room, or would you land in that big empty cornfield just north of us?"

Art first became interested in flying because he wanted to find a good place to fish. "My wife and I had heard that there was some pretty good fishing up around the Apostle Islands," he said. "The only trouble was that to get there meant

* *Runways are given numbers that correspond to their compass direction. The final zero is omitted. For example, east is 90 degrees, so a runway going east is called Runway 9.*

ten hours of hard driving." There were no Interstate highways in the early 1950s. There were scarcely any roads at all in the far north country where the really good fishing was, and to get to the Apostle Islands he'd have to drive through all of Wisconsin to Lake Superior. "Well, I was bellyaching about how I hated to drive, and someone said, 'Why don't you fly?' " Art was not one to sit around thinking about what he might or might not do. "I looked around and found a man named Bob Ellis, who would fly us up there." He and Vera packed their fishing and camping gear and drove up to Ellis's place in Wisconsin to meet him for the flight in his four-place airplane to the Apostle Islands.

From the first moment of flight, Art loved it. The landscape seemed to drop away, revealing a great plan that had been hidden by the cluttered world around him. Ellis had pointed out things along the way with his tilted wing. "He let me handle the stick just enough to give me the fever," Art said.

"We were up there by nine-thirty in the morning, and we fished all day and had a shore dinner that night. The next day we fished until about four in the afternoon and cleaned our fish, and we were home in bed that night and had eighty pounds of lake trout in the freezer." By the following week, Art Galt was looking for a flight instructor. "I saw that was the only way to go."

Every few minutes as he talked we could hear the sound of an airplane taking off. The state Department of Transportation counted 54,000 operations in 1989, which means, speaking in averages, that approximately every ten minutes an airplane lands or takes off from Galt, all day, all night, every day of the year. Sometimes we call it Galt International, especially when we have to wait in line to take off. But in the early 1950s it was nothing more than a wide and gently rolling pasture behind the house. Within a week after the Apostle Island trip, Ellis dropped into the pasture in his Piper J-3 Cub to begin their lessons. Soon afterward, Art bought his own Cub, a small fabric two-seat airplane, for about $700 from a local boys' school called Todd's.

Ellis was an old barnstormer from way back, and a pilot of true fundamentals. He taught the Galts some rather unorthodox basics of flying. For example: If your engine fails at night, never land north or south or east or west, because that's the way the fences run, and instead of running through a fence just once, you may find yourself running the full length of a fence, causing much more damage to airplane and body. Ellis taught Art and Vera never to wear their seat belts—they were useless. Art followed the advice until one day when he had his first experience with real turbulence. He found himself pasted to the ceiling while the airplane tried to descend on an elevator shaft of cool air. When he flew out of the shaft, the plane rocketed upward again, taking Art down so fast that, as he put it, "I nearly got the stick up my ass. From then on, I wore my seat belt."

When Art talked Vera's daughter, Wilna, into taking lessons, Chuck, Wilna's husband, was at war in Korea. "We didn't tell Chuck about it," Art said with a mischievous smile. "He came back one winter when we were flying off of Wonder Lake." Wonder Lake, a mile east of the pasture, was the largest clear space around; it was common practice to land on frozen lakes in those days.

"Why don't you get Wilna to take a ride, Chuck?" Art suggested.

"She'd never do it in a million years," Chuck said. "She's scared to death of Ferris wheels."

"Oh, go ahead, give her a try," Art said. "Everybody else is doing it."

"I'll talk to her," Chuck said, "but it won't do any good."

To Chuck's surprise, his wife agreed to take a ride with the instructor.

"So Chuck strapped her into the Jeep—that's what we called the Cub—with Ellis and watched his wife take off. They flew out of sight and landed at a different part of the lake." Ellis got out and stood on the ice to await the conclusion of the practical joke, while Wilna flew the airplane back alone. She landed right in front of Chuck. At first he couldn't tell what he was seeing. Then, as he came closer, he looked inside and saw that no one else was there. "He just about fainted," Art said.

"Where's the instructor?" Chuck asked in alarm.

Wilna looked around and said, "What, honey? What instructor? Did I have an instructor up there? I must've dropped him somewhere."

Of course, when he got back from Korea, Chuck wanted to take lessons, too. "We have twelve licenses in the family now, with grandchildren and one thing and another." Chuck became a captain with Eastern Airlines. After fighting in Korea and serving twenty-six years as an airman, he was forced to retire when he slipped on a patch of ice in his own front yard a mile south of Galt Airport and broke his ankle so severely that he could no longer depress the brake pedals. He died of a heart attack in 1992.

Student pilots today could expect a less eventful courtship than Art Galt had with Ellis's Cub in the 1950s. Ellis was an aviator in the old mold, known for feats of daring. Art told me that Ellis once drew a circle in the snow on Wonder Lake with his wingtip without breaking the wingtip light. Ellis would fly straight across Lake Michigan in his tiny fragile Aircraft with his dog hanging out the open window lapping up the summer air. "Eight feet off the water," Art insisted.

The landing area in the pasture was short enough—only 600 feet. But during the winter, ice and snow would make it shorter still. In a tail-wheel aircraft there are several stages to taking off. First the aircraft rolls down the runway on all three wheels. Then the pilot lifts the tail off the ground by pushing the stick forward. When the airplane gains flying speed, the pilot pulls the stick back, lifting the nose. But on that short patch of frozen grass, Ellis didn't have the time or patience for all of that nonsense. He would have Art hold the tail off the ground before he started rolling. Then Ellis would lock the brakes, run up the engine to full power, and signal Art to let go of the tail. The Taylorcraft would take off almost immediately and climb away, shuddering at the limits of its modest abilities.

The fishing trip that had inoculated Art with the passion for flight took place in the summer. It was winter before he made his first solo flight. "We went at it pretty slowly at first," he said. Slowly, if not carefully. Art's solo flight departed from Power's Lake. In the winter the lake freezes and makes a nice landing area. A first solo flight is supposed to be a well-planned, carefully thought-out event. Instructors and students may wait weeks for just the right weather. But when Ellis decided it was time for Art to solo, there was no stopping him.

"It was blowing so hard that Ellis could barely stand up," Art told me. In the excitement of his first solo flight, Art forgot to change the pitch trim from landing to takeoff attitude. The trim tab on the horizontal tail surface of an airplane sets the angle at which the wings meet the oncoming air. On the approach to landing, the trim is set nose up in order to slow the airplane and put it closer to the stall. "So when I took off and gave it the gun, the airplane climbed like a homesick angel," Art said. A steep climb on takeoff can result in a stall, and a stall fifty or sixty feet off the ground can result in the death of the pilot.

"We used to fly in any kind of weather," Art said. "The day I got my license, I went to Rockford with Vera and it started to snow. I nearly lost my way. That's when I learned you couldn't see ahead in snow, only down. And I really did follow the road home." Art smiled and said, "I Follow Roads—IFR."

One day Ellis let Art take off despite bad weather moving in. Art flew toward Rockford and encountered a wall of blackness not five miles west. He returned to find Ellis standing there with his arms folded, tapping his foot, waiting. "I was wondering when you were going to notice that," he told Art.

Art took his FAA practical exam at Janesville, Wisconsin, and was awarded a private pilot's certificate.

"How did you do?" I asked.

"Everything worked all right," Art said, imitating the taciturn farmers he had learned to live with, who met him out there in 1949 with their sour looks and suspicion and their perfect and serene willingness to watch him and his whole operation sink into the bog that once was Mama Schranz's farm.

It was never Art's intention to start an airport. In the bitter winter of 1949, with his new bride, Vera Davis Chizek, his only intention was to start a family farm. Vera had three children of high school age from a previous marriage. They had nothing when they arrived in mid-January, five people in a war-surplus Jeep, nothing to speak of that was useful for farming at any rate—no animals, few machines, and no knowledge or skill connected with crops or land or the husbandry of animals.

Before a month was out, that frenzied wind came up, gaining momentum over the unchecked reaches of the cut-down cornfields, and it blew against the leaky clapboard house until the old coal furnace was working continuously, pumping out heat and trying to catch up with the falling thermostat. The more the wind blew, the harder the furnace worked. The harder the furnace worked, the more the wind blew. There was only one radiator for the whole house and an expansion tank in the attic. The more coal the furnace burned, the more water it pumped into the attic tank, and the more the northerly wind seemed to fan the fire. Then one night, at the height of the blizzard, the old tank popped its relief valve and overflowed right through the ceiling and down onto Vera and Art's nuptial bed. When Art discovered where the water was coming from, he couldn't help himself, he just sat down and laughed, and Vera stood over him with her arms folded saying, "What are you laughing at? It's not funny."

Art went to agriculture school at the local high school on the GI Bill to learn what he thought he'd need to know. He laughed now thinking of how naive he was. "The neighbors were no help at all," he said. When he asked even such a simple question as what kind of tractor he should buy, one neighbor told him, "Well, let's see here. . . . Some of 'em like a red tractor. Some of 'em like a green tractor, but I don't know. You might either like a red one or a green one, see, so I couldn't really say."

Art bought a three-plow Oliver tractor with live power takeoff for $8,000, a lot of money then. It was bright green. The neighbors came to view the impertinent monstrosity. There was no secret made of the fact that his new neighbors wanted to see Art Galt stumble and fall. "When I got the three-plow tractor," he told me, "they all came over and admired it. 'Glad you got a big one like that,' they said. 'Well, why the hell didn't you tell me?' I said." They all just smiled and shrugged.

In fact, those same neighbors who had attempted to discourage Art from becoming a farmer were soon watching with a certain inexplicable curiosity and longing as those crazy Galts began landing airplanes on the grass there by the house. It was the most confounding sight. Why would any sensible farmer want to have those machines going in and out of his pasture?

Art would bring fresh fish from his trips to Lake Superior, and he would share the bounty with his icy neighbors. By and by, they began to see that he wasn't such a bad sort after all, even if he did perform this kind of witchcraft of aviation. Some of them even went for rides with Art and Vera and found themselves inextricably caught in the spell of flying.

Word spread about Galt Field. A few fliers from the county and from just across the border in Wisconsin began to ask permission to fly in and land there. When someone would ask to park an airplane on his land, Art would think about it for a while and then allow as how it would probably be all right.

A single airplane is like a bird on a wire: It attracts another, then another. One pilot told another, who told another, and pretty soon a line of airplanes had begun to form against the fence on the north side of the Galt pasture.

"Of course, it was just a regular pasture," Art said, "so when we'd go through a fresh cow pie, the wheel would zip up a brown streak on the wing." Art hung an electric fence to keep the cows away from the airplanes. He began to keep a fifty-five-gallon drum filled with gasoline under a big oak tree by the fence. It had a stirrup pump, and there was a notebook in a wood-and-tar-paper box beside it, so if a pilot took fuel, there'd be a notation, such as "Took 8 Gallons—Sue." Even though there are electric pumps and line boys today, who pump gas and wash windshields, many of us still pump our own gas and write our names on the sheet when no one is around.

They bought a radio when such gadgets came into fashion among pilots. It was a huge contraption filled with glowing vacuum tubes and rheostats and crawling with soldered-on wires, and it came jammed into two heavy steel cases that sat side by side and plugged together with a cable thick enough to use for the electric chair down at Joliet. "We had the radio up here in the house," Art told me. "It was really funny when we first started as a business. Vera and I would sit up here and wait, watching for airplanes, and if we saw one, we'd say, 'Do you think they're gonna land? Do you think they're gonna land?' " The heavens proved extravagant, and the flinty sky above the yellow farmhouse on the green plains filled with the barking of Continental engines.

By 1954 Galt Field was a full-fledged grass-strip airport. The Galts' became a popular weekend gathering place. "The people would congregate right there in the house.

We'd come home from church on Sunday and we couldn't even get in the kitchen. There'd be eighteen or twenty people having coffee." Today some of those same people—and a lot of new ones—can be found in the briefing room. Somebody brings a coffeecake or doughnuts—home-baked or from the bakery in Woodstock—and there's always coffee brewing. On a winter day, when the wind is strumming down off the great plains through the corn stubble and piling up the snow around the hangar doors, and Carla's husband, Steve, big and bearded as a mountain man, can be seen out with a plow on the front of his '36 Ford truck, striving to keep the drifts back long enough for some stout-hearted aviator to take off or land, the back room is often filled with people talking and telling stories about their gut-flushing narrow scrapes in this or that classic aircraft, which could only have been survived by dint of exceptional piloting skill and positive grit.

But most of the people who spend their weekends talking in the briefing room at Galt Airport have no real idea what daring with an airplane was like in the early days. When Art first began to fly Piper Cubs, he had no lights, neither on the airplane nor on the ground. Nevertheless, he and the other pilots landed at night on the cow pasture—no runway, no lights, no seat belts, no radio. "We did it on a moonlit night," he said, "and we put newspaper on the barbed wire fence so that we could see the damned thing and land. That's pretty primitive stuff."

The main east-west runway, 9-27, went through several phases before it reached its present paved condition, but "finally we leveled the strip properly and put bank run gravel down one foot deep and then crushed stone on top of that and then blacktop Sealkote over that. Eventually that didn't work so well either. It started throwing pebbles and wearing through, so we put two inches of hot mix down and then Sealkote on top of that, which is approximately what you see now," he said. There are now two runways at Galt, one made of asphalt, running east and west, one made of mowed grass, running north and south. They meet to form an imperfect L-shape on the land. "Then we started in building hangars. We'd build one hangar and then another, and so on." By the early '60s there were four rows of hangars in addition to the shop (the old shop, which burned in 1984).

Art built his first big hangar by hand. He dug with a hand-operated posthole digger. Then he erected the hangar structure around telephone poles and put up corrugated steel siding and giant sliding hangar doors. It became the first shop, just across the runway from the present flight office, which was the second airport structure he built—built with his own hands, board by board, shingle by shingle.

One day, long after it was completed, some McHenry County officials came out to the field and saw his hangar and frowned in dismay. Standing on his runway, sweating in their suits and squinting up at the summer sky, they said, "You never got a permit for that."

Art said, "That's right. What are you going to do about it?" He wasn't fond of the idea that he would have to ask someone's permission to build on his own farmland in the United States of America.

The county officials agreed that they couldn't very well ask him to take it down, and they went away scratching their heads about what to do. The point was of strictly academic interest after the building burned to the ground, and Art left it down because the runway, which had been gradually extended farther and farther west as the airport grew, had now come uncomfortably close to the shop.

Before long, pilots were clamoring for night landing privileges, but there were no lights, and it was too expensive to have someone else install them. Art mounted a chisel plow on a tractor, rigged a curved length of conduit on the end of it, and threaded plain electrical wire through the conduit. Then he paid out wire into the ground as the chisel dug the trench. "We put down the whole line in half a day like Christmas tree lights," Art said delighted at having outwitted those who would take his money.

The office was built across the runway from that very first hangar on the south side. Next door to the office—and attached to it—Art built a second hangar, almost a block long, for housing airplanes. On top he had a man paint the name of the airport in ten-foot-high red letters. It, like the others, was constructed out of corrugated steel siding and telephone poles. It now houses eight aircraft, including mine. It has a dirt floor, and clouds of dust rise and settle within it as the breeze blows between and under the doors. Birds nest in the rafters and their droppings dry on our Bahama Blue Dacron wings with the white sunburst on top. In fact, in the spring it's like an aviary in there, where hundreds of sparrows are breeding, and the sound of their pleas for food is deafening. A great field of sunflowers grows just southeast of the hangars, and in the summer their heads swell and tip over and nod with every breeze that happens by. They are like an immense herd of yellow beasts grazing on the sunlight that falls all around.

"We had the radio up in the kitchen at the house before we built the office and hangars. That first hangar and the office were built more or less together, and we took one hangar space and set that aside to make a restaurant." Art put in a stove, sink, tile, vent hood, a counter with stools, and a nice linoleum floor. "We operated it for five or ten years that way with no problems. We had a gal who made two pies a day. God, those were good pies," Art added.

When they had the restaurant, Vera was the cook. Art recalled many days when they had twenty-four plates and forty-eight people, and Art washed the plates twice to get through one seating at lunch. A lot of people miss it now. It's been gone for more than ten years. It would still be there today, Art says, except that one day the Health Department came in from McHenry County and decided to inspect.

It wasn't as if there had been a problem. The Galt Airport Restaurant had operated for years without complaints. But when the Health Department officials came in, they immediately spotted some pretty serious hazards. The counter had a strip of stainless steel running around the edge of its Formica and plywood top. The Health Department man said, "Mr. Galt, that stainless steel is put on with screws. Now, you see, the slot in those screws can collect dirt, and that's a health hazard. Germs can accumulate in there, bacteria and fungus molds, and we don't know what-all. Now we can't have that, can we? You're going to need to remove that strip and refinish that counter properly."

Art said, "Well, I don't know. For the last ten years it's been doing all right."

"I'm sorry, Mr. Galt. Those are the rules."

Art said, "Okay, well, I'll tell you what. Why don't you get the hell off my property, because this restaurant is closed permanently as of today." Art told that story one Sunday afternoon in the office when pilots were crowded in paying their gasoline chits, and one of them overheard him and said, "Yeah, Art, but a cheeseburger sure would go down good right about now."

"We got the community to accept us as an airport and not complain by having hangar parties," Art said. "We'd have some liquor but not a lot. Mostly we'd have punch, and we'd put out hay bales to sit on. We'd have a band and Vera would make sandwiches, and we'd take anybody up who was willing to go for an airplane ride—that was the big thing, free airplane rides and dancing."

On summer nights they would hire an orchestra and people would fly in from as far away as Land O'Lakes, Wisconsin, and the neighboring farmers would come with their sons and daughters to meet Vera and Art's son and daughters and to watch the bonfires burn high and eat chicken and cornbread and homemade pies.

There was a young boy named Steve there at the hangar

parties. He came from Greenwood, just a short bike ride down Greenwood Road. At night when the orchestras were playing and the people were all spilling out of the warm light of the maintenance hangar with food and drink and with the laughter dying across the cornfields and everyone taking turns dancing, it seemed that he lived in a magical dream.

Steve would have done just about anything for a ride in one of those airplanes, but he was still too young; he needed his father's permission. The smell of wood smoke and gasoline drifted on the smooth night air. Dance band music mixed with the tremulous cries of fear and delight, and the mechanical hammering back beat of the Continental engines spread across the darkened somber fields as the airplanes hung their mysterious moving lights among the moon-streaked clouds over the undulating oily waves of Wonder Lake.

"They came in droves and had a hell of a time," Art said. "Now, they could hardly talk against us after having such a good time, could they?"

When the parties were over, Steve would come drifting back on his bicycle and hang around and wash airplanes, "as well as an eight-year-old can help," Art said. Steve hoped and prayed, and finally one day his father sent a note of permission and Art Galt consented, and Steve had his first ride in a Beech Bonanza 35, a fine and fancy airplane if there ever was one. It was everything that Steve had imagined it would be. He looked down on treetops. The things he knew in his world were suddenly shrunk, the barns and buses and roads and fields, just as they had been for Alice in Wonderland, as if he'd taken a potion. The people almost vanished altogether, although he could see them there if he looked carefully, tiny as they were, waving their arms up at him. He was up and they were down, and they were all watching him go.

Today Galt Flying Service, Inc., has grown into a corporation owned by Art and Vera. GFS owns about half a dozen aircraft (depending upon whether you count the ones that aren't flying because their motors burned up or because they were crashed and aren't yet repaired). The whole operation nets about $50,000 a year after expenses and taxes. Meanwhile, the land is worth more and more as developers eat up the surrounding farm fields and knock together Sheetrock shanty communities with wishfully pretentious names such as Lake Moor Emperial Estates.

In assessing the operation, Art said, "If I can sell the hay in the field and then rent the pasture and rent the whole farm as a game farm for hunters and then set aside land to the club that shoots doves—that field of sunflowers you see back there—then I can make ends meet." I asked him about the hunters, and he said, "Oh, it's twenty-five guys with shotguns, and they blast away in there, and when there are no more birds left, they go in and divide them up and then they wait until more come in."

That winter Art had been taken to the hospital with internal bleeding. At first no one could determine what was wrong with him, until he admitted that he had thrown away his pills—medicine that was meant to prevent internal bleeding. "They were too damned expensive," Art told me, "and I figured, once I finished the first bottle, what was the point? I was feeling fine."

"Do you feel up to flying?" I asked. It was only his first full day back on the job since leaving the hospital, and I had found him in the front office keeping busy. Now at the question Art turned his eyes inward as if to check himself. Then he smiled that mischievous smile of his. "Your plane or mine?" he asked.

"Your choice," I said.

"Well, I don't feel up to flying my own plane, but I'll go up with you," he said after a moment's consideration.

I told him to wait inside where it was comfortable, that I'd inspect the airplane carefully before our flight. I said, "I'd hate to kill you after you survived that hospital."

Outside, I pulled back the big metal hangar doors, my shoes sliding in the puddles that had formed from the sun melting snow on the roof. There in the darkness the blue airplane sat back on its tail wheel, nose cocked skyward, yellow foam cowl plugs in the air scoops to keep the birds out. I pulled on the prop to get the 1,600-pound airplane—a 7KCAB Bellanca Citabria, registration number 36250—to roll itself out into the sunlight where I could examine its imperfections with the hope of finding the one that might hurt us. I had learned that looking the airplane over carefully before every flight is a tedious and unrewarding job most of the time. It's the same old airplane with the same old blemishes, and nothing is ever very wrong. Almost never.

Once I was going out to fly a twin-engine Beech Baron. It was night, and we were in a hurry. The pilot who was going to show me how to fly the Baron, a young airline pilot, had already peeked into the cowlings, but at dusk the light can do funny things. Against his insistence that we get going, I decided to fetch a flashlight from my flight bag and inspect the two engines more closely. When I pointed the beam inside the left engine's cowling, I saw straw. "Hey," I said. "Straw."

"Straw?"

"As in cows and chickens and horses." I reached in and pulled out a handful. "Straw."

"Straw," he muttered as I opened the cowling to reveal that some enterprising bird had made a nest about the size of an old-fashioned Easter basket in there, tucked in among the cylinders where it was nice and warm. We would have had just enough time to take off and climb out over the south end of the city before it caught fire.

But today I found nothing about the Citabria that seemed likely to knock us out of the sky, and as I checked the oil and sampled the fuel, I noticed that I had begun to sweat inside my layers of clothes from the exertion of hogging the airplane around. Art stepped out onto the ramp and started to climb in.

He lifted himself halfway up onto the metal step to get in and then hesitated. "Where do you want me?" he asked. "You know, the back seat is the pilot-in-command seat."

A placard in the Citabria called for the pilot to sit in the front seat, but I figured it was just like Art—if a sign told him to sit in front, he'd certainly want to sit in the back.

The issue of weight and balance is of more than passing interest. Flight is a delicate, some say precarious, balance of four forces, all of them constantly changing. The pilot is the controlling influence at the center of those forces, like a bear balancing on a ball. The weight of the airplane holds it down through the force of gravity. The thrust of the spinning propeller forces it forward through the air, just as a ship is driven through the water by a screw. The air rushing over the curved top of the wings creates a third force, called lift, which works against gravity. The faster the propeller pulls the plane, the faster the air flows over the wings, and the more lift the wings produce. That's why there are runways, so that we can run down them and get the air moving over the wings. But the airplane resists being moved through the air, too. Drag is the fourth force, and the faster the airplane moves, the greater drag becomes. The Four Forces: Gravity, Thrust, Lift, Drag. If thrust overcomes drag and lift overcomes weight, the result is flight.

With Art behind me, I strapped in. "You ready?" I asked over my shoulder.

"Yep," he said, putting on his headset so that we could hear over the engine noise.

I shouted, "Clear!" and then pressed the small silver starter button on the instrument panel, and with one labored revolution of the propeller the engine caught and spewed forth heat and fire and wind in our direction. I could smell the exhaust and feel the air blowing over the cowling as the ship shook and strained against the brakes.

With the coming of a midwinter thaw, the ramp had begun to crowd with people and airplanes. I switched on the radio and dialed in 122.8 for the Unicom, FAA jargon for Everybody Talk At Once. I could hear calls coming in from all over the midwest, an electronic Tower of Babel. I ignored the radio and taxied out. Art and I found ourselves lined up behind five other airplanes.

We taxied to the eastern end of the runway and were waiting on the run-up pad, listening to the raucous congestion on the frequency saying, "Galt Traffic, Galt Traffic, Galt Traffic."

I asked, "How does it feel to have your name called over the radio about six thousand times a day?"

"Pretty darned good," he said, laughing through the intercom.

I took off and climbed out into the pattern.* As I turned back over the field, I saw a deer grazing on Runway 18-36, the north-south turf strip, and as our sound footprint hit her, she leapt as if she'd been struck by lightning and ran into the high scrub pine, oak bush, and poplar, which grew in clumps amid the geometric cutout shapes of farmland.

Art pointed out the boundaries of his property and his three lakes, Lake Vera, Lake Art, and the nameless lake still waiting for a reason to be called something other than the north pond.

"You have the airplane," I said, giving the controls to Art and putting my hands up to show him that I was no longer flying. He eagerly took the stick, saying, "I've flown this plane many times before," referring to a time almost twenty years earlier when 36250 had been a Galt Flying Service

* *The landing pattern at most airfields is made up of a series of four left turns, beginning from takeoff and ending when we turn onto the final approach, lined up with the runway once again.*

club airplane and was let out for rent and used for instruction.

Art flew us north of Wonder Lake to Wilmot Mountain, an area popular for its ski slope, which to the midwestern mind was mountainous. Art angled over the ski area, and we looked down and commented on the parking lot: It was jammed with cars. Lines of yellow school buses dominated one side of the lot, and the dazzling array of multicolored cars glittered in the sunlight as we moved our shadow across them. On the slopes the lifts were busy, and the black dots of skiers careened erratically down the trivial swell of the land. Those people evidently thought it was a mountain. Art remarked how people crave silly things. They were going to all that bother and expense to slip on the snow for a few seconds, while we were burning expensive avgas in order to turn in circles above them. We concluded that there is no explaining people.

Art banked away and flew like a horseback rider, turning his steed this way and that, playing with the feel of flight. He tipped steeply left, then right, and for a moment I thought he was going to pull a couple of barrel rolls.

As we returned to the landing pattern, Art kept up a running commentary on what he saw below. He looked down and saw the shadow of our plane following a highway, and he laughed. "Isn't it fun when you can see your own shadow? I like to make it follow a road. It's kind of a game." And I understood that Art Galt had succumbed long ago to the compulsion of flight. Somewhere back in those wintery days with Bob Ellis out on the frozen lakes, doing insane things with primitive airplanes, those two men had fused The Impulse in themselves and had caught it and rendered it inert. Pilots say a lot of things they think are clever. Most of them aren't that clever, but they are sometimes true. One such aphorism is this: There are old pilots and there are bold pilots, but there are no old, bold pilots. Art was once bold, flying a single-engine airplane over Cuba to Haiti with no navigational radio—bold like Lloyd or just plain crazy. But Art passed through the fire, and had finally been annealed.

He looked down for a long time in silence at the endless rectangles of crops and then said, "I've been here forty years, but I never get tired of looking at it. Isn't it beautiful?"

THREE

APPROACHES

THE COMING OF DAWN was almost imperceptible. A faint gray light spread upon the low hills that surround Galt Airport. The cold had returned, and now the corn stubble poked through snow, which had fallen during the night. A turbulent wind blew from the northwest, as dark and vagrant clouds hunched over the hills munching on a stand of naked trees. A wood frame building, which resembled a control tower with an orange wind sock on top, stood watch over the flight line where single-engine Cessnas and Pipers waited, tied down with muddy nylon ropes in rows out on the white and frozen grass. As gusts of wind hit them, they shook like horses left too long in the fields. They were not shiny airplanes. Most of them had a weathered appearance, their once-brilliant blues and reds and greens now scoured and faded by the ceaseless buffing of the wind.

Parallel to the flight line were ranks of rusty corrugated

steel hangars as long as city blocks. Their sliding doors—great sheets of metal fixed on wooden frames--sounded like stage thunder as they rumbled in the wind against their rails.

I stood in the second-floor office in the square frame building sipping coffee and waiting for the weather to lift. The room had windows all around, as a control tower might have. The office was cramped by the clutter of desks and file cabinets and cardboard boxes. Facing north, I could see the first students of the morning taxiing out in their Cessna trainers. They would motor slowly down the runway toward the east; I could hear them on the radio speaker across the room, declaring their position so that no one would land on top of them. At the far end of the field, more than half a mile away, they would turn around and rush toward us, still silent in the snowscape, and wobble into uncertain flight, the fragile wings kicked this way and that by the wind. At last they would clamor past the office window, their tiny and pitiful racket as triumphant as a child's string of firecrackers tossed into the air.

They wouldn't leave the landing pattern this morning for fear of losing the airport. But since the instructors weren't paid unless they flew, some of them would drag their students up in nearly any kind of weather, saying, "This is good practice for you. If you can land in this wind, you can land in anything." Or: "Now, don't ever do this by yourself, but . . ."

Out the west windows I could see the maintenance hangar, a great gray metal building called the shop (the new shop), large enough for five airplanes, and beyond that, in a field overgrown with dried thistles and dusted with snow, a kind of hillbilly heaven of antique rusted trucks and tractors, old airplane wings and tails and motors in various stages of disintegration. Farther still beyond that, closer to the main road, was an old yellow barn with a concrete silo attached, the gray shaft of concrete gripped by the black veins of naked vines. In the middle distance: three rusted wire corncribs which had once stood in a neat row. Although two had been crushed and tossed aside in a storm, one still stood mysteriously intact, as if to prove the defiantly illogical nature of Nature and its random, unaccountable calamities. Between the three corncribs and the barn was the hog shed, peeling yellow paint, abandoned now for more than a decade. On one side of the driveway that ran past the farrowing pens, a bulldozer was frozen in rust and snow, its scoop slightly raised, as if it were the victim of a spell cast upon the whole place, the yellow house, the yellow barn, the yellow shed, even the shattered gray-green carcass of a World War II B-17 Flying Fortress with weeds growing up through its ribs and nothing but spiders dropping on silken bungees from its bomb-bay doors. For someone who just happened by, it would be difficult to tell if this was an airport that had once been a farm or a farm that had once been an airport.

Behind me at her desk, Carla talked to pilots on the radio. "Six Fox Sierra, wind at Galt is north eighteen gusting thirty-five, and it looks like they're using either end today." Either way there would be an uncomfortable wind across the runway.

Carla hung the microphone on its hook beside a speaker on the wall between the photographs of her son, Chance, and her husband, Steve, and another photograph, equally prominent, of their yellow airplane in the act of landing over the pines at Galt Airport. It was an old Cessna 170, which she referred to as "the family car."

The airplane whose pilot Carla had been addressing as 6FS* on the radio appeared out of the mists. It was a miracle that would have been easy to miss: something being created out of nothing. The airplane simply materialized with no fanfare or ceremony, and what was not there before all at once existed, as divine and inconspicuous as an amoeba being born in the sea.

* *An aircraft's call sign is always pronounced digit by digit, and the letters are given according to the official phonic alphabet. Thus, 1237U is "one two three seven Uniform" and 6FS is "six Foxtrot Sierra."*

The plane landed, and the two Cessna 152 trainer planes took off again, dipping left and right in the stiff wind, and began grinding their way around the pattern like toys on a wire.

Directly across the east-west runway were the ruins of the original maintenance hangar, or shop, which had been left exactly as it was after the fire, its corrugated metal roof and walls curled up where they had melted. Certainly human beings have had a hand in shaping this place, but there has been a curious fatalism in the way that Art has allowed Fate and Nature to co-produce. He has always seemed to know that there were other forces at work here, and he's made no attempt to deny them. His overt, almost defiant, statements in leaving the battered corncribs where they fell, the frozen bulldozer gaping at the wind, were more than mere acts of neglect. Art has never shied away from work—he literally built the farm and the airport with his own hands. No, what Art left undone was left carefully, like the silence between notes in a symphony.

Carla sighed at the pile of invoices on the desk before her. Galt Flying Service, Inc., was a flight school and a repair shop. It sold gas and oil and assorted pilot supplies. More than 200,000 gallons of gasoline were pumped in 1991. GFS provided parking for airplanes, either transient or permanent, either outside or in a hangar. Galt had seven airplanes and rented them for a total of 7,800 hours in 1991. In other words, speaking in averages, a Galt airplane was flying not quite every hour of every day of the year. For such a small airport, Carla had a lot of invoices. "So. Are you going to fly or not?" she asked me.

"Nobody's paying me to go up in this weather," I said. And then I thought, well, actually, it might be a good day to practice blind flying. And then I thought better of it. "Where's Steve?"

"He's out in the shop," she said. "Where else?"

Bill Tate, an instructor in his early twenties, came in to

check the schedule with Carla. Bill was tall and thin and had dark hair. He wore prefaded jeans and Reeboks and a white and gray sweater. Bill looked as if he belonged in a movie about a fighter squadron. His walk was cool and loose, and he flipped a pencil as he sauntered in and sat down to look at the weather computer. The report looked something like this: RFD RS COR 1251 M8 OVC 11/2SF 927/29/25/ 3619G30.

"You going up?" I asked him.

"Not in this," Bill said. "Ground school today. Mucho ground school."

"What about those guys?" I asked, pointing to the 152s.

"That's Jay and Brett. They're coming in. It's too low. What about you? You going up?"

"I don't think so," I said. I could feel myself being drawn toward flight. There was something—definitely something—in the idea of going into those clouds with a little airplane strapped onto me. But I gave it up. "Nah," I said. "It's too low."

I descended the stairs from the office to the flight desk and said hello to Jay Pettigrove, the curly-headed chief flight instructor, who had just landed. Jay now sat at the scheduling desk behind two glass display cases placed in an L-shape to provide a demarcation between the public and employee areas—in front of the flight desk or behind the flight desk—though people walked behind the desk and helped themselves to what they needed, and the cash register and merchandise cases were never locked. One morning I found the register drawer sitting out. It was full of cash. No one was around. All was quiet. I called out for Carla, and she answered from the office upstairs, "Good morning, Laurence."

"Carla, did you know there was a drawer full of cash sitting out here?" I asked.

"Oh, yeah, why don't you put it in the cash register?" she called.

In the glass display cases were fanfold charts, fuel testers, flashlights, logbooks, textbooks, plotter-computers, and sheet metal screws for replacing the ones that fell out of airplanes as they rattled through the sky.

I could hear the wind humming against the picture windows that dominated two walls facing north and west, giving a view of the ramp and runway and parking lot. The lot was nearly empty, and only a few students straggled in.

Jay glanced up from the schedule on the desk before him. He had a disheveled appearance and always looked as if he needed a new wardrobe and a haircut, but he was meticulous and organized when it came to instructing. He was one of the few flight instructors I knew who took notes during flight.

"You going up?" Jay asked me, thumbing through a gray steel box of three-by-five cards, which were scribbled with the names and telephone numbers of the members of the Galt Flying Club. On the front of the box was the number of the Hebron Crash-Fire-Rescue Squad, which had only been used twice, once for Lloyd and Scotty, once for the shop fire.

"Probably not," I said. "I don't know. I got a briefing for Kenosha. There aren't any pilot reports of icing."

"You're right on the ILS for Runway Six," Jay said.

"Yeah," I said without enthusiasm. "So what are you going to do?" I asked.

"Sim rides today," he said, referring to the instrument flight simulator, a device in the back room for practicing flight by reference to the instruments. IFR means instrument flight rules. The world is crisscrossed by an invisible spider web of electronic signals that connect points of interest, say, Indianapolis and Champaign. Instruments on board the aircraft receive those signals and guide us from point to point so that we can zigzag from anywhere to anywhere.

Like chess players, we sit for hours studying dials that barely move, while we barely move the controls. But after what seems an eternity of sweaty, trembling concentration, we appear at the end of a runway at some distant place. It's a game of intellect, and if we don't play well, we can be sublimated into the very clouds themselves and never reappear. On a single-engine airplane, a single vacuum pump runs the critical instruments that keep us right side up in the clouds. One day I saw Bob Russell, the airport manager and chief mechanic, carrying a new vacuum pump in a plastic wrapper on his way out to the shop, and I asked, "What's that?"

"A time bomb," he said.

"What?" I asked, taken unaware.

"Yeah," he said. "Because just when you get into the clouds, they quit." And he went off to install it on an airplane.

I pulled my coat around me and hurried across the parking lot to the shop on no particular errand. It was a gray metal cube of a building with a greasy concrete floor and a colossal door that curtsied across a horizontal crease and lifted away like aluminum skirts gathered up by steel fingers. As I entered, I was greeted by the whine of a drill, which ricocheted around the big open space and came screaming down from the rafters like an electric hawk. A faint and oily light filtered in from somewhere, illuminating three small Cessnas in different stages of disassembly. An aircraft engine on a hoist sat in one corner, and the airplane from which the engine had been removed had scrap iron chained to its nose to keep it from tipping backward onto its tail. Some of the walls of the hangar had been covered with a kind of chicken-wire mesh, and here and there scraps of plastic sheeting kept the wind out. High up by the roof, rectangular holes had been cut in the steel siding and fitted with translucent yellowed green plastic material to admit a kind of dingy curdled light, which mixed with the harsh fluorescence of industrial fixtures. The room smelled like fuel and urethane.

It was there, in the dark glare of the shop, amid the seeming chaos of mysterious mechanical undertakings, that I found Carla's husband, Steve Nusbaum, a bearded man in a leather vest and greasy jeans, wearing battered blue Velcro sneakers and a threadbare seed cap that read, obscurely, "39395." Steve was tall and rangy with a salt-and-pepper beard that grew completely untrimmed, mountain-man style. When I entered, he looked up from his work at a table fashioned from plywood and sawhorses and glared suspiciously at me. He looked like a moonshiner who had just been discovered in the most secluded part of the woods.

"What's this?" I asked, indicating a fifteen-foot-long skinless fuselage, which sported a shiny blond wooden propeller and sat back comfortably on new tires but had as yet no wings.

"A *Stork,*" Steve said and continued to work on the tube-steel frame with hands so rough they looked as if the fingers had been welded together at the knuckles. *Stork* was the name that he and his partner, Don Ericson, were going to use for their miniature single-place aircraft. Like a work of art, it was all original hand work. When I first saw it, the *Stork* was barely a skeleton. But in its strange incipient qualities, I could see the promise of flight, as in a newly hatched dragonfly. The original Fieseler *Storch* had little in common with its namesake, except high lift and slow flight. "In 1943," Don told me, "one of these flown by a German colonel picked Mussolini off of a hilltop and got him away to Northern Italy."

Just behind the pilot's seat an ominous-looking canister was fixed to the frame. "What's that?" I asked Steve.

"A parachute," he said. He was not a man who gave himself over to voluble discourse, but I stayed and pestered him until he showed me how, in an emergency, the pilot could pull a red knob, and a ballistic device would fire the parachute right through the Dacron skin, bringing the airplane and all its contents, living or otherwise, gently back to earth.

Don Ericson, a local pilot and industrialist businessman from an airfield ten miles south of Galt, had lost his pilot's medical certificate to a heart condition. He could no longer fly commercially produced airplanes—not legally. Anyone can fly an ultralight aircraft without a pilot's license or a medical certificate. So Don, who was a smiling pixie of a man with an elfish grin and a snap-brim cap concealing a slightly bald head, a man who spoke quickly and confidentially, as if he were letting us in on a secret, and always with a smirk and a friendly laugh, had begun to design the *Stork* ultralight aircraft as an attempt to get back into the air after being grounded. Now with Steve's help and tight-lipped encouragement, Don was refining the design, and they were actually fabricating the prototype. Don had the engineering expertise, the equations, but Steve had the practical know-how and the skill of having built or rebuilt many airplanes by hand. One day I watched Don compare notes on model airplanes with Steve's 14-year-old son Chance. Chance had all the models and Don had all the history. As Chance brought out more and more of them, Don became more and more excited. "Oh!" he would say. Or: "*Well*, now!" And: "When I was a kid, I built one of these." He narrated how one particular model went up and up and caught a thermal and crossed the river, "And I never saw it again." He had wanted to build a real one ever since.

Yet no one asked why Don would bother. All conversation about it began from the assumption that he had to get back into the air. And most of the people involved in the effort looked at it as a necessary test, as in a mythical story, a rite of passage; and they were only too glad to help the hero of the tale.

But viewed from the outside, Don's course of action seemed much less clear. He did not need to go anywhere, so the aircraft could not rightly be viewed as a mode of transportation. He did not fly for a living, so it would represent no income. On the contrary, it represented quite a substantial expense. Why did he need to fly then? To entertain himself? He could have bought a boat. He could have golfed. I have a friend who in his sixties races cars, a sport for which no medical exam is necessary. And my friend has only one kidney. Don could have raced.

But even granting that Don must fly, why didn't he buy an ultralight airplane? No. This went deeper. For Don was being pursued by something, no more or less than Lloyd had been.

Don had told me that store-bought ultralights would not do for him. They simply did not have the qualities of a real airplane. His would be a real airplane, but it would also fit the FAA's definition of ultralight.* Even after all this, Don's explanation seemed flimsy. I felt that his quest went beyond what logic could support. It was evident in his unbridled enthusiasm, in his gleeful concentration on the task of figuring out the plan for his airplane, that Don was setting out to shape and craft a fitting image of himself, like Queequeg building his own coffin on the deck of the *Pequod*. And in the act he would renew and redefine his life. His heart had been taken away, and this would be his new heart, with rudder pedals and a silver parachute. This *Stork*, like the German original, would pluck him from a hilltop in a daring escape.

When I came upon the *Stork*, most remarkable to me was not the airplane itself but the childlike temerity of the men who were making it with their hands. I had always thought of airplanes as arising from sophisticated research projects at some secret headquarters out west (or east). Real airplanes were created somewhere else by someone else. And yet here, among the cow pies and cornfields, was an airplane as real as any, being born in this unlikely manger scene, the big airplanes like cows breathing warm life onto the baby. How appropriate that they had called it the *Stork*. And there were Steve's hands, with their stigmata of grease and the scabbed-

* *Ultralight is defined by Federal Aviation Regulation (FAR) Section 103.7. The craft must not weigh more than 254 pounds empty. It can carry no more than 5 gallons of fuel. Its top speed cannot exceed 55 knots, while landing speed must be 24 knots or less. Once a vehicle meets those requirements, it is not considered an airplane, and no license is required to fly it.*

over scrapes and cuts on the scarred knuckles; those very human hands, which trembled when he tried to quit smoking Camels, were raising—out of the elements of the earth by a power just as mysterious as rain—an apparatus that would fly. Their innocence struck me more than their boldness. It was the same innocence, I reckoned, with which someone first hollowed out a log and set forth across the infinite sea, casting adrift without the hint of a question about where to find land again or the tremor of apprehension for a safe return. What we celebrate as heroic vision is more often a deadly naiveté for those who don't make it to the celebration.

"When will it fly?" I asked.

"Maybe April," Steve said.

"Who will fly it first?"

"I suppose I will," he said, not looking up from his work, a Camel dangling from his lips, smoke curling up across his frown, seemingly unimpressed with the notion of sending his one and only body up in the contraption. Certainly greater minds than his and Don's had created machines that failed to fly. Some of them were fairly recent, too. The first P-51 Mustang fighter plane ever built had crashed. The first B-17 bomber ever built had also crashed. The first P-38 Lightning twin-engine fighter ever built had crashed. The first X-15 had crashed, too.

I stood there with the growing sense that I needed to fly. The craving for food or sex, for music or travel or a swim in the sea, is no different. Steve asked me the same question: Would I fly today? But I found myself inexplicably giving him a different answer.

"No. Yeah. Maybe so. I don't know," I said, trying to understand the process that was taking place inside me. Surely I believed that I had a choice in the matter, and surely, somewhat earlier, I thought I had made the choice not to fly in this weather. Perhaps I shared with Don that peculiar compulsion. I found myself telling Steve, "I was thinking about going over to Kenosha and just shooting a couple of approaches."

"Pretty scummy out there today," Steve said, buried in his work within the wing.

"Yeah," I said. "Just right for approaches."

My ten-year-old daughter, Elena, had refused to fly with me until I earned my instrument rating. Since she was five or six, she had been telling me that airline pilots, the kind she flew with on her way to Grandma's house, had instrument ratings, and that if I wanted her to fly with me, I had to get one, too. Consequently, I had earned my instrument rating the previous year, and discovered that I had inherited from my father a flair for flying on the gauges. But it took constant practice to remain sharp, and it was not an endeavor to be taken lightly. Once I got myself up in the clouds, I would have to make a successful approach—a rather complicated technical procedure that led to a glorious moment when I'd burst out of the clouds over the runway. But going into the clouds represents a big commitment: Once up there, I can't stop to close the baggage door if I forgot. I can't take a coffee break or go to the bathroom. If it's bumpy, I can barely stop to wipe the sweat out of my eyes. Sometimes, without explanation, pilots find themselves upside down in the clouds and simply come spinning back to earth. Those crashes are usually written off by the government body that investigates them, the National Transportation Safety Board, as disorientation accidents, although a lot of pilots believe they are the result of that idiotic vacuum pump, the Time Bomb, which fails in flight, taking away the primary reference instruments with no bells or whistles to tell you there's anything wrong. Whatever the cause, thoughts of those accidents always give me pause before I blast off into the clouds in just any old kind of weather, in just any old mood, in just any old bucket of bolts. One instructor told me, "Whenever someone comes to me and says, 'I want to learn instrument flying,' I put them in a big galvanized garbage can, and I give them a flashlight and about a dozen needles to thread, and then I close the lid and start throwing rocks at the garbage can. Because that's what single-engine IFR is like, and anybody who wants to do that on purpose is crazy."

Even so, I found myself drifting back from the shop and standing behind the flight desk thumbing through the schedule to see what was available in the way of IFR airplanes.

I believe that certain people—Lloyd and Steve and Don and I among them—fly once and are never the same again. The question is whether the effect is something particular to the flying or to the compulsion of the person and whether that same person would have, like Toad of Toad Hall, fallen into the thrall of something else had the circumstances been different. Kenneth Grahame in *The Wind in the Willows* described how Toad, overcome by his enchantment for a motorcar, actually stole one:

> The next moment, hardly knowing how it came about, he found he had hold of the handle and was turning it. As the familiar sound broke forth, the old passion seized on Toad and completely mastered him, body and soul. As if in a dream he found himself, somehow, seated in the driver's seat; as if in a dream, he pulled the lever and swung the car round the yard and out through the archway; and, as if in a dream, all sense of right and wrong, all fear of obvious consequences, seemed temporarily suspended. He increased his pace and as the car devoured the street and leaped forth on the high road through the open country, he was only conscious that he was Toad once more, Toad at his best and highest, Toad the terror, the traffic-queller, the Lord of the lone trail, before whom all must give way or be smitten into nothingness and everlasting night. He chanted as he flew, and the car responded with sonorous drone; the miles were eaten up under him as he sped he knew not whither, fulfilling his instincts, living his hour, reckless of what might come to him.

I do not mean to say that anyone who learns to fly an airplane is an addict. For many people it is merely a pastime or a profession, and an airplane is simply a tool, like a halberd or a hypodermic needle. But there are those of us who fly—I mean who really fly a lot—and with a mad insatiable passion and all the time thinking and dreaming of it with that tingling in our fingers and toes, yearning for the feel of the stick and rudder and with a deep socket in our bellies that can only be filled by G-force and swirling mists, and I believe that we perform our feats of daring in the service of altered brain chemistry. It is precisely this *Impulse* that has been the cornerstone of aviation since the very beginning. Why else would someone throw himself off a cliff with a pair of homemade wings strapped to his back, while the certainty of death and the hope of flight struggle for dominion over his leaping heart? The Impulse. A mystical disease of the mind which overwhelms our will and propels us against all good sense not simply into flight but into more and more dangerous and audacious methods of rocketeering, controlled falling, death leaps, and fiery plummets to earth. The Impulse: It's the only explanation.

So it was that I stood on the ramp that snowy foggy day looking longingly at the sky, seriously considering going up "just to see what it's like." I had no destination. Yet I craved flight so desperately that I was on the point of risking all just for the pluperfect sensation of having done it.

I believe it's the same impulse described in Yeats's poem "An Irish Airman Foresees His Death."

Nor law, nor duty bade me fight,
Nor public men, nor cheering crowds.
A lonely impulse of delight
Drove to this tumult in the clouds.

In essence, he's saying, "Hey, all this stuff about politics and war and love of country is all bullshit: I'm doing this because it's fun." Or as the Great Santini said, "It's better than dying of piles." Yeats again, saying the same thing:

I balanced all, brought all to mind,
The years to come seemed waste of breath,
A waste of breath the years behind
In balance with this life, this death.

There are people who become legends by dying and there are people who become legends by living. Amos Buettell, owner of Crown Industries in Hebron, Illinois, did both, and Russell, especially, was one of the keepers of his legend. Russell liked to talk about Amos's Pitts special, which had such a big engine that the exhaust flames burned the Lexan window out of the floor between Amos's feet as he flew in aerobatics competition. Better than any historical figure, Amos conformed to Russell's ideal of the perfect aviation story, and often at lunch or on break, Russell would tilt his head back and look at the ceiling and say, "Boy, Amos could fly." Amos also was the perfect embodiment of the obsessed pilot, perhaps even more so than Lloyd had been. There was a time in the early 1980s when Amos Buettell's presence dominated Galt Airport. There used to be a big framed color photograph of Amos on the wall in the briefing room, but his legend grew so large that someone actually walked away with it.

I found myself nosing around the blue-and-white Cessna 172 Cutlass, taking a fuel sample, tightening little screws that were always coming loose, preparing it for flight. One of the line boys came out and said, "Are you going to take the Cutlass?"

"Yeah, I'm just going over to Kenosha to shoot a couple of approaches." There: I had said it. I was going after all. How could I do it? Why would I do it?

Even as I checked the rudder, the wheel wells, the Pitot tube, I could not walk my way mentally through the logic that had taken me this far, that I was freezing out on the snowy grass, trying to take a collection of bolts into the air on a day such as today. And yet I plunged heedlessly on, swept away, bewitched.

"Okay," Greg said. He was one of the line guys. He began to walk away, calling back across the ramp, "Want me to put you down for two hours?"

"That sounds fine," I said.

I filed my flight plan and rolled down to the end of the runway, still thinking that this might not be such a great idea. As I sat at the end of the runway running up the engine, I half hoped that something would go wrong. If I had a mechanical problem, then I could turn back and not have to go. I'd have something to talk about. There was always apprehension, a longing to go back, a sudden sense of loneliness in the desperation of it all, which laid bare our deeper motives. At the beginning of many flights, I was very eager to take to the air, but even then there was always something held in reserve, some occult sense of peril, well hidden from myself and from those around me.

I think my greatest fear was ice. Dr. Boone Brackett, my instrument instructor, liked to fly to New York to attend the opera. Dr. Brackett was an orthopedic surgeon, a lawyer, and an airline transport pilot, a man well read in science, literature, and the arts, compact, somewhat bald, forceful, quick-witted, sometimes wearing a beard and always with a gruff Texas accent. He had been a combat surgeon in Vietnam and wanted to go to the Gulf War when it started. On a moment's notice, he and his daughter had flown to Germany to see the Berlin Wall come down. His favorite routine involved sewing someone up on Friday night, rushing out to the airport on his motorcycle (which he had once driven to Alaska with his sons), flying his twin engine Baron to New York, taking in a weekend of opera, and then rushing back to Chicago just in time to see patients on Monday morning.

When he first began his shuttle from Chicago to New York, Dr. Brackett had a single-engine Cessna Skylane 182RG (for retractable gear), not very different from the aircraft I was about to fly, and one night he was coming back late on a Sunday, in pretty solid weather with his pretty solid girlfriend, when they entered an area of ice that had not been forecast. Up in the higher levels of the atmosphere, where the temperature is well below freezing, sometimes moisture exists that has not yet come out of the vapor stage, but it is supercooled. The presence of almost any object will cause it to form droplets—a dust particle, for example, or smoke. An airplane wing works nicely, too. Two problems develop rapidly when water, being supercooled, comes into solid existence as ice just as it touches the airplane wing. Water weighs a lot, for one thing. And ice works like magic clay, molding and shaping a new wing, changing its aerodynamic characteristics. In fact, a nicely curved wing that flies can turn into a square wing that doesn't fly in a matter of one minute in heavy icing conditions.

So it was that Dr. Brackett flew into some deadly place over Pennsylvania. He had begun to notice that he needed more power just to stay level. The airplane was slowing down. He added power and nose-up trim to compensate. Sometimes ice can form in the carburetor and close off the throat like diphtheria, so he pulled the carburetor heat to keep the engine from coughing. He looked out the window at the wing struts and felt his heart cease and then begin again as he realized that his airplane was being transformed into a gay and decorative confection: Ice had formed a frosting that winked and sparkled every time his wingtip strobes popped off in the murky nighttime clouds. All at once a chunk let loose from the spinning propeller and exploded on his windshield. The unbalanced propeller shook the airplane so hard Dr. Brackett thought the engine would come loose from its mounts, and then another chunk hit the fuselage like a cannon shell. "It was like we were taking flak," he told me.

In the end, he had the throttle pushed all the way to the fire wall, and they were still going down. That was when he realized that he had no approach plates for Pennsylvania. An approach plate shows how to line up on the electronic beam that leads us down to the runway. ("Well, I didn't intend to land in Pennsylvania. I intended to fly *over* it to Midway and go home!") He called the air traffic controller on the radio and told him that he was in trouble and that he needed an airport with an ILS, an instrument landing system. The weather was low, and he had to shoot an instrument approach blind if he was going to have any hope of landing on concrete and not on the side of a hill in the forest. One thing was certain: He was coming down.

"That air traffic controller saved my life," Dr. Brackett told me. "Do you know what he said that saved my life?"

I said I could not imagine.

"He read me the frequency of the ILS and turned me onto a course that would intercept it." Then Dr. Brackett's radio antennas iced up so that he couldn't hear the controller. The ILS is a radio beam, like an extension of the runway in the air, and in order to fly down that beam, the on-board receiver must be tuned to the correct frequency. "I wrote the frequency on my leg, because I had already dropped my clipboard I was so nervous. I dialed in that ILS and rode it down with the stall warning horn blasting and the power on full, and I honest-to-God didn't think I was going to make it. But when we broke out, there we were, right over the numbers, and when I landed about eight hundred pounds of ice fell off onto the runway. I mean, we were *loaded*." After that, they taxied to the ramp and took a look at the plane. It was encased in ice. "I couldn't believe the thing flew at all," he told me. "The ramp guy came out and took one look at the airplane, and he said, 'Did you land like that?' I said, 'Yeah, but we left half the ice out on the runway.' "

"Then what did you do?" I asked.

"Oh, I had 'em haul it into a hangar and melt off the ice. Then we took off and finished the trip."

Dr. Brackett figured that the worst was over. "How bad

could one trip get?" he asked me. After that, sometimes when I'd call him in the operating room, he'd answer the phone by saying, "Lone Star Airlines."

So it was as I sat on the end of Runway 27 at Galt, preparing to cast myself into the clouds that wintery day, that I thought, Well, if Dr. Brackett can do it, then I can do it.

I checked the magnetos, and they were normal. I pulled the carburetor heat to make sure the RPM's dropped, indicating that heated air was being fed to the venturi. I turned on the heater for the Pitot tube. I checked the propeller; its pitch is controlled by a knob on the instrument panel. I checked the vacuum pump, the Time Bomb, the only source of power for the gyroscopic instruments that are meant to keep us level in the clouds. The attitude indicator, for example, displays an airplane that moves in reference to an artificial horizon line. Whatever the make-believe airplane in the round glass docs, thc rcal airplanc docs, too. It's so simple that a child could do it. So why do people get killed trying to fly the artificial airplane?

Sometimes the Time Bomb goes off and the vacuum system fails. Then the gyroscope winds down and the little airplane tips slowly and sadly over, and we don't notice, because we've become hypnotized by the drone and the darkness and the swirling mist outside. We innocently follow the little airplane over, over, tipping, tipping, down and down, failing to notice that our compass is going around and around as our airspeed increases. Then it's too late; we're in a graveyard spiral. Suddenly we get all excited and pull back to stop the spiral, but we're going so fast that we pull the wings right off the airplane.

By and by I ran out of things to do on the ground, so I took off. The cornfield stubble and fenceposts whipped past on my right, and the rows of parked airplanes snapped by on my left. Eventually I noticed that the nose wheel was trying to come off the ground, and I lifted gently back on the yoke, and the airplane wobbled into a crabbing, lurching, wind-blown ascent.

I reached for the landing-gear lever, a little toy wheel on a metal stud, and lifted it out and up and listened while the clumsy wheels made their slow crunch-thunk-hammering transit into the belly. I glanced out the window to see that the wheels were gone and lifted away over Art Galt's yellow house and the pine trees at the next-door farm across Greenwood Road and saw the clouds coming at me fast. I set the power at twenty-five inches of manifold pressure and 2,500 RPM. Then I put my attention inside the cockpit and set the little artificial airplane in the round glass window for about 10 degrees nose-up. I spun the trim wheel to hold the plane in that attitude and glanced up to watch myself vanish into a cloud. The thin and swirling mist reminded me of the white fatty fabric of flesh seen through a microscope. I could see through it into a darkness beyond. The spaces closed around me. I found myself in a rushing whiteness that took my breath away, even though I could feel nothing, not even a bump, not even a change in sound as I plunged in. It was as if I entered the ghost of a living white tissue. I felt myself disappearing. I felt a chill as my body came apart, molecule by molecule. I can only look at the whiteness for so long, and then I have to return to the world of logic and order presented by the instrument panel or all will be lost in the delirious transubstantiation of the clouds. My brother Philip calls it Rapture of the Shallow.

The courage is not in the flying—never in the flying. It is in accepting ourselves as this small in a cloud so large and accepting the cloud as so small in the larger sky and the sky so small in the region of space we call home.

Now I hunched over the gauges, keeping the little airplane level, watching the directional gyro to keep on course, and scanning my altitude, airspeed, vertical speed, occasionally glancing at the engine gauges to see that everything was in the green. I called the air traffic controller to open my flight plan to Kenosha. "Chicago Center, Cessna five one nine two Victor just departed Galt Airport, out of one point five for three thousand."

A woman's voice reported back, "Cessna nine two Victor, radar contact, three west of Galt, climb and maintain three thousand, turn right zero six zero, vectors for the ILS."

"Nine two Victor," I said, "right to zero six zero and up to three." I rolled into the turn, watching the little airplane bank inside the glass like a child's Christmas toy that snows when it's turned upside down. As I turned, the directional gyro spun clockwise to north and then northeast. I perceived a brightening in my environment and looked up to see what was happening. I was simply moving closer to the top of the cloud layer, where more sunlight filtered through. I was like a fish swimming from the depths of the ocean toward the surface of the sea. But I knew from the controller's instructions that I would never reach sunlight; the tops were at 6,000 feet. There was no point in going higher for the short flight, only twenty-two nautical miles, or ten minutes in the Gutless Cutlass. In fact, Kenosha's ILS localizer went more or less over Galt, and when we practiced approaches in nice weather, we flew this beam right from takeoff.

The controller cleared me for the approach before I had gone much farther than the Wisconsin border; and by the time I had reached my assigned altitude, I was already setting up for the descent, like the shuttle from New York to Washington. I slowed the airplane by putting the nose up and reducing the power. When I reached the final approach fix, I put the lazy crunch-thunk-hammering landing gear down and began my descent down the glide slope—a second radio beam. The localizer provides lateral direction; the glide slope provides vertical guidance. The system is so accurate that I could descend to the exact spot on the runway where big white lines had been painted and then defaced by black tire marks. On the instrument panel, that process is managed by keeping two needles centered on an inscribed

"O," which we call the Donut. One needle moves left and right, the other up and down—localizer, glide slope. The trick to a good approach is to have everything set up well ahead of schedule and then simply sit there, monitoring the needles, changing as little as possible. Pilots who like to fiddle with things make lousy approaches. Lazy pilots who like to watch the world go by tend to make nice smooth approaches. Most really good pilots move slowly all the time. You can see it in their walk. Their hands hang limp at their sides. Their heads turn slowly when they look left and right. In the clouds, a pilot can induce vertigo simply by tilting his head back to throw an overhead switch. Then the inner ear suddenly and insistently begins saying, "We're upside down. No, really. We're truly, for real upside down—hey! Wake up! Your instruments are all broken and you'd better turn this stupid plane right side up, or we're going to die!" And sometimes we listen to that evil voice. And we turn the plane, only to discover that now we're *really* upside down and we don't know how to fix it. The instruments don't work upside down.

Like Zen monks, we try to learn this essential lesson of life: Start slow and taper off. No sudden movements. Always believe the instruments. Of course, believing them is what kills us when the vacuum system fails, because then the instruments *are* lying. It's a cunning, baffling, and devious system.

I tried to concentrate on not doing anything as the white world swirled around me and the engine noise, now reduced to something that seemed like quiet, churned along. I went through my checklists, routines designed to ensure that I was ready for the world below. I watched my altimeter revolve like a clock ticking time in reverse. There is an Einsteinian quality to the ride down a glide slope in the clouds. Nothing moves, and yet I was clipping along at better than a hundred miles an hour. I seemed suspended in time and space. I had no faith that I was going to reach some sort of reality, a destination—certainly I didn't believe that there was an airport down there. I was in the white tissue of a beast I could not describe, seeing molecules of cartilage flinging past the window, cruising through its sinews, screwing through the web of its flesh in my smoking machine.

I felt a jolt. Sometimes there are just jolts, but we're never enlightened as to their meaning or origin. We say they're currents in the air, but they could just as easily be tendons we cut as we screw our way through muscle and bone.

There was one last consideration to my instrument approach before I could land. There is a minimum altitude beyond which we can't descend unless the runway is in sight. Yes, after all the wizardry and gadgets, the radar and technology, it all comes down to the eyeball, and that's true whether I'm in my friendly little Cessna or a Boeing 747 lumbering home from London. If I reached that altitude and I could not see the runway or its lights, then I would have to miss the approach. I'd have to pour on the power and climb back up and go somewhere else.

Most ILS approaches have a minimum altitude 200 feet above the runway, which is extremely low, since a typical descent rate is 500 feet per minute or 100 feet every twelve seconds. At 200 feet, we have less than half a minute to make a complete change in plans, reverse our direction from down to up, and get out of there safely. If we are off the localizer to one side or the other, we are closer to obstructions than we ought to be. If we have botched the approach and we are not near the runway, we have no idea what might be beneath us. As a consequence, part of preparing to arrive involves preparing to leave.

As I flew down the ILS, I wondered about the weather. I had to get back to Galt. (I realize that makes no sense, going to all that trouble just to turn around and go back, but that's the essence of general aviation.) Galt Airport has an instrument approach, but it is a cruder style of guidance called a VOR approach, which provides lateral information only. If the clouds were low enough, I might not be able to return at all. And if Kenosha was below its minimums, then I'd have to go somewhere else where the weather was better. The perfect flight is like the perfect crime: It doesn't exist except in novels.

The altimeter unwound down and down, showing 500 feet, now 400 feet, now 300 feet, and I felt my heart sinking as I tried to decide what I would do. It's easy to see how the elements of a bad decision can assemble themselves out of our idle musings: I don't have my toothbrush, I need to get home, I'm going to break out of the clouds any minute now, I'll just go a little lower . . . Out of the corner of my eye I saw a flashing light. I looked up from the instruments. The white fog burned my eyes as my strobe light flashed from the tip of my wing. I looked back at the gauges. That flash again. Was it my lights or something on the ground? I looked down at what I hoped was earth, and all at once the mists whirled into a vortex and split like fabric.

It looked like an electric rabbit running away. It vanished into ragged cloud, then reappeared, then ran away again. It happened over and over. The flesh of the beast unraveled around me. I was caught in a tissue of gray for a moment as the lights screamed out their directions to me, pointing, pointing, pointing the way, and then I sprung free of the vapor and came dripping out of the clouds over the sequenced flashing lights of Runway 6 at Kenosha Airport. It was as if the ether itself had sweated out a black cinder, and I rode it down toward the steaming earth.

I was in a kind of dun netherworld of weak light and misting rain that streaked my windshield and teared back toward the sides of the aircraft, as if my pretty blue Cutlass were crying with joy for our good fortune to have arrived at Kenosha, Wisconsin, where we had no business being on a day such as today, where we would do nothing more than drink a cup of coffee and take off again. Oh, joy! What a stupid idea!

I controlled the nearly irresistible urge to push the control wheel over and dive for the runway. The ILS went almost to the ground, and we were meant to follow it all the way down, the better to avoid pointy things sticking up at us. I left the airplane alone, and it did quite nicely without my help, flying all the way past the houses and farm fields and the rainy winter world, where it was obviously warmer by the lake, for this was definitely water on my windshield and not ice. We squatted over the white fixed-distance markers and I pulled back on the yoke to stop our descent rate. The airplane skimmed along above the concrete for a while and then gently touched down.

I'd had a grand plan to make many approaches and practice holding patterns, and it had been all very glorious and elaborate in my mind when I'd conceived it, but I abandoned all that and launched again without delay.

This is the way it goes sometimes: I had flown no more than five minutes out from Kenosha toward home when the clouds parted and a ray of light shone down on me as if I'd become part of a Rousseau painting I once saw in Paris: a scene of 1907, a Wright Flyer just over the river where fishermen were fishing, *Les Pêcheurs à la Ligne*. That dragonfly had barely hatched, and Henri Rousseau caught it on a cotton canvas not unlike the one that covered its wings. He had caught, too, in the tipping, precarious angle of the ship, the reckless, dire, and urgent impulse of the whole thing, which was opaque to so many people, just as a craving for heroin would be opaque to most.

I could see the winterscape below. I could even see in the distant vapors the traces of Wonder Lake on the shores of which Galt Airport lay. There was a hole in the clouds the size of McHenry County, and I flew within the grace of it, looking out the window at the ice-fishing shanties on Wonder Lake.

Closer to the airport, I passed over Art Galt's land, dotted with lakes. There were measureless sources of water here, pushing up from within the soggy earth beneath the ice.

About 15,000 years ago, when the glaciers melted, they left a carpeting of gravel and rocks several hundred feet thick all across that area. And in that retreat, low hills of stone were dropped in steaming heaps like so much dung from a dying animal. Now it is possible to climb them and view the whole area from the treetops, just as we do when we lift off in an airplane, that first delicious glimpse when the mantle of the earth drops away and we see what seems like the whole of creation and we are filled with that dangerous illusion of elation and wonder at our own sovereignty.

As I banked into the pattern, I could see people fishing on the frozen eastern half of Lake Vera, a pond Art Galt created with a bulldozer from a natural spring pushing up out of the ground. He named it after his wife. As I banked over the snowy scene, I saw a child fall on the ice, and once again I was struck by my intoxicating perspective. On the ground we rarely see more than a block or so in any direction, and that which our vision encompasses is small, close, discreet, and personal. As soon as we lift away and clear the tops of the trees, our view opens to encompass whole counties full of people and houses, rivers and fires, and all their heroic calamity in a single glance. Here is a riding ring where people do dressage in the summer; and there is a house burning down; and there a deer runs across the open road, barely missing a truck. No wonder Satan sought to tempt Christ by taking him to a high place and showing him the view.

In the office, in response to questions about how it went, I shrugged nonchalantly and said, "Oh, it was all right. Nothing to it. No big deal." But I lied, of course, for effect. It was the deal of the century. I had gone when I didn't have to go, and I had no idea why. It seems that something more powerful than I was had hold of me, and it left me with the gnawing, uneasy sense that although I had come down out of the clouds, the danger had not passed.

FOUR

NO JOY

THE NUMBER-ONE hangar was just outside the flight office. Most of the time it was closed, but not long after I first came to Galt, I saw a gray-haired gentleman roll away the big metal doors. I came closer; hiding in the shadows I thought I saw a blue airplane with stars on it, and I moved closer, wondering why an airplane would have stars on it. The man grabbed hold of the propeller, like a farmer taking a bull by the nose, and with a great effort he dragged it out into the sunlight. He might as well have rolled away the stone on Easter morning. Even though it was the humblest of all the sport airplanes, the first time I saw John Fountain push his Bellanca Citabria out of the hangar I was mesmerized. It had the lines of an antique, sitting back on its tail wheel, high wings attached kitelike over a kind of guppy-shaped fuselage. It seemed friendly somehow, eager to fly, and not at all forbidding, as some aerobatics aircraft were. There was something frivolous and childlike in the conceit of having put stars on its tail, as if it had been designed for play. It was sky blue, which the manufacturer called Bahama Blue.

For looking at his airplane, I almost missed the man who owned it. Except for the small detail of wanting to fly upside down, John was a conventional man. At seventy, he was retired from his career as a bank officer. He and his wife, Mary, lived in Crystal Lake, a fifteen-minute drive from Galt Airport. He drove a Lincoln Continental and golfed with pretty serious intent. The difference between him and everybody else who fit that description was that John had flown Corsairs with the Marines in World War II, and somewhere along the line he tested positive for the inverted flight virus. There was no cure. John told me, "My wife regards my flying with about as much relish as she would regard my having a mistress," which was oddly reminiscent of what Nancy Hughes had told me about Lloyd's love affair.

I began to lie in wait for him. Off and on for several months I cadged rides. I rode in the back while he flew, and now and then he let me handle the controls. I was amazed that anyone could perform such maneuvers with an airplane; it seemed as if by thinking alone, John was able to cause the airplane to screw itself into the sky and dance like one of those thirteen-year-old Russian gymnasts.

One of the first times I went up with him, he handed me a little white three-by-five card and said, "Why don't you read me these figures while I'm flying so I don't have to look down."

The card was scribbled with hieroglyphics. It showed angles, curves, lines, and arrows, all filled with a mysterious urgency of motion, laid across a grid and numbered from one through ten.

"What is it?" I asked.

"It's Aresti Key," he said. "It's a system of cryptographic notations developed to describe the figures for competition." And he explained each one: spin, Immelmann, 270-

degree turn, Split-S, Half Reverse Cuban Eight . . . I sat in the back seat studying the scribbles as John took off and climbed out over Galt Airport.

Suddenly I looked up from my card and found myself upside-down over midfield about half a mile above the airport, stupidly trying to read those nonsensical words—Immelmann, 270 turn, Split-S—to the elderly banker in the front of the plane, all the while solemnly hoping that he knew what he was doing.

I looked out through the plexiglass roof of the airplane. I hung from my seat belt. During aerobatics one isn't nicely and effortlessly carried in those unusual attitudes of flight. That stuff hurts. The belt cut across my lap in a vicious way. I tried to plant my feet firmly on the floor, but they kept falling away and folding my knees around my cheeks. I saw the numbers come into view: 27 painted in white on the end of the runway directly beneath us. A little Cessna landed far below.

We flew along level, inverted, as I watched the Cessna taxi to the ramp. For a moment I forgot where I was, hung there like a carcass on a sling. John closed the throttle, pulled the stick, and the nose cut the horizon. We were pointed at the middle of the runway, the wind noise rising as we gained speed.

"Half Reverse Cuban Eight," I said, and John began pulling out of the dive, harder, harder, harder. I felt my hands and head grow heavy with centrifugal force; acceleration robbed my brain of blood. Finally we were horizontal, upright. I sat once more, a feeling of relief about my midsection where the belt had tried to chop me in half. John flew straight and level for only a moment, then pulled rapidly to a 45-degree upward angle, rocketing toward the sky. On the way up, he unexpectedly rolled inverted and continued up, up, finally pulling over the top, as if to make a loop. My knees hit me in the cheeks, and then my feet fell heavily to the floor once more, as we returned to upright flight. Now we crossed directly over the runway from west to east. I could see Wonder Lake not far ahead.

There followed a loop, a Half Cuban Eight with two points of a four-point roll, a hammerhead turn, and a 90-degree turn. I had reached the tenth maneuver on my card. "Roll," I said, and the improbable but undeniable fact of earth and sky switching places seemed so outrageously funny that I laughed out loud. In subsequent years, as I learned to fly those same figures, first from John and then from other instructors, I gave many people rides just as John had given me. I learned that it wasn't unusual to hear the passenger cry out for joy involuntarily in the middle of a figure. One passenger asked, "Why do you bother with sex?"

As in so many disciplines, what looks simplest is often the most difficult to do well. The roll seems easy. The plane simply rotates around its longitudinal axis. One wing goes down while the other goes up, and around we go. All the while, the nose stays pointing in the same direction, and the airplane returns to level flight without a bobble. When I was ignorant of aerobatics, I could not imagine what shoulder-wrenching, gut-snapping work it was to hog that airplane into submission during a roll.

One instructor told me, "The roll is everything. If you can do the roll well, you can do anything." I had no idea what he was talking about until I began practicing seriously and realized that I could not roll the stupid airplane. Not really. Not correctly. Not well. Not gracefully. I'd come out with the nose pointing 15 degrees to one side. I'd lose 300 feet of altitude without having any idea where it had gone.

Learning the roll made me realize that I had flown for ten years without understanding flight or the controls that made it possible. As the plane tips over, it begins to fall from the sky; like a cup brimming over, the wing spills its precious lift. The controls seem to forget what they were meant to do. Left is right, up is down, and sideways is a shuddering cry for help.

The only cue to safety in the roll is the relationship between the pilot's eye and the horizon, the union of earth and ether. We don't usually see the horizon when we are on the earth, because the earth is cluttered with trees, houses, trucks, vending machines, and marching bands. But once we are clear of the clutter, the horizon is always inexplicably at our eye level, whether we are standing on a roof or flying in the stratosphere. It rises to meet us and always tells us, if we look carefully, whether we are falling or climbing or level.

If we must see the horizon to roll, and if the horizon is obscured near the ground, then a roll near the ground is a dangerous maneuver indeed. And yet year after year, time after time, pilots are tempted to try that victory roll. It looks easy. It feels like it's going to be easy. It is not.

John Fountain sold me half ownership of Citabria 36250. He showed me basic maneuvers, and we practiced together. I hired an acrobatics instructor to help me take the next step: to polish each maneuver and then to put them together into a sequence.

Bob Murray was a young Air Force A-10 pilot who had his own instruction service at Rockford. He was short and well built and had dark hair and a soft, ironic smile. I always thought he was laughing at me, but it was just his manner. His circumstance was that of an acolyte or a monk in his hermitage. Murray slept on a futon in a neatly kept little room in the back of an airplane hangar at the Rockford, Illinois, Airport.

Murray's life was narrowly defined. He walked a few feet to the ramp to get an airplane. He flew away somewhere (or as with me, nowhere). He landed again and taxied up to the place where he lived, and then he walked a few feet back inside to eat or sleep.

I felt I was doing badly from the start. As we sped down the runway for takeoff, I lifted the tail, and the gyroscopic effect of the spinning propeller turned us left. I countered with right rudder. I was nervous, because Murray was watching, and I wanted to do well, so I overcompensated, and we went wobbling and wavering in a drunken S-turn down the runway and finally struggled into flight. I was feeling vigorously maladroit.

The practice area was next to the Byron Nuclear Power Plant, which sent a brilliant and stupendous white cloud of steam thousands of feet into the atmosphere, so that I had the uncomfortable sensation that I was at any moment about to be swallowed by that great white nimbus of foam. Murray asked me to do a few loops and rolls, and it seemed that I went wallowing all over the sky. He asked me for a spin and a Cuban Eight, and by the time he was prepared to comment, I felt convinced that I had acquitted myself very poorly indeed. He sat behind me, so I couldn't see his expression, but it would not have betrayed his feelings anyway; he had a narrow affect. Now when I heard him, I heard him through the intercom headset, all frosted with static. We had not stopped our maneuvering; Murray had simply started his assessment of my flying in the middle of a figure, so I was both listening and attempting to fly at the same time.

"Well," he said, "judging by the way you're flying . . ." He paused, and I cringed, expecting to hear the verdict pronounced: *You should never fly aerobatics again.* I was drenched in sweat, attempting to keep the aircraft under control through what I was certain was turning out to be a pathetic and ungainly L-shaped loop. Finally the words passed through that fine wire that connected us, and I heard not my imagination but his real voice say, "I see no reason that you can't compete this year."

I was at the top of the loop, upside down, and looking back over my head, past the top of Murray's head, to the far horizon above us, trying to level my wings so that the plane ran around the circle like a toy on a track. As I came down the other side of the loop, accelerating rapidly, pulling off the power to avoid racing the engine, I heard him say, musing to himself, "You should compete in the first contests of the season."

I was pulling now, pulling with both hands, trying to find that sweet spot in space, to reconnect with my own turbulent trail and hit the bump on the bottom that would tell me that my loop had been round. Wait a minute, I thought. The first contest of the season was only ninety days away. Besides, I was afraid to try those maneuvers alone. What if I got stuck upside down?

I went home trembling at the thought of doing those maneuvers by myself, never mind in competition. I remembered my first lessons, my first solos, my first cross-country flights alone. The first time I flew to Galt it was in a Cessna 150, and I had not flown in eight years. I considered getting the airplane safely on the ground at the end of the fifteen-minute journey to be a large and exhilarating experience, and I wanted to go to a party and tell everyone about it. Now it had been some years since those nervous days, but I was brought right back to that level of inexperience by my attempts to enter the world of acrobatics. I could not imagine that I might go upside down alone and not perish for my audacity. I thought if I got up there, inverted, I would never get out. I would become mesmerized and simply plunge to the earth. And of course I always thought of my father (The Captain, we called him) and his spinning plunge to earth.

On the way home I saw a boy on a bicycle deliberately leave the smooth and comfortable roadway to ride into a drainage ditch. On the way down, he picked up enough speed to send him zooming up the other side. He turned back at the top of his arc and pointed the bike into the ditch again. Once more he made the figure, and then again and again. All at once I saw that he was making Lazy Eights just the way I do warming up for aerobatics practice in the Citabria. And I remembered doing that same maneuver when I was ten years old back in San Antonio, Texas. I recalled how my bike had become part of me—how I knew, as if it had nerves, where every edge and curve of it was as I sped through narrow spaces. The tips of my handlebars were as sensitive as the whiskers of a cat—I never hit anything accidentally. And now I was trying to make my airplane that sensitive, too.

During my second lesson I made it through the Sportsman sequence. The International Aerobatics Club prescribes sequences of figures to be flown at contests. Sportsman is the usual level for beginners, but it was brutal. There was no time to think. One figure followed the next with blinding speed, and I was dripping sweat when we were done. Murray taught me to use right rudder in the left roll during inverted flight. It fixed my disconcerting tendency to fall into an inverted spin at the top of an Immelmann.

That afternoon I went home, and my five-year-old daughter, Amelia, asked me to teach her to ride her bicycle. As she worked at it, I realized for the first time that her bike with its training wheels and my trainer, too, both had stars on them.

Later that evening I was helping Amelia to learn numbers. She told me, "I hate four. I can never draw four."

I said, "I know. I can never draw an Immelmann," which is half a loop followed by half a roll.

I said I had an idea about the four that might help her.

"What?" she asked, and there was a challenge in her voice.

"Make an L," I said.

"L is easy," she said, and she drew one on the page.

"Now put a vertical line through the bottom part of the L," I said. She did. Her face lit up with a smile. It had worked. She had made an effortless figure four.

Amelia grinned at me. I grinned at her. We were fearless.

One day Bob Murray and I had a short-field landing contest. The idea was to see who could get the airplane stopped in the shortest distance. We were using Murray's Piper Arrow, a complex airplane with retractable gear and flaps. (There was a handle like a parking brake between our seats, and by pulling it up, the pilot could extend the flaps, providing more lift in slow flight.) I went first and managed to get the heavy airplane stopped on the big runway at Rockford before reaching the first taxiway intersection. I looked over and grinned at Murray; he would have to do something dramatic to beat me. I sat back then as he flew the approach. I felt smug and secure in my victory as I watched him. He'd practically have to crash to beat me. He came in full flaps, balanced on the edge of a stall, way behind the power curve, and as he flared for landing, he grabbed that handle and dumped off all the flaps. With our extra lift gone, we dropped like a stone from about five feet up. It sounded like garbage cans being thrown down a fire escape, and Murray stood on the brakes. It was a hard and ugly landing, and we came to an abrupt and ungainly stop in a cloud of blue smoke, but it was shorter than anything I'd done. I had concentrated on making my short landing *pretty*, and now I understood his lesson: This was American Zen. Winning counts. Everything else is bullshit.

Weeks went by, and I practiced hard. Murray seemed able to identify my mistakes and tell me the hand or foot movement that would correct them. Maneuvers that had baffled me before fell into place, like Amelia drawing a four. I began to gain confidence in my handling of the airplane. My rolls were staying on a point, and I was holding altitude. My loops were getting round, and my wings were staying level throughout. I had learned to recover from a spin on a precise predetermined heading. I had begun to talk about buying a Pitts Special for more performance, more competitive edge, and anyway, my friends Gerry and Howard had them. I wanted to be one of the gang.

Murray had smiled that thin smile and allowed that perhaps I ought to consider flying the Citabria for a while longer. "It'll make you a better pilot," he said. I understood that he was saying as politely as he could, "You're not ready." Even so, he could probably see the wild look in my eye and was no doubt afraid that I might go out and buy a Pitts on impulse, so one day he took me aside on the ramp and said, "I have to give you this speech. I wouldn't feel right if I didn't say this to you."

"What is it?" I asked. The weather had grown warm, and we sat beside his hangar, watching his cat torture a ground squirrel in the shady spot beneath an airplane's wing. The cat had no interest in eating it, nor even in killing it. It was a game.

"I had this student last year," Murray said, leaning back in a lawn chair and putting his feet up. "He was a level-headed guy. He was a good pilot, serious, cautious, you know. I trusted him. I trained him in our two-place Pitts, and he bought a single-seat Pitts to compete in. Well, a month or so after he got it, he happened into De Kalb Airport—you know De Kalb, about thirty miles south of here? He stopped for fuel, I think. And the guys at the pump, the line boys and such, they were talking to him, saying, 'Hey, do something on takeoff. Do some stuff for us.' You know the kind of things people say when they see you come in with a Pitts. Well, he took off and tried to pull a victory roll right after takeoff." Murray's student had taxied to the far end of the runway to take off back toward the pumps, where the line boys were waiting excitedly to see what he'd do. "He crashed and killed himself right there on the ramp, practically in their laps. And I can't explain it. I mean, I know *you* wouldn't do something like that, because you're a smart guy, and you seem level-headed, but I had to tell you that, you know what I'm saying? I mean, he was level-headed, too." Murray stripped a long piece of grass and put it between his teeth. He tilted his head back and looked at the sky through his Ray-Ban Aviators. "God. Imagine saying that to somebody, you know, asking somebody to do a roll for you, and then seeing them coming right at you and crash at your feet and then watching his flesh bubble off the skeleton. Those boys must have felt terrible. Just awful."

I told Murray that I'd never do a roll on takeoff. But of

course what I thought was, I'll never do it until I get good enough. It's The Impulse again, guarded like the grail, in the secret heart of so many pilots. Long before the Wright Brothers, people were willing to die for the nameless essence of a particular flight. Early flight was often nothing more than hopeful falling as they leaped inexplicably from cliffs on sunny days when they could have lived peacefully on the ground instead. The story is as old as Icarus. Pilots may be driven by dreams, but they are governed by physics.

The whole sequence had begun to come together, and I had made two decisions. First, I was going to Grain Valley, Missouri, to learn how to fly a Pitts at The Great Planes Aerobatics School with the best instructor in the nation, John Morrissey. And secondly, I was going to try to make it to an early-season contest in Texas. I called the contest director down in Edna, Texas, to make arrangements to fly there. He told me to look for him when I landed, but he said, "Once things get started, I'll be jumpin' around like a queer in a weenie factory."

One day I took my father up to Oshkosh, Wisconsin. I climbed to 10,000 feet. We watched the details of our world grow faint as we climbed more and more slowly toward the pulsing blue-white of the sky. I felt afraid, holding my father's life there, as if I dangled him by the end of that control stick, that piece of plumber's pipe, so high above the earth. I felt that to swing him so defiantly in the face of Fate was perhaps too much, given his history. Something had pursued him, too, and it had caught him when he was a crackerjack pilot in his early twenties, caught him and tore him to pieces.

We found Paul Poberezny in the big gold Experimental Aircraft Association hangar preparing to make the first test flight of a newly built replica of the *Spirit of St. Louis*. It was largely made out of sheets of polished aluminum, and where the workers had bothered to make the corners as pressed-straight as the collar of a brand-new white dress shirt, they had also buffed into the surface a pattern of overlapping circles, to give the whole thing an art deco appearance appropriate to the time of its original design. The floor of the cockpit was plywood, but it had been sanded and varnished so carefully it seemed as extravagant and rich as parquet. The crew was putting the finishing touches on it when my father and I arrived.

My father and Paul, the founder of EAA, were about the same age, and they shook hands and immediately did what those aviators do: began to talk about some wicked old airplane they both knew. It was there in the hangar at Oshkosh, watching him talk to Paul, that I finally understood what I was seeing. It was only because he was my father that I hadn't recognized it before. I always recognized it easily in perfect strangers. My father had that certain fighter pilot stance and that certain fighter pilot slowness I had come to know so well. He had not actually made it to the fighters, but that was his intended destiny, and he'd flown twenty-five combat missions, which must have counted for something. Moreover, he had come closer to death than any of the other aviators I knew, except the actual dead ones. No, he definitely had the walk, and he had the talk, and he'd had The Impulse, too, before it was burned out of him on that last mission.

Suddenly I saw my father as a man apart from me, apart from the family, a figure out on a ramp squinting at the sky, assessing the wisdom of movement, and holding still on account of his wisdom. He told me that the most terrifying flight of his life had not been in combat but had come after the war, when a young DC-3 pilot flew him back from England, ignoring my father's warnings about thunderstorms approaching over the Atlantic. They flew right through them, and the wings of that old Douglas prop plane made great excursions up and down as the airplane threatened to shake itself apart. My father thought, What a crude burlesque of history it would be to die now, lost at sea, after surviving that unimaginable fall from the heavens.

I had arranged my flight with Paul beforehand, but he was busy with his *Spirit of St. Louis* test flight and had misunderstood what I wanted. He thought I wanted to fly his plane, when in fact I wanted to fly with *him*. It was the same sort of misunderstanding my father and I had been having for forty years.

Jerry Walbrun, the legal counsel for EAA, took me up in North American 51D, which had the word *Paul* painted on the side and *Col. Paul Poberezny pilot* painted underneath the canopy rail. Just before my flight, as I shrugged into my parachute, I walked past my father and asked, "Would you rather go, Dad? I've already flown a Mustang."

He said, "No, you go ahead," and I understood that The Impulse was truly gone for him.

I strapped into the back of the P-51 Mustang, and we blasted off out of Oshkosh. Jerry had been giving other people rides all day, and he was kind of inured to it. Besides, he had owned a Mustang for a while and had put 1,000 hours on it. It was maroon, he said. He sold it. The man who bought it crashed and died in it. It was such a common Mustang story that I didn't even react when I heard it. After World War II, the government had sold so many surplus Mustangs (about $1,500 each, then) that it wasn't even very interesting if a pilot simply bought one and killed himself in it in a kind of *ordinary* fashion. A pilot had to do something really spectacularly stupid to get on the books. One man removed the auxiliary gas tank behind the pilot's seat and placed a platform there. He put his three-year-old child in his lap and put his two other children and his wife on the platform in the back, with only one seat belt among them. Then he flew to 20,000 feet in bad weather and became hypoxic from lack of oxygen. His P-51 dove straight down and went into transsonic flight, disintegrating before it reached the earth.

P-51s were crashing at a rate of eight per year, which is to say that flying in a P-51 could be considered one of the most dangerous rides you can take, if you are prone to statistical thinking. But I looked at it another way: I'd better get in all the rides I could while there were still a few left. Either way, I observed with an oddly detached curiosity that I didn't mind at all the idea of dying in there. It would, I thought, be a fine way to die, given that death, like landing, is mandatory. I thought of people saying, "Yeah, he died in a Mustang," and I thought, Well, better that than "He got hit by a gravel truck."

But Jerry's ride was uneventful and workmanlike. He flew out west of Wittman Field and performed a few loops, barrel rolls, and so on. Then on the way back in he requested a high-speed fly-by from the tower and a military overhead approach. Jerry dove the airplane until the airspeed indicator read 350 knots, and then we exploded down into the pattern, past the tower in a blur, rattling windows, and we were on the ground before I could say, "Did you remember to put your gear down?"

We stood around the ramp, Paul, Jerry, my father, and I, and now we were joined by a little man I had almost missed as he stepped out of the Mustang when Jerry had taxied up earlier. His name was Eppo, and he had flown across the North Atlantic in a bathtub. It was the first transatlantic flight in an ultralight, and from the photos it looked just like a bathtub. Jerry had taken him for the same zoo-train tour of loops and rolls in the Mustang, and Eppo was beside himself with joy. Here was a man who had performed a feat of navigation akin to Lindbergh's, a man who had faced death in every form that an aviator might imagine, cold and watery and windy and lonely, and yet he was dazzled by a few rolls over this bland Wisconsin farmland.

As my father and I returned to Galt, an hour's flight south, we watched intersecting chevrons of contrails turning red in the western sky. The railroad tracks that once criss-crossed the continent in rusting lines of steel, now rusted in the stratosphere as evening descended.

I had enjoyed being out there on the ramp talking with the heroes. They were bound together by their willingness to do something that no sane person would do, and I stupidly wanted to be just like them.

FIVE

GOLDEN HANDS

I ARRIVED BEFORE 8 A.M. to find Art Galt playing tennis with "Doc" Francis P. Klocek, a dentist from Woodstock. It was 24 degrees, and they both wore parkas. A large tear in the middle of the net had been crudely woven together with a length of clothes line, but the court was otherwise in fine shape. "This tennis court cost me more than the whole place," he told me once.

Art was serving and acquitted himself admirably, even encumbered as he was by layers of shirts and sweaters beneath the parka. The National Weather Service promised snow, but so far the day looked fair. In the background I could see the B-17 that was being rebuilt by a group of hopeful young people, but it looked as if there had been a terrible crash and the aircraft had slowly disintegrated as it ploughed through the lawn and came to rest against the house and barn and garage. All Army green and ripped to pieces, with silver aluminum innards showing, it was a sight such as I had seen only once before, in a photograph of my father's B-17. By the time the photo was taken, weeds had grown up through the cockpit, which still lay as it had fallen, cut in half alongside the railroad tracks near the Peiffer family home in Neuss; and the little German children, who were using it as their playground had no idea what terrible murals blood had painted on the insides of the clouds.

Approaching the front office, I could see Steve and Carla through the plate-glass window that faced the parking lot. As I entered the building, they were standing at the flight desk sipping coffee. There was a large banner printed by a computer hanging over the flight desk: "Lordy, Lordy, Carla's Forty!"

"I tried to keep it a secret," Carla told me, "but somehow it got out. And the boys were pouring cement that day, and now it's written in *stone*."

When I asked him what he was going to do this morning, Steve grumbled, "Aw, I was going to replace that cylinder on the Aeronca, but they're busy in the shop, and I can't get in."

Steve's 1941 Aeronca Defender was used by Galt Flying Service for teaching pilots to fly airplanes with tail wheels. "Didn't it have a fairly new engine?" I asked.

"Yeah, I put it on there with nine hours when the last one burned out." Someone had flown away with the oil drain plug open, and the flight ended in a bean field not far from Galt. Luckily, the airplane wasn't hurt. "But there's been this knocking noise. Russell said it was the number-three cylinder, so of course I took off the number three, and it was perfect. But I busted the oil wipe ring while I was taking it off, so I went ahead and ordered a whole new set, which I'm going to put on there as soon as I can get into the shop. Then I'm going to take the number-one cylinder off and see what's up."

"So what are you going to do?" I asked. Steve took a sip of

coffee from his giant green plastic driving mug with the no-spill lid.

"Oh, I've been working on the two-place *Stork*," he said.

"The two-place? What happened to the single-seat *Stork*?"

As we talked, Bill Tate, Jay Pettigrove and Brett Hansen, another young instructor, were working over the schedule with a couple of students. One was not making progress. Bill was trying to establish whether or not she was going to be able to fly today. She hadn't flown alone for months and was unsure of her skills. (So was Bill.) The conversations, phone calls, and general moving about of people, went on as Steve and I talked, leaning on the glass-case counter sipping our coffee. Every now and then a pilot would come in, check the anemometer, then look outside to what was clearly a contradictory condition—wind blowing the trees around, airplane wings rocking, someone with her hair flying straight up from her head as she checked the fuel on a Cessna 152—then glance back to the anemometer and comprehend that the instrument did not work.

Steve explained that Don Ericson had decided that he wanted to have nothing to do with the two-place *Stork*. He did not want the liability. He was going to be happy just to have his own airplane to fly. Steve, however, still had ambitions. And as he talked about the two-place *Stork*, he became animated once more with the dream of flight, the dream of creation. "The cockpit is twenty-six inches wide," he said, "which means it's just as wide as my Aeronca," which is about as wide as a bar stool. "It's tandem seating, and the door comes down just like this, so you can get in the front or back." He drew me a schematic on a scrap of paper on the counter. "I've been drawing this all month now," he added. "I'm just to the point where I could build an airframe, and I've got the workshop in my barn all set up. All I have to do is hook up the heat." The airplane was going to have a ballistic parachute, as the single-place *Stork* did, for a safe recovery in case of a major structural failure, midair collision, or ditching in the mountains. Steve said structural failure was unlikely, since he was designing it for aerobatics. Despite the fact that Don wanted to distance himself from the project, he had agreed to do the stress-loading calculations. "And they came out great," Steve said. "Eighty percent safety factor."

In the background, Kurt Marunde, another instructor, had joined in to help in lecturing Bill's reluctant student: "Nobody can make you go. If you want to finish up in the spring when the weather is warm . . ." he trailed off, and he and Bill exchanged a glance. They thought the woman was a loser because she had been at it so long and was irregular about making it to the lessons. The woman, who appeared to be no older than high school age, looked glum. I knew the feeling. She wanted to go, but there were other things: She had work, she had family, she had a thirty-knot cross wind. She had fear. The instructors, on the other hand, sometimes found it difficult to understand. They were like the seagulls, which I had watched most of my life on the shores of Lake Michigan, turning and turning over the waves, always in flight, even in a blizzard. Nothing deterred them, because if they didn't fly they didn't eat.

The reluctant student eventually left, telling Kurt and Bill that she'd resume her lessons in the spring. Many people took lessons for a while and never finished. They discovered that flying was simply not for them or not what they thought it would be. Perhaps they discovered that it wasn't like learning to ski or sail, that it demanded so much more than they had expected it would, that it pulled pieces out of you and kept them. There was always an adequate excuse to stay on the ground. Like a religious conversion or love itself, flying requires a fundamental change in the way we perceive the world. The very nature of that change attracted people prone to obsession: They were most likely to be converted and hence to finish.

Art came in, and I asked how he did in the tennis game. "Oh, the Doc always wins," he said. "Because he keeps score."

Every day there was a crowd for lunch in the briefing room. The instructors and mechanics usually brought something from home. The men who had mothers or wives often came with their food in Tupperware containers, which could be stored in the big brown refrigerator behind the bar. Now they drifted in to reheat their food in the microwave oven, which sat between the refrigerator and the sink. Today Bill Tate had a container of spaghetti and meatballs, which he heated quickly between lessons and ate right out of the container while standing behind the counter looking expectantly across the room at the rest of us, where we sat on the couches by the plate glass windows overlooking the ramp.

"Why don't you sit down?" someone asked him.

"Nope," Bill said through a mouthful of food. "Got a student."

We were all eating and watching the action on the ramp through the picture window. It was what we had instead of television. A man was trying to start a Cessna 150. The plane had not been preheated, and it wouldn't start. He got out and pulled the propeller through several times, then climbed back in and tried again. This time it worked. But instead of taxiing away, he stepped out and left the airplane running on the ramp. A collective groan of disapproval went up.

Russell remarked that he knew the man from another airport. "He wants to do all his own maintenance," Russell said disdainfully. There are always a few pilots who attract attention by their dangerous, destructive, or death-defying patterns of behavior. We always remark that they won't last long, but it seems to be part of the etiquette not to mention the problem to the person directly, where it might do some good.

"A guy at Pal-Waukee was cut by his own propeller the

other day," Russell said. "The line boys said they saw him pulling the prop through and paid no attention. Next thing they knew, they could hear his screams. Evidently the prop caught, came around, and cut his hand off. Did he scream! They took him to the hospital and the doctors got it sewn back on all right, I guess."

"I hate hand propping airplanes," Lee Nusbaum said, expressing a nearly universal sentiment. In his big dirty-colored fur coat, with his shaggy brown hair sticking up, Lee, who was Steve's half brother, looked as if he lived in the mountains of Alaska.

Russell launched into a story about a pilot who prop-started his airplane. He had his girlfriend sit in the cockpit which may have been thoughtful for her but did him no good whatsoever, since she had never seen the inside of a cockpit before, and didn't know where the brakes were. The pilot set the parking brakes, but only one of them caught. Of course, he couldn't tell quite yet. The airplane was difficult to start that day, so the pilot reached inside and put the throttle to about half power. It started all right. That was when he found out about the one brake being set, because the airplane began to go in a circle. The pilot took hold of the strut, thinking that he would stop it, but the airplane overpowered him and began dragging him around and around. Meanwhile, in the cockpit, the girlfriend was in a panic. She tried to stop the plane, but in doing so, she inadvertently set the throttle wide open, which dragged the man around faster and faster, until he could hold on no longer. He let go.

Russell got to making noises like an airplane, "Brrrr-Bump! Brrrr-Bump! Brrrr-Bump!" as the airplane ran over the man again and again. Someone who happened to be on the airfield, conveniently filming all of this with a movie camera, drove his van into the path of the airplane, bringing the drama to a halt. Now with visions of that escapade in our heads, we took a vote and elected Lee to go out and stop history from repeating itself.

□

It was a beautiful day to fly, but I decided to leave the Citabria in the hangar and wait until it was warmer. It's too easy to crack a cylinder with a small airplane on a cold day. A much better day for ice skating, I decided.

Although I had wintered on Wonder Lake before and had seen people skate and even drive snowmobiles and ice boats on it, I had never done it myself. This year I finally bought a pair of skates and went out. I could see the cracks where tectonic plates of ice met one another, six or eight inches thick.

At first I had the sensation that at any moment I might fall through. Weighted down by my skates and my water-logged clothing, I understood that I'd go plunging to the bottom. That fear was helped along by the marvelous and terrible sounds the lake made as I glided across the surface. It sounded like electronic thunder, designed to be the background for a thriller film where someone is about to die mysteriously. It was the ice nudging its many edges against one another. My whole first tour of the lake was fraught with anxiety and considerations of what I must do if the illusion that held me up abruptly vanished, for I believed more firmly in its ability to vanish than its ability to abide.

I had lunch, rested, and then, late in the afternoon, as the sun was lowering over the trees, I went out again.

This time I went farther out, to the middle of the lake. The deep, reverberating explosions coming from within the belly of the lake were ominous and menacing, but somehow I had come to the conclusion that they would not harm me.

I skated backwards, remembering how after being rusty. I gained speed, which now and then ended abruptly when I hit a patch of snow. But after a while, I forgot there was surface and relaxed with the idea that I was not going to fall through. I forgot about the deep of it. My skates, the wind in my face, the electronic music of the shifting ice, and the play of late light through the trees—that was all there was. In the end, I loved it. I didn't want to stop. I had begun to believe in the ice.

The experience was very much like learning to fly. At first I thought I'd fall through. Now there is only the airplane and the sky. The process took a long time, though.

I don't think I've ever been more frightened than on my first solo flight—frightened and thrilled and proud all at the same time. It had been a normal day with my first instructor—let's call him Tom—who happened to be an escaped mental patient, I think. He did frightfully dangerous things with students on board.

At the time, I didn't have the experience to be able to judge such things, so I trusted Tom. We were practicing takeoffs and landings at a small airport called Campbell (Charlie 81) a few miles east of Galt. After a few uneventful tours around the pattern, Tom asked me to stop the airplane on the runway.

"Right here?" I asked.

He opened the door and hopped out. "Go ahead," he shouted over the noise of the propeller. "Take it around a few times."

"What?" I asked. But he slammed the door.

I taxied back, taking care not to kill him with the airplane. My predicament was not yet real to me. It was so far outside of my realm of experience that I could not grasp its significance. I pushed the throttle forward and the little airplane began to roll. Immediately I wanted to stop it, but I did nothing, frozen with fear at the controls. One doesn't have to do much to get an airplane to take off, not if it's a Cessna. In fact, other than keeping it from running off into the grass, there's nothing to it. My mind was locked by panic, but I didn't have to be able to think to find myself in the position where the plane was actually lifting off the ground. It was at that moment that everything in my life became clear to me.

As the earth dropped away, the tree line fell like a skirt,

exposing the warm, bare beauty of the world to my view. At once I understood my thrilling and dreadful plight.

My predicament, of course, was that I was off the ground and not at all certain that I would ever regain my hold on the earth. But it was a deeper affliction that put me there: We live in a culture where the great majority of people are taught that everything is someone else's fault. No, it's still more fundamental than that. We are taught that only experts can know anything. Science (so the mythology goes) is the key to understanding the world in which we live, and only scientists can understand science. We therefore cannot understand our world. Medicine, which keeps us alive (or so the mythology goes), is the secret of the physician, who speaks in Latin. Government is a spooky secret, and we grasp only bits and pieces as they are stolen from the state. Reporters have to sue the government to learn anything. The whole system seems designed to keep us in ignorance, while at the same time imploring us to "sit back, relax, and enjoy the flight," as the airline captain says, the invisible captain, whose disembodied voice on the public address system assures us that, although we can't possibly understand what's going on, we had better submit.

Bumper stickers say, "Shit happens," but when shit happens to us, it's someone else's responsibility, and we sue them. Our whole world is labeled with warnings to remind us that we're not responsible for our own well-being. The lid for the Styrofoam coffee cup that we get at the doughnut shop is stamped with a warning: "Caution! Coffee May Be Hot! Sip With Caution!" We have become so used to our own stupidity that we've forgotten that coffee is *supposed to be hot*. The disease of abdication has overtaken our culture, and like the pod people from *Invasion of the Body Snatchers*, we are left without volition, expecting someone else to do, to say, to be. We forget. We wander about like ghosts, plaintive, longing, unfulfilled, dreaming of imaginary conquests.

It was precisely that realization which struck me like thirty milligrams of Biphetamine as my perky little Cessna 150 leapt off the ground without any coaxing at all and began climbing away from the field where my slaphappy instructor stood shaking his fist at me in gleeful lunacy. As the craft clambered up and away, dragging me along, I understood fully that it was the first time in my life that I had been forced to take full responsibility for myself in a real sense. I could scream and holler, I could call on the radio, but only my own two hands, my own skill and good sense, were going to get me back on the ground to live another day. If I did not take responsibility for myself right then and there and forever after, I was going to die. It was that simple. And the fairy tale that had been my life came to an abrupt end.

I was shaking, fevered with fear. My hand on the yoke trembled badly. I could barely pick up the microphone to t-t-transmit my p-p-position. I maneuvered downwind in a lurching, preposterous imitation of a turn, and as I saw the airfield passing away behind me, I felt as if it would disappear, vanish forever, leaving me stranded out there over that hostile landscape of towns and towers, silos and steeples and roads. How would I ever get back down? It was like the feeling I'd had once as a boy, climbing a tower too tall and finding myself stuck up there, welded to the steel ladder by fear. Now I was afraid that the slightest movement of my muscles would send me tumbling out of the sky. Moving my hands was like trying to move a dead man. I was in rigor mortis, only I was watching it happen to me.

I turned back, of course, and I survived to tell about it. In fact, as a solo flight, it was utterly ordinary. My instructor climbed back in the airplane. "How did it go?" he asked.

I said, "Oh, nothing to it. It was a piece of cake. No problem. Blah, blah, blah . . ."

When Tom was fired from the flight school, my solo privileges were rescinded, and my new instructor gently suggested that I get a bit more training before I went around alone is a conveyance as demanding as an airplane.

□

Out on the ramp I noticed Colleen, one of Bill's students, preparing a blue Cessna 152 for flight. She drained fuel, peered into the gas tanks, and ran her finger over the propeller of the airplane called 485.

John taxied out with Jay Pettigrove in the front seat of the Citabria to practice aerobatics with him. I watched them lift off, tilting in the turbulence, and a few minutes later they were back on the ramp. It was our mysterious fuel leak again. The Citabria had been leaking fuel now and then, but not consistently, and although many people had volunteered for the research team, not one of them had succeeded in explaining the problem. Now Russell and Bob Buchik and Jim Liss, Jay, John, and many others were drawn into solving the mystery. We unscrewed fairings and peered inside at the black tubing, but it was about as enlightening as looking at the guts of a dead rat.

Since I couldn't fly until the Citabria was fixed, I decided to walk down to check the north-south turf runway to see if it was usable. As I stepped out into the parking lot, a semitrailer was just pulling up the drive delivering a new airplane engine. I passed the semitrailer, watching them lift the pine-slat wooden crate from the flatbed and place it in the battered, rusted Jeep pickup truck. Lee drove. The poor truck seemed barely capable of carrying the airplane engine and shuddered away, bottoming out on its old shocks as it hit ruts in the taxiways. Art had come out to watch, too, and as we stood there, the Jeep disappeared around the hangars on its way to the shop, where the engine would be uncrated and put back on the nose of the pitiful noseless airplane 18F (called *Fox* or *Foxtrot*), which sat ingloriously behind the shop now with scrap steel hanging from its front end, like a bad boy who had been put in a corner to wear the dunce cap. It was the Cessna 172 that the club depended on the most because it was the only one good enough for instrument training. The other one, 1237U (called Uniform) was, as the instructors said, "a real roach."

The way 18F came to be out of commission was that Brett Hensen had been training an instrument student, making approaches at Fond du Lac, Wisconsin, Airport, when *Foxtrot* lost its crankshaft and went dead about 4,500 feet up. At first Brett handled the situation as he would have handled an emergency training session, so accustomed had he become to training students in the loss of engines: "Okay, now, slow the airplane down a little bit, you're going almost ninety, and your best glide is sixty-five, that's it. Good. Okay, now I'd say turn off the gas, here, and go through your checklist. We're not going to get a restart, so let's go to— Hey, wait a minute!" And he thought to himself, This is real! Brett grabbed the controls, saying, "My airplane," and took the airplane directly to the airfield.

He was talking to the center at the time, and when he reported that he had lost his engine they said, "Uh, Roger, sir, cancel IFR with me or call flight service on the ground, you may contact the advisory frequency now."

It was just one more reminder that the thin veneer of clearheadedness, science, and reason in which we cloak aviation form not a safety net but an illusion. And like a shaman using magic to treat pneumonia, it's certain to fail us just at the moment when we need it most.

Now Brett could see that, too, and said, "No, no, no, my engine is out. Would you please forget the clearance?"

"Do you want the equipment, sir?" they asked, calm as ever.

Brett thought, Well, at least they could put out the fire. Watching the airport come up underneath him, he said, "Well, yeah. Why not? Of course I want the equipment."

Later Brett told me, "If we hadn't been shooting approaches, we wouldn't have made the field."

They were met by fire engines on the runway, and *Foxtrot* was deader than a Christmas goose, but the pilots were all right.

□

I returned to the office and stomped my feet to warm them. The aviators were at the counter in the briefing room as usual—there was almost always some group of pilots there. John Fountain stepped up to the counter with his cup of coffee, and we began talking about the Cuban Eight and the hammerhead, and then the wind dropped below twenty, and we all gathered around the broken anemometer in front of the flight desk to see if somehow it had healed itself and was telling us wind speed and direction again.

We went out and studied the wind sock. The wind was down the runway.

We returned to the briefing room. I said it looked like flight might be possible, and then it was the same old story again, like two old sots talking themselves into just a little nip from a cheap bottle of gin.

John said that it wasn't such a bad day after all. "They seemed to have fixed that fuel leak," he added.

"Maybe we ought to go up," I suggested, "just for half an hour."

"We could work on that hammerhead," he said.

After all, it *was* a beautiful day. And one little flight wouldn't hurt anything.

I asked John to fly the front seat so he would be most comfortable and have the best range of vision. Then he would have the best chance to perform the figure well, and I could watch.

Soon, with the smell of gasoline still strongly present in the cockpit, we were circling high over Galt, and John was lining up on an easterly descending line, accelerating through the bumpy air, and the little blue plane shuddered all over with pleasure as we approached 150 miles per hour pointed at the earth. He leveled the plane for a moment to establish the horizontal line required for proper judging of the figure in a contest, then pulled back sharply. I could feel my hands and head grow heavy as if I'd been injected with a sedative. Even my cheeks tried to stay behind as the earth disappeared and was replaced by sky. I looked out the left window to regain my bearings. That point when the earth turns into a vast and featureless blue screen is precisely where a passenger will become disoriented, anxious, and ill. But a quick glance out the side window will show the flat knife of the wing's edge turning neatly around the horizon, and we instantly recover a sense of where we are.

Far below us, Bill's student Colleen, whom I had seen inspecting 485 earlier, was about to make her first solo flight. She was ready. She knew the material. She was one of his best students; and with him on board the aircraft, she had just shown him two perfect landings. Her fiancé was there to witness the event. He and Bill decided to sit in the truck to watch.

Colleen rolled down the runway and performed her engine checks in the distance. They could barely see her.

Now I looked back over my head, through the plexiglass top of the fuselage, and I saw the earth come toward us and Colleen at the run-up pad. Down, down, we came, floating now in our seats as we seemed to crawl like a roller coaster car down the back side of the loop. The pile driver of the sedative had turned to the floaty weightless feel of opium. John pushed the stick, and gravity seemed to grab hold and fling us against our belts. We were inverted, going down at a 45-degree angle. He was aiming at a farmhouse. I saw John's shoulder jerk, and we rolled and were upright again, still diving toward the farmhouse. He let the plane accelerate for another moment, enough to establish the symmetry of the figure but not enough to damage the airplane, then pulled out of the dive. We were horizontal. We were level once more.

Below us Colleen was lining up for her first takeoff, as Bill and her fiancé watched. The wind had calmed down considerably, but it still switched now and then to the north. Even so, Colleen had landed in worse cross winds, and she was a good student. Colleen started the run. The little Cessna accelerated in a straight line for a hundred feet or so, and then suddenly wobbled, swerved, dipped, and—like a dog that's broken its leash—ran right into the grass, sniffing, sniffing, down the hill, and over onto its nose. The old blue airplane went up, stuck its tail in the air, and tipped onto its propeller. The nose wheel was sheared off, the left wing dug gruesomely into the earth, and the airplane ground to a horrible wrenching stop.

John and I were oblivious of the events unfolding below. He had pulled into the second half of his Cuban Eight and was explaining what he was doing. I was trying to learn, and one more student taking off in one more Cessna was not of much interest to me.

Bill vaulted from the truck and ran. As he reached the plane, he saw Colleen crawl out. To prevent a fire, he shut off the ignition and master switch. Her fiancé arrived a moment later and took Colleen into his arms. She was shaken but uninjured.

A quarter of an hour later, when John and I landed, I noticed the airplane off in the grass, but I didn't realize how damaged it was. There was always so much junk around that I didn't pay that much attention to it.

In the office, everyone had gathered around Colleen: It was nothing. That old airplane will be fixed in no time. You'll be back flying before you know it. Colleen's fiancé took her to lunch and urged her on, but Colleen swore she'd never fly again.

The FAA sent an investigator, who looked over the situation and advised Colleen not to let it throw her. "Get right back on that horse," the woman told Colleen.

After everything quieted down, I found Jim Liss out behind the shop lifting the broken cowling down from the back of the red truck. He had hauled 485 back to assess the damage.

"Well, for starters," he said, "the fire wall is shot. The engine will most likely have to be rebuilt because it was stopped when the prop hit the ground. New front gear. That whole left wing is trashed. Look here." He showed me where the wing had buckled. "That spar's bent," he said. It was a major wreck.

Russell had bought a Cessna 150 that was struck by lightning. Now Liss was going to put it in going order to take the place of 485.

Russell came around the side of the shop and looked over the situation.

"How long, Bob?" I asked.

"Six months," he said.

Returning to the office, I found Bill sitting behind the desk promising everyone who would listen that he was going to get her back in the air again. He was the instructor. It was a matter of professional pride. But he didn't look happy. He could have lost his instructor's certificate. She could have lost her life. And Galt had lost a valuable airplane, which produced income like a money machine all day long every day of the year.

Bill had Colleen flying again that same afternoon.

When John and I walked into the office after our flight, Colleen was at the desk. "How are you?" I asked.

"I'm smiling," she said.

"You're breathing," someone else said.

She went solo a few weeks later. She earned her license and married her fiancé, a pilot for United, who has encouraged her to keep her skills sharp. They fly together regularly in the Cutlass. A year and a half later, 485 was finally repaired and put back on the line.

SIX

UNUSUAL ATTITUDES

It is not likely that aerobatics competition will ever be covered on television. It doesn't make good pictures. Cameras cannot capture it. In fact, there aren't even very many spectators at the contests, which take place all over the world throughout the summer and fall. The press scarcely covers the main events at the U.S. Nationals in Denison, Texas, or the World Aerobatics Championships—the Olympics of precision flying, held every two years. The Nesterov Cup does not rate a single line in the newspaper.

When people think of precision flying, they think, perhaps, of the Air Force Thunderbirds. Perhaps a few people think of "stunt pilots" and air shows. A stunt pilot is someone who does stunts with an airplane for the motion pictures, for example, crashing a plane through a barn. The loop, roll, and spin are *figures* (as in figure skating), which certain airplanes are designed to make. An air-show pilot presents a series of figures close to the ground, often with smoke, to alarm and delight people who, it seems, are already sufficiently convinced that flying is dangerous without having to see it done upside down ten feet off the ground. Some pilots, such as Patty Wagstaff, fly both in air shows and world competition. Some do stunts as well.

International Aerobatics Club competition is precision flying taken to its highest level. At least that's what the IAC tells us. They even have a book that tells how each maneuver should be flown. The flights do not appeal for the approval of an audience. The figures are flown for a panel of judges. There are five levels of skill, Basic, Sportsman, Intermediate, Advanced, and Unlimited. (Most of us begin with Sportsman, because that's the way pilots think. I believe that the IAC invented the Basic category to prevent pilots from beginning at the Intermediate level.)

Watching forty airplanes perform the same sequence of figures over and over can be a bit numbing. The figures are flown well away from the ground so that no one gets killed. A Pitts Special against a blue sky looks like a fly on a television screen. If forty airplanes fly for fifteen minutes each with no breaks, the process takes ten hours.

Competition pilots like to boast that no one has ever been killed during an IAC competition, which is true. That's like saying that no combat troops have been killed during a Memorial Day parade, which does not mean that it's safe to be a soldier.

The least hint of warm weather signaled the beginning of the aerobatics season at Galt. Although the weather just a few hundred miles south of Lake Superior in northern Illinois could go from blizzard to balmy and back again in the space of a day or two, we were like swarming insects: always there waiting. There was a lot of work to be done before the contest season.

Gerry Molidor, for example, would take his Christen Eagle (a two-seat Pitts) apart and clean it and check it and put it all back together again. Gerry, bright-eyed, always ready with a smile and an enthusiastic handshake, had short brown hair with gray beginning to sparkle evenly through it. A United Airlines captain, Gerry was thin and fit and had regular features. His physical presence was slight and light, but he had a polished, almost political, demeanor of sincerity and camaraderie. When fathers brought their small sons by to look at his dazzling multicolored biplane, Gerry would call them Tiger. "Hey, Tiger, how's it going? You like flying?" Some years ago, I followed Roger Penske and Rick Mears around for a racing season. (Mears has won the Indianapolis 500 four times.) Roger's chief mechanic told me, "Roger likes to get everything spic and span and then go out there and blow their doors off." Gerry was the same way.

Sometimes Gerry's wife, Kathy, could be seen standing on the ramp with his three children, Sarah, John, and Gerry, Jr., and the tiny white fuzz-ball dog, Pittsie, watching Gerry make 200-mile-per-hour passes low over the runway. Gerry was carrying on the tradition begun in the town of Volo in McHenry County, Illinois, by his grandfather, Joe Molidor, who at the age of sixteen in the year of 1916, built a Marionette Monoplane from mail-order plans he had purchased for a dollar. Joe Molidor drove a horse and buggy into town for parts. Exactly seventy years later, Gerry built the fanciest aerobatics airplane there is: the Christen Eagle. Within two years, he went on to win all of the most prestigious aerobatics contests within a day's flight of his home field. Gerry Molidor had golden hands.

As I entered the hangar, I had almost stepped on Howard Stock, who was sprawled beneath the cowling of his red Pitts Special. The Pitts is the most popular aerobatics airplane in the world. Some were made by Christen Industries (now Aviat) in Afton, Wyoming, and some were built by amateur aircraft builders from blueprints. Aviat also makes kits for building Christen Eagles such as Gerry's. Howard and his father, George, built their single-seat Pitts in the late '70s.

The day grew warm, the hangar doors were open to the breeze, and people began dragging metal folding chairs out to watch the airplanes. There were even a few bugs beginning to investigate the open Coke cans as the lunch hour approached.

Howard was a national IAC judge, head of the Rules Committee, a serious competitor, a USAir pilot, and a longtime member of the aerobatics community. When I asked if he would teach me aerobatics, he told me that he no longer gave instruction. "In fact," he said somewhat sadly, "I really don't give rides much either, because I've lost a lot of good friends recently." He thought about that for a moment and then added, "I've really kind of backed off lately. I lost a couple of good friends right at Galt." He meant Lloyd Hughes and his son, Scotty. Howard had been out flying at the time Lloyd crashed. Howard invited me to talk to him, to join the local IAC chapter in Chicago, and generously offered to critique my flying for me—that is, to stand on the ground and watch while I flew.

Now Gerry and Howard were performing the annual maintenance on their airplanes. "I like to touch those things that I'm going to be hanging from up there," Gerry said. Naturally, they explained their actions in terms of safety and obligation, but Aladdin probably said that about his lamp, too.

It was true that the hardest flying of all would be done by the aerobatics pilots, and their peculiar and impractical craft would take the worst punishment. During the coming season, some of them would fall apart—some in the hangar, some on the ramp, and a few, with catastrophic results, in the air.

As Gerry removed his brake lines, he said, "The day you roll the airplane out of the shop, it's all downhill from there." He looked sadly at his white and seemingly perfect fire wall, seeing some defect there that was invisible to the rest of us. "Even putting it together starts destroying it," he observed, stumbling as if in total innocence upon an immensely important and universal concept, and then moving right along, as if he had picked up the Rosetta Stone and skipped it into the sea without ever knowing what he'd held in his hands.

We had been working on the problem of getting permission to practice our aerobatics directly over Galt Airport, which was a slightly delicate political problem that involved convincing the FAA that we weren't going to embarrass them by dying.

IAC competition is conducted in a 1,000-meter imaginary box. Markers on the ground tell the pilot if the airplane is going out of bounds. The only way to know if the figures are performed well is to have someone on the ground watch. The most practical way to do that is right over the airfield, so that pilots can take turns observing and practicing. It might seem foolish to perform spins and loops right over an active airport, and in fact, it might be. Nevertheless, that is how aerobatics are practiced. The bottom of the aerobatics box is above the top of the landing pattern, and we hope that pilots watch for each other. Because our airplanes take such a beating, we like having the airfield right under us in case something breaks and we need to land quickly.

Gerry wanted to approach Russell cautiously and with an organized plan for our practice box, "so he doesn't think we're a bunch of air-show pilots," he said, indicating the clear distinction made between us ("never had a fatal crash at a contest") and them (who die in droves). It turned out that Russell had no trouble adjusting to the idea. In fact, he liked it because it attracted people to the field. They wanted to come and see if we'd kill ourselves.

Gerry asked me, "Wouldn't you just love to know what goes through their heads the moment before they have that lapse in judgment? You just get into a Pitts, and you've got all that power at your fingertips. I mean, one flick of the wrist, and it's done. It takes so little effort." He was talking about *The Impulse*. Most people involved with flying use the vague rubric of *safety*, but that doesn't begin to express the intent of what we were saying. Gerry was actually asking a question like this: "Wouldn't you really like to see the face of your adversary just once?" We knew that something invisible was pursuing us.

So whenever we gathered for practice, eventually the talk would turn to safety, and we'd give ourselves *The Lecture*. Like a tribal group making incantations against a force it cannot comprehend, we chanted the litany of safety: Never roll on takeoff. Howard was our high priest, but Gerry was the one who gave The Lecture. He'd say, "You know, just one accident could spoil everything. Now, we don't want these people thinking we're air-show pilots or something."

I knew he had seen something, somewhere in his past, but he didn't say what it was at first. I knew he'd eventually tell me. "So let's not do anything foolish," Gerry would say. "All right? All right?"

I'll never forget the first time I saw Mark Peteler. It was a windy Sunday in that almost-spring season, and Mark came storming out of the sky in his red Pitts Special, skittering down the runway as if he'd go into the grass before he finally came to a stop. Then in that twitchy, jittering way a Pitts has of taxiing (like a nervous dog sniffing gopher holes, and they're all just so yummy that he can't decide which one to dig up), Mark made his way around to Gerry's hangar. The plexiglass bubble popped open and out stepped this tall, bespectacled, almost academic-looking fellow wearing shorts and an oversized bold-print softball jersey and sneakers. He looked like Buddy Holly. But he was a level-headed guy. He was sensible. He was a banker.

Gerry introduced us and I asked, "How was that cross wind?"

"Pretty scary," he said. "You know, people always say you

should never use brakes landing a Pitts, but if I hadn't used brakes, I think I would have ended up in the grass just now." We talked about aerobatics, and I explained to him where I was in my development as an aerobatics pilot. He said he had had about one hundred hours and two years in his Bellanca Decathlon when Jim Batterman's wing folded in flight. After Batterman died, there were no aerobatics schools between Michigan and Kansas City. It was not easy to be an aspiring aerobat and live through the aspiration period.

When I met Mark, he had put thirty hours on his Pitts and felt, to use his word, *comfortable*. While he put number-ten sheet metal screws on his new nose spinner, he invited me to climb in and see how it fit. I carefully stepped on the black tread on the wing and lowered myself in. The parachute had conformed to his body, taken his own sweat pattern like the imprint of a fossil in limestone. It was as intimate as slipping into someone else's shoe. I was really down there, too; it seemed as if only my nose peeked over the cockpit rail where the canopy bubble slid closed. I sat there for several minutes listening to my heart race at the mere thought of being alone aloft in that, that— Well, what was it? It looked like no other airplane. It was a factory S1S, a $33,000 *piñata*. It was a wicked, playful, and contrary parody of an airplane, like what I imagined would have happened to the work of the famous Mexican sculptor Candelario Medrano had he turned his attention away from automobiles and started making little high-colored papier mâché airplanes.

Gerry was smiling to himself, watching me, as he sat on a crate before his Eagle biplane, using a hair dryer to shrink the white plastic cover over his new brake lines. He laughed at me and called out, "Sure looks good on you." I could feel nerves growing out of my hands and taking root in the wingtips, as Mark closed the canopy over me and shut me into that bubble of aromas. It was sexy, the animal smell of Mark—all his old fear and exhilaration trapped in there—mixed with the nylon, the aviation fuel, the dope and oil, leather and smoke. I could feel the hairs standing up on my neck at the idea of trying to land the thing. I felt the tremendous power in the fingers of my right hand to release like a bolt cast from a cloud this red thunder with the flick of my wrist. I *wanted* it. I resolved that I would go to Missouri and learn how to fly the Pitts with John Morrissey.

As I slid the canopy back, the fresh air hit me and broke the spell. No wonder people get into trouble flying these things. I was already in trouble, and I was still parked.

I could see Mark through the cabane struts as I began to climb out. "You know," he said, "Jim died right over the practice area with a student on board. That could have been me." It could have been me, too. I had been on Jim Batterman's schedule before he died. We never had the chance to fly together. "That plane just has too much wing for hard aerobatics." He was telling me that because my Citabria was essentially the same aircraft with a smaller engine. Mark and Gerry were trying to convince me to buy a Pitts. Gerry would say, "Come on, can't you see it? Four of us—you and Mark and Howard and me—we come storming out of the sky in formation, *arrive* at these contests. Man, you drive a Pitts, you're one of the gang. You're in the Air Force."

By the end of the day we had all flown and hung around the hangars. We had received The Lecture and flew a little bit more and drank some Cokes. At one point Mark and I went to the flight desk for a Coke, and he warned me not to step on a board with nails in it. He was a level-headed guy. Eventually the sun drew down the western sky and it came time to go home. Mark had only recently bought his red single-seat Pitts, and it was still pretty new to him. He'd flown a couple of contests the previous season, some in his old Decathlon, some in his new Pitts. And now as the sun started to settle and grow long shadows behind the flight line office, Mark said he had to get home, and he climbed into that tiny cockpit and strapped himself into his parachute and then into the harness. He started up and taxied out, and we watched and waved as he took off. Just as he cleared the trees at the end of the runway, he pointed the nose about 30 degrees up and flipped the plane into a quick roll. It was so fast and delicate that we would have missed it if we had blinked. "God damn it," Gerry said. "Mark—what the hell?"

That night Gerry called Mark. "What the frickin' hell were you doing rolling on takeoff, Mark?" Gerry asked.

"I don't know," Mark said. "I just did it. I didn't even think about it. It was just like—I don't know—this *feeling*. I took off, and it felt so good I just rolled. I'm sorry."

Gerry gave him *The Big Lecture*. Mark knew it by heart, of course, but he sat still for it anyway. He knew he deserved it. He had succumbed to our greatest fear: that we would be flying out like that, 120 knots or so on the up-line out of Galt Airport or some little weedfield, bean-patch, nowhere strip way out in the middle of America, and we'd just be *overtaken* by the invisible spirit, that demon that's always hovering so close to our shoulders, and we would not even be granted the time to make one last wish or to decide if it's a good idea or a bad idea. We'd simply find ourselves rolling. A Pitts rolls 240 degrees per second. Three quarters of a second, that's all it takes to get inverted. There's not a lot of time to say, *Well, maybe I shouldn't be doing this.*

That evening I stopped at the bar in the briefing room and sat for a moment, drinking a Dr. Pepper. The lights were down. The place was deserted now. Outside the ramp and fuel pumps were bathed in floodlight that flickered in some sort of mist that had begun to move in. I could faintly hear an airplane passing somewhere overhead.

The briefing room was an open area where the restaurant used to be and where C & S Ultralight School (the initials stood for Carla and Steve but they say the C also stood for their son Chance) still had its counter and display cases with a few instruments in them. I had never seen a sale made. I had never even seen the cases opened, and the ultralight school no longer existed for all practical purposes.

The briefing room was paneled in pine, and there were a few lockers on one wall, remnants from a boys' gym. Flying helmets had been left atop the lockers after most of the ultralights departed when the craze of the '80s ended. Now the helmets were filled with cobwebs, and in the dim light they vaguely resembled gaping red and blue and yellow papier mâché skulls, irreverently gleeful in their mock solemnity, like Mexican Day of the Dead decorations.

I faced a wall that had been hung with fading photographs in dime-store frames, and I couldn't look at it without being reminded of a similar wall in Pancho Barnes's bar from *The Right Stuff.* For one thing, most of the pilots in the photographs at Galt were either dead or trying very hard to achieve that distinction. One of the photographs didn't even bother to show a pilot. It featured three Pitts Specials arranged fanlike on the grass tie-down area with their tails pointed provocatively at the camera like some sort of techno-pornography. It was a little like looking at a snapshot of three empty beer cans. But such is the totemic value of the Pitts that someone in this place of almost religious procrastination had taken the trouble to pay for the eight-by-ten enlargement of the photograph and go to the dime store and buy the frame and find a hammer and a nail and put it up in that position of prominence.

One of the airplanes no longer existed. A Galt pilot took it to Harvard, Illinois, about ten miles west, and was practicing aerobatics over Phil Dacy's airfield there when he put the little Pitts into an inverted flat spin. He couldn't get out and made a big dry crunch as the construction of tube and fabric hit the cornfields like a *piñata* thrown out of a tenement window.

The sheriff in the next county called, asking if anyone at Galt knew a pilot who flew a red biplane. One of the Galt instructors jumped into an airplane and flew out to Harvard to have a look. He saw the red airplane below, upside down in a field. "The plane looked as if it hadn't even been damaged," he said. But when he landed, they found the pilot hanging in the straps, dead.

I went up to the office and found Art sorting his mail. Art Galt's mail: It was not a dozen letters, not even a dozen-dozen letters. It was a mountain of envelopes that rose to a height of eighteen or twenty-four inches from the center of the rather large desk and slid off the edges onto the floor like a place where the tectonic plates of communication had met and buckled.

"And that's just the tip of the iceberg," Carla had assured me the first time I asked about it. She pointed out the white garbage bags beneath the desk. Art—the owner, the founder, the boss—forbade her to throw away his mail, and so instead she periodically swept some of it off into white garbage bags and put them beneath the desk. Occasionally someone would sneak a few out to the dumpster in the driveway between Art's house and the cow barn, but as long as there were a few bags bulging with unopened mail, piled like sandbags in a bunker, Art seemed to feel safe.

I perceived in Art's relationship to his mail the true secret of the airport itself, as well as the secret of Art's life out there on that odd, unkempt, mismatched, mutant farm. For one thing, Art's ruthless independence was reflected in his refusal to be cowed by the deluge of mail. We all receive it. His mail was no different from anyone else's. But most of us slip it into the trash, out the back door, under the bed. Art let it pile up to its true height and then faced it resolutely.

He did not ignore the mail. He was not a shirker of duty. He went to the office every day, driving his Oldsmobile down from his sprawling yellow farmhouse a hundred yards away, which he could see from the office window, docked like a great golden flagship at the departure end of Runway 27, bound in place by the ribbon of Greenwood Road and a cornfield that stretched to the northern green infinity. Art sat each morning and actually opened mail. Of course, he couldn't open it *all*, but he tried to do his part. It wasn't unusual for me to find him sitting there, as I did on that night, completely hidden behind the mountain of mail, with a steel letter opener, smiling secretly. "I've been officially declared a winner," he said, and then he laughed that crazy laugh of his, as if this were all part of a wild, mad, outrageous joke—all of it, the farm, the airport, the office, the people coming by, all the endless farms rolling around him like so many whitecaps, and the great growing pile of mail, placed before him like a mythical never-ending task. He never complained of his crazy destiny, to sit and calmly open the envelopes one after another. He even read the contents. "Look," he said, calling me over to look at a forgery of an official document, "this Presidential commission is waiting on my decision."

After we had talked for a while, I said good night and went out.

The cold mist was beginning to clear. Thin remnants of the last low clouds formed a pattern like the hammered floriation on the metal ceiling of an old drugstore. The west wind drew a mossy pennant of cumulus across the sky like a dark flock of geese and slowly revealed a misshapen moon. On my way out, I walked past the smashed-down corncribs around the side of the shop where I had parked my car. I stopped to look at a blackened skeletal sculpture of tube steel that lay in the weeds. The gas tank was a pool of melted aluminum; it had the spermy silver-gray look of candlewax. The rudder pedals, front and back, were bent harshly forward. The wooden wing spar had been burnt to charcoal. It was all that remained of Lloyd's Starduster. He did it on takeoff with a four-inch movement of the stick. And looking at it there—all that remained of him and Scotty and the lime-green biplane—I had this thought: He did it to me. Not just to Scotty and Nancy and her other children. He did this to all of us. And it made me angry that he should be so careless as to leave that gruesome legacy.

SEVEN

TRUE WARRIOR SPIRIT

THE LEGACY MY FATHER LEFT ME was a terrible one, too, even though he didn't quite die. In May of 1988 I went to Randolph Air Force Base to see him decorated for some flying he did during World War II. After the ceremonies and the TV cameras and even a cake with the image of a B-17 squirted on it in gunmetal-blue frosting, my father was invited to tour the base, and I went along. As we walked around, I found that I wasn't paying much attention to what the officers were telling us about the history of the base. Without knowing what was happening to me, I was falling under the spell of the jet airplanes that were tearing past overhead, drowning out our conversation. Before the end of the day, I had decided that I needed to fly one of those little jets. Trying to be casual, I asked the base commander, Nick Kehoe, "Who do you have to, um, *know* to get a ride in one of those?"

"Being the son of a senator would help," he said bluntly.

"How about being a journalist?" I asked.

"You'd have to get an assignment," he said.

Within the month I had an assignment from *Harper's* magazine, and as I look back at my notes now, it's clear that I was possessed. I wrote, "A child in a cold soap bubble, rising on a column of flame, climbing into the sun." I wrote, "Thin clouds stream across the sky as I watch a mysterious celestial spider weave its blue web across the huge horizon and spew the tangle of those shiny lanyards out at us as we come on and on. Nothing else matters anymore." It reminded me of the notebooks of experimenters at the turn of the century who gave themselves opiates to unlock the muses. Only I was burning kerosene and pulling G's.

After an eight-year hiatus, I was launched back into flight, and for the next two years, while I was earning my instrument rating and commercial pilot's license, I cadged as many rides as I could, looking for a way to get upside down in an airplane again. I flew in an OA-37 and an F-4D Phantom, a couple of Mustangs, a Falcon, and even a Dolphin twin-jet helicopter. I went out in Apaches with the 82nd Airborne and up to Camp McCoy, Wisconsin, in Hueys, rock and rolling at treetop level, night assault maneuvers, listening to Elvis on my Walkman, as we drove on up the bad guy's tail, feeling sorry that I'd missed the Vietnam War.

But it wasn't the military experience I was after. It wasn't even jets. Those rides only galvanized my resolve to fly aerobatics for real. For real meant I had to own an airplane. I had to have the freedom to go out to the airport by myself on a quiet, clear morning when the air was calm and the grass was still wet, to sit in the hangar and commune with my airplane, to touch it and look at it, smell it and feel it, and then quietly mount it and ride out there looking for mastery and power.

It was around that time that I met those young IAC competitors at Galt—Gerry and Howard and Mark. I instantly recognized my bond with them. They were just as I imagined my father must have been when he was a young lieutenant and flew in the war. I had seen photographs of him and his flying machine when he was lean and young and had a Clark Gable mustache and a look of gleeful sorcery. They were like that, those young IAC pilots, like bullfighters. They were the acolytes of death.

My father was a twenty-three-year-old first lieutenant when he became a lead pilot in the 398th Bomb Group in the old Army Air Force. He drove B-17s and dropped bombs on German people. One day, returning from a mission, he was hit by flak. His radios were blown out, his fuel lines cut, two of his four engines were lost, and his navigational instruments were gone. In addition, he was above the clouds. The plane was going to go down, and he told his crew to prepare to bail out while he took a whack at the clouds.

Here is how my father told the story: "I was flying pilot for the Air Commander, Captain Scott. We decided that our plane would not make it across the Channel, so we let down through the clouds. We were lost, but fairly certain that we were over friendly territory. Under the clouds, visibility was very poor, maybe a quarter to half a mile. Our compass was gone. We flew in several unknown directions looking for a place to land. By blind luck someone on the plane saw a flare, so we headed toward it. It turned out to be an airfield. We spent the night in a hotel in Brussels. The next morning I was awakened by a terrible noise. I thought it was the end of the world. It turned out to be large numbers of people with wooden shoes running after a streetcar."

It was about that time when my father became bulletproof. He and his friend David Swift, another bomber pilot, had sworn in blood or beer that they'd sign up to fly P-51s the moment they finished their current assignment in B-17s. Both had requested fighters straight out of pilot training, but the world had needed bombers. Jean Miller, the lieutenant's commanding officer, told me, "Your dad had a flair for flying on instruments, and that's what I needed. He was a terrific weather pilot." My father told me that he hated flying in the clouds.

It was my father's twenty-fifth mission, scheduled to be his last before he went into Mustangs. The 398th Bomb Group departed at dawn in waves that layered the land around station 131 at Nuthampstead, England, with fumes and smoke and shook the neighboring farmers as they crawled from their beds. The 398th joined with the 91st Bomb Group and others to make up a grand 209 B-17s, each with a ten-man crew; and escorted by 171 P-51 fighter planes, they all cruised out over the English Channel toward Germany. And they were all following my father.

At 140 miles per hour, it was nearly lunchtime in the rural towns and villages around Düsseldorf before the air-raid sirens began to sound. (More than four decades later, my father and I went back to Germany to learn some of these details.) Farmers scattered for the concrete bunkers that served as bomb shelters. The gunners of the *Flakbataillons* ripped the covers off their 88s and started moving ammunition into place. It had snowed the night before, and the world was brilliant white beneath a low overcast. But there was one lady of eighty years, a certain Mrs. Peiffer, who refused to leave her lifelong home near the railroad yards in Neuss. "Let them drop their bombs," old Mrs. Peiffer said, or words to that effect. "My home is my castle. You go and hide. I am sitting right here." And she sat in her farmhouse by the railroad tracks, where the snow had fallen the night before, and she sipped her bitter coffee and awaited bitter fate.

Nearing the target at 27,000 feet, the crew was cold and cramped. The planes were not pressurized or heated, and my father took his oxygen through the rubber mask strapped to his face. The ride to the target could be as long as five or six hours, depending upon the route, which often led them far out of the way to give the impression that they were headed somewhere else.

The bombs were armed and ready to go. The target was a rail marshaling yard at Neuss, now an industrial suburb of Düsseldorf. The bombardier would fix on the target and drop smoke markers along with his bombs. The other planes would use the downward spiral lines of smoke as aiming guides.

Two minutes from target, they saw flak: a careless watercolor tinting the sky. The closer they came, the more accurate the operators on the ground became with their triple-A. A gunner in another plane recalled, "Puffs began appearing off the wingtips, and we could hear the shells bursting and the metal spraying off the airplane. We could smell the powder."

There was a stunning concussion. Like water pouring through a hole in the hull, blackness swept in. Everyone was floating. Four crews in four planes thought they'd been hit. But in the lead plane, ten souls shifted out of their shells, like planets knocked from orbit, and the lieutenant's world went silent.

Light returned. The young lieutenant looked out. Beyond the inboard engine, the left wing was no more. It appeared as if the invisible beast pursuing him all those years had leaped up, snapping now, and had taken a bite off its end.

The airplane pitched and tried to buck like a horse. The lieutenant grabbed the reins to gentle it down, but it rolled into a sickening somersault—out, over, onto its back—and gravity grabbed the silver ship and flung it toward the earth.

Alarm bells rang, Klaxons sounded, and a slipstream whine tore the air like a wounded cry. The lieutenant turned to his air commander, Colonel Frank Hunter, who was sitting in the co-pilot's seat, and shouted over the noise, "I guess this is it!" But if Hunter answered, my father did not hear it.

The old seat-pack parachute was an uncomfortable rig. My father (with that marvelous disdainful certainty of the aspiring fighter pilot) kept it under his seat. He couldn't reach it without unstrapping, but then the centrifugal force of the spinning plane was so great that he was thrown against the instrument panel, which closed off his oxygen hose. How many G's would it take to rip an old-fashioned B-17 in half?

Spinning there, unable to move, the lieutenant thought of his girlfriend back home. He thought of his mother's sadness, and a great sadness entered him.

He lost his wing at 27,000 feet. He lost consciousness somewhere in the clouds. He never left the plane.

Five miles below, Mrs. Peiffer waited as the black shapes of ships rumbled overhead above the clouds. The nearby *Flakbataillon* guns rocked her house with their detonations, and the shells burst high and away, exploding pomegranates of smoke in the atmosphere. Then one of the planes came fluttering away from the pack, a broken silver cinder falling in two pieces. Somewhere in the clouds, the aerodynamic forces had torn the plane in half. The wings and cockpit turned and turned like the helicopter of a maple seed, and the tail section spun straight down into the earth. The cockpit landed in the snow against the railroad tracks just beside Mrs. Peiffer's garden.

The farmers came out of their shelters and laid the young American bodies out in the snow in Mrs. Peiffer's garden. When they discovered the pilot, crumpled up in the cockpit but still alive, they sent for a priest. Their compassion, face-to-face with the enemy, didn't square with the propaganda. It never does.

The lieutenant awoke half in a dream and found himself down by the rudder pedals. He was happy, he said, happy that he was alive. He saw a German soldier stand upon the wing and point a pistol at his head. The soldier was cursing in German. He was going to shoot the wounded officer. The lieutenant could not speak or move. The German pulled the trigger. Nothing happened. The soldier began working the slide on his pistol, trying to make it function, when his superior officer stepped up beside him and asked, "What's this? A live one? We can't shoot him. He's an officer. We have to interrogate him." He had his men lay the lieutenant out in the snow next to his air commander. Some of the local Germans still claim to this day that Colonel Hunter, the air commander, died while receiving absolution, although others also claim that my father was smoking a cigarette using his broken arm. Most of the ones my father and I met were six or eight or ten years old at the time.

The lieutenant, in and out of consciousness, awoke lying in the snow, spitting up blood. He told me that at first he thought he was dying of internal injuries, but then he realized that his nose had been cut nearly off and he had been swallowing blood. He said he felt an almost hysterical joy at the realization that he might live. "But it might have been the morphine," he said. He looked over to see his air commander. Hunter was there. The lieutenant felt a sense of relief and asked a soldier if the commander was OK. The German soldier felt Hunter's neck, searching for a pulse, and shrugged. "*Kaput,*" he said, and the lieutenant felt his heart sink.

A kilometer away, others attended the dead in the tail section. Some had arrived from the clouds with no arms or legs.

The farmers carried the pilot into Mrs. Peiffer's kitchen, and she gave him bitter coffee. Someone else held a cigarette to his lips, just like in the movies. The soldiers called a truck to take the sole survivor to the prison camp.

"I wasn't really in pain until the truck began bouncing over those rutted roads," my father said. Then as all the shattered bones began to grind in that bag of flesh, that once-youthful body, my father cried out for mercy and longed to pass out again.

A French surgeon, also a prisoner of war, received my father and wired him together somehow in that basement dungeon. They survived on Red Cross cigarettes and a kind of soup made of potato peelings and other garbage left from the soldiers' meals.

When my father's plane went down, no one saw parachutes. The crew was (reasonably) presumed dead. Colonel Jean Miller, commander of the 603rd Squadron, had completed the paperwork for my father's promotion and for a Distinguished Flying Cross (for the stunt at Brussels). But the paperwork lost its way.

In San Antonio, where my father was born, his sweetheart waited with Rosa and Agustín González* to hear news of the lost pilot. It came in the form of a telegram informing them that he had died in combat. The long slow months of winter gradually turned into spring. Anne Marie Mosher went back to her home in St. Louis, where she worked as a teacher. When she visited San Antonio, she would sit in the backyard under the moving shadows of the pecan tree on the red and whitewashed wooden lawn furniture watching Rosa tend her garden, where figs and tangerines, peppers, avocados, and cactus grew in flowering profusion. Hummingbirds drank at the pomegranate blossoms, hanging in the air by mysterious invisible threads, the same forces of flight that had taken her man away. Some people in the family mourned the lost pilot. But my mother and his mother refused to believe it.

One day Agustín was sitting inside listening to the enormous old Philco radio, a piece of furniture the size of a refrigerator, when he heard the news that the war had ended. Agustín, who was only five feet five inches tall, picked up the great brown stegosaurus radio and carried it out into the backyard. He strung a cord to power it and turned it on and grabbed the young girl who was to marry his son, and they danced out there, among pomegranates and humming-

The spelling of my name is another legacy of sloppy Air Force paperwork.

birds, and with the great century plant blooming behind them and the music playing at full volume, they danced now, around and around in the grass, around the whitewashed lawn furniture, among shifting patterns of sunlight and shade, until the neighbors came out to see what this mad Mexican man and his beautiful young companion were doing. A phone call came. The lost lieutenant had been found.

My mother and father had seven sons, as if they were trying to replace the dead crew, and all during our childhood my mother celebrated January twenty-third as if it were a holy day, the miracle of falling angels, the day the lieutenant was shot out of the sky and lived. She refused to believe it was a chance occurrence. To her it was divinely prescribed. She would make a cake and a special meal, and we would all sit down to recognize that on that day some unknowable and invisible force had placed its warm hands around the fragile envelope of my father's body and soul and held them together during that 27,000-foot fall from the heavens. Some divine breath had blown away the blue and living spark, which should have set the fire to consume all the fuel and all those armed bombs, which had taken the ride down with the doomed crew. We were always reminded that *we wouldn't be here,* except for that mysterious power. It was the power of his mythology, shaped by my Irish-German mother, that dominated my childhood, as if we lived in the shadow of a dormant volcano. Reality was made of mere events, like so much clay. It was the power of the storyteller that gave it life.

In 1987 my father happened into a reunion of the 398th Bomb Group. He wasn't one of those old aviators who was obsessed with his history. In fact, it was my mother, not my father, who talked about the crash. But the reunion was in San Antonio that year, and my father happened in. A bunch of the boys were whooping it up, lying and drinking, just as they had in Nuthampstead. My father joined right in and happened to remark that he might have been the oldest first lieutenant in captivity.

"What do you mean, Freddy?" Colonel Miller said. "I promoted you to captain!"

It was only forty-three years late, but the captain's bars and the DFC were presented at Randolph Air Force Base, February 22, 1988, in a special ceremony that made national news. The whole family was there, babies and grandchildren and four generations of Mexican-Americans. My father couldn't wipe the grin off his face, always a handsome man. The crash had cut off his nose, but one of the German soldiers had put it back in place as he lay there in the snow, and miraculously it had grown back perfectly. He had a stainless steel screw holding his elbow together, but today if you met him, you'd never know that he belonged to that exclusive club of sky divers who don't use parachutes.

The Air Force had the captain's bars and DFC mounted on a plaque (every military pilot has a plaque), which had been inscribed with the mystifying caption: "True Warrior Spirit." My brothers and I, all grown up by then, had gathered around the plaque more than once, reading that legend over and over, trying to understand what connection there was between those words and our father. True Warrior Spirit? Him? The guy over there taking a nap on the couch? The one reading *The Nation* and watching public television? The one who never taught us to fly?

In the years after the liberation, the wrecked shell of that B-17 Flying Fortress became a favorite play fort for the local children. Decades later, by coincidence, the land was turned into a park, and the town erected one of those wonderful, complex, megalomaniacal German playgrounds there. During the dedication of the playground, my father planted a tree there. He met a gunner from one of the *Flakbataillons* that had been shooting at him that day in January 1945. The German soldier, now an old man, returned my father's silk survival map and some other items that he had taken when he and fellow gunners ransacked the wrecked B-17. Their wives had made baby clothes out of the silk from the parachute they found under my father's seat.

My father told me that when he was back in San Antonio, still recovering in a military hospital, he and another crippled aviator sneaked out to Stinson Field and talked the owner into renting them two Piper Cubs. Despite their obvious disabilities (they were both on crutches, and the other man had drop foot), the pilots were not only able to persuade the owner to rent them airplanes, but to his amazement and horror the wounded officers went up and staged a dogfight over the field. No, not even the war, the moist and intimate nearness of their own deaths, seemed capable of dispelling The Demon that pursued those acolytes. (No wonder Lloyd returned to find his fate in that Starduster.) But somehow, finally, my father overcame it, as many old aviators do. By the time I was born, my father showed no interest in passing along the aviation legacy to any of his sons. He neither taught us how to fly nor took us flying, nor even took us to an airport to get the smell of airplanes in our nostrils and the clatter of them in our ears. He had been an aviator in the war, and my brothers and I had the photos and stories to prove it. But for all we could see of that character in the father we were presented with each morning at breakfast, we might as well have been studying a butterfly that had turned into a caterpillar.

Perhaps he thought that if he didn't mention it, I wouldn't notice. But like someone with a genetic disease, I was driven to flight, invisibly, insidiously. By the time the '60s had ended, I was an airplane whore. I would shamelessly befriend anyone who had a flying machine. I begged rides and obnoxiously demanded to handle the controls. It was disgraceful.

In 1979 I was a journalist writing about issues of airline safety when four friends of mine were killed in an air crash.

At the crash site I saw what I suppose was them and 269 other people in various stages of dismemberment, the unspeakable carnage caused by the disintegration of an American Airlines DC-10. I was supposed to have gone on that flight to the American Booksellers Association Convention in Los Angeles. I had refused to go because I believed then as I believe now that the DC-10 is an unsafe aircraft. My friend and boss, Shel Wax, had teased me about my unwillingness to go. Shel boarded with his wife, Judy, whose book, *Starting in the Middle,* had just been published. Two other friends, Mary Sheridan and Vicki Chen Haider, both editors, went with them. The flight lasted 31 seconds.

I had been working a job I didn't like and had been drinking too much. It was not a very happy period of my life. But in some strange way my reaction to the disaster surprised even me. It motivated me so powerfully to finish my private pilot's license that I even quit drinking in order to fly.

It wasn't until my first long cross country flight that I found myself back in the airport bar drinking beers when my instructor came in and asked me how the flight went. I said that everything had gone smoothly, which was a lie. The first leg from Chicago to Peoria had gone without a hitch, but as I left Peoria, I went 180 degrees in the wrong direction and became lost. I managed to get myself home, but not without a certain amount of help from controllers and a lot of fear.

By the time I actually received my license from Art "The Terminator" Solberg, the examiner who flunked me the first time, I was a timid, uncertain, and phobic pilot. Just going up at all took an enormous effort of will to overcome my fears, and more than once I taxied out to the end of the runway to find that I simply did not have the courage to take off. I reported some sort of malfunction and taxied back and parked the airplane. My plan to conquer aviation was not taking shape very majestically in those days. Eventually there came a day when I chose to drink rather than fly—I knew I couldn't do both or I would surely die. And after one particularly difficult experience of taxiing out and being unable to take off because I was afraid, I simply went back, tied down the plane, and didn't return.

My medical certificate lapsed. My skills went out of date. The year was 1980. The following year, I managed to convince myself that the new obligations of starting a family were the real reason that I let flying slip out of my fingers.

In 1988 that unlikely set of circumstances surrounding my father's decoration for heroism and his promotion to captain led me back into flying and directly into aerobatics. I had quit drinking some years earlier, and as I grew more and more sober, some unseen force seemed to be pulling me back into aviation without my even realizing it. I became involved with kites for a time. Well, I suppose *obsessed* is a better word. I wanted to fly on them, but they weren't quite big enough. I started making kites. I built them bigger and bigger. I dreamed of taking off on one of them. I went to a hang glider school in San Diego to see what that was like. Something baffling was happening to me.

After my father's ceremony at Randolph, Nick Kehoe arranged for me to fly jets with his 12th Flying Training Wing for my magazine assignment. The base Aero Club let me take aerobatics lessons in a T-34. While I was out there doing cloverleafs over Hondo, it suddenly hit me like an epiphany: I had been meant to be an aviator. This was the secret life that had been snatched from me in some way that I would never be able to explain. But there was still time. If I hurried (or if I moved really slowly) I might still regain some of it before it was too late.

I had a lot of recovering to do. When I returned to flying, all the memories came rushing back: in a Cessna 150 on the end of an immense runway, all alone with the smell of that cheap plastic Cessna interior and those familiar fumes, looking at a mile of empty concrete, which beckoned at me to come on, come on, push that throttle forward. This is going to be fun. . . . I was still petrified when the white line dropped away beneath me. Those first flights to Galt left me dripping in sweat, and all I had to do was land.

But I was lost to the world of aviation and aerobatics. I knew that the fear was secondary now. My life had changed. I needed training from a proper instructor and a lot of practice, but I knew I'd get through it. I took my lessons with Bob Murray at Rockford, and that gave me the confidence to fly aerobatics alone—something I never dreamed I could do in those first anxious days after I had been returned to flight status. But it wasn't enough. I needed a Pitts and an instructor I could trust not to kill me.

John Morrissey, the coach of the U.S. Aerobatics Team, was fifty-one, but he looked forty. The moment I saw him, I understood that I was looking at the genuine item, not just a fighter pilot but what fighter pilots call a real G-Monster. Tall, blue-eyed, big-boned, fit, he had been annealed by the fires. Wherever he stood, it seemed that he was going to stand there forever, planted like a bronze statue. He moved slowly or didn't move at all. He looked at my shoes and said, "Don't you have any soft shoes?" He meant that I had to feel the rudder pedals. I was about to learn that flying a Pitts was like trying to play guitar with your toes.

John's hangar was large enough for five or six airplanes, but when I first arrived, I saw only two: the red-white-and-blue Pitts S2A, and a Luscombe Silvaire antique, in which his wife, Anne Marie, gave instruction. As we passed it on our way in, I admired it, and John said, "That's a freedom machine, a hundred knots at four-point-five gallons per hour."

I touched the propeller of the Pitts, and John said, "Never touch a polished metal prop." I felt like a dunce. I had the wrong clothes, and I knew better than to touch the prop: Acid in the sweat from my hands would leave a mark, which would slowly etch the metal. But I was falling under the spell of the machine. Now I saw how neat everything was. There was even a coffee can under the oil breather tube of the Pitts to catch the drips.

John's tools were neatly laid on a carpeted workbench. The radio played classical music softly. The high hangar roof beams were bare wood supporting galvanized steel. At the back was an L-shaped couch and John's reclining chair upholstered in camel-color velour. The chair was for his bad back. He had ejected from a fighter plane. I asked if he'd been hurt. "Hell, yes," he said. "I broke my taint."

"What's your taint?" I asked.

"You know that place between your balls and your asshole, and 'tain't balls, and 'tain't asshole? That's your taint."

I felt as if I were in a strange dream. My father had come back as a fighter pilot and he was finally going to teach me to fly. Even his wife's name was the same.

Whenever I flew with the Air Force or National Guard, I would wonder at how they sat around and did nothing for so long before they went up. There seemed to be no reason to wait, but now I understand: They were preparing their inner selves in a way that even they might not understand. They were doing something extremely important—they were *not* hurrying. As John and I sat doing nothing, talking idly, I had that same sensation. The plane was there. The sun was out. I was ready to fly—at least I thought I was. And yet it seemed that John would never rise. Our view was of silver hangars against the almost-silver sky and what must have been a green field of grass once upon a time, now struck like a coin with the hard imprint of silver concrete. It was a warm, pleasant day, and it seemed we could have sat there forever as John went on with his briefing, talking about the coefficient of lift, drag ratios, and asymmetrical airfoils.

When he finally seemed ready to fly, he reminded me that "we don't have to go through that whole dick dance with the radio," because there was no control tower at Grain Valley Airport (3GV). He said, "I'd rather eat a yard of shit than talk to the tower."

John stood, and I followed his lead and stood, too. I thought he was going to sit down again, he looked so relaxed, but then he walked toward the Pitts, and so I walked toward the Pitts. I offered to help him push it out, but he declined, taking hold of the drag wires on the tail and pushing it into the sunlight as if it weighed nothing at all.

John said, "Well, if this doesn't peg your fun meter, what's the point?"

Most pilots can look at almost any airplane and study it for a while, and conclude, "I can fly that." But when most pilots look at a Pitts, they say, "How could anyone fly that thing?" Just sitting there, it looks as if it's breaking the rules. Aviat's chief test pilot recently came to the midwest to deliver a new Pitts, and when he landed, he said, "Boy, I used up every inch of that hundred-and-fifty-foot-wide runway getting down."

A normal plane wants to stay level, but that works against aerobatics. Within the vicious parentheses of its wings, the Pitts pilot flies an extremely unstable airplane. It is its very instability that gives the Pitts its tremendous maneuverability. It wants to tumble, and that is, by definition, aerobatics. As one of my early instructors told me when I said I wanted to fly a Pitts, "That damned thing doesn't know whether it's right side up or upside down."

The front seat had no compass, no needle and ball. "If you don't look out the window, you can't fly aerobatics," John said. I would have to learn the feel of being centered in a turn. Centrifugal force would pull me straight down in my seat, while lift pulled the airplane around the turn.

Just before takeoff John said, "Remember: big engine, little airplane. Keep your eyes on the Big Gorilla, which is the edge of the runway. I can save you from most things, but you go off there, I can't save you. That's one, and the other is if you put on the brakes. Do not touch the brakes."

I took off. Well, I started to take off, and then John saved me from crashing his beautiful stars-and-stripes Pitts. The machine seemed to claw up the runway in big chunks, howling and nosing this way and that, angry, eager, an uncontained explosion of directionless energy. Nothing I could do with the rudder pedals seemed to work—as the Aviat test pilot said, I used up every inch of that runway. I felt John take over behind me, and then the Pitts grabbed the air with both hands, growling, and lunged itself into flight. I was a Mexican peasant, and I'd been riding a burro all my life. Now I was on the favorite at the Kentucky Derby, and someone had just opened the gate.

He gave me back the controls and suggested that I fly around and get the feel of it. It was like driving a spike through the meat of the air, a piercing weapon.

I have noticed in so many disciplines that a true master returns us to basic moves. In the movie *Karate Kid* the old master made his pupil scrub the floor, wash the windows, and polish the car. Murray had taught me to perform the whole IAC Sportsman sequence, which was good in its way; it was fun, and it built my confidence. But with John Morrissey, I went back to learning to crawl. At first he would not even let me do an entire roll.

The first time I rolled the airplane, he said, "That's way too fast for your level of proficiency." When I was a kid, I went to work in the factory of the great trumpet maker Renold Schilke. He agreed to give me lessons and a place to practice if I swept his floor. On the first day he listened to my playing, I did my fanciest numbers for him. He told me to practice whole notes. I had been shocked and humiliated: Whole notes were for beginners. I wanted to play high and fast. After all, that's what a trumpet is for, isn't it? But from then on, any time he heard me playing high and fast, he'd burst into the room and shout at me, "Whole notes! Long tones! Breathe! Breathe!"

John touched my shoulder softly as we flew. "That's the amount of pressure you need on the rudder pedals," he said.

There was a very good reason that he wanted to make sure I could roll the airplane before he let me go any further. It was the same reason that Gerry gave us The Lecture. One of the most common accidents for an aspiring aerobat, especially a Pitts driver, is the crash that usually occurs when we try to make a victory roll immediately after taking off. We see it in air shows. It looks easy. We try it. It turns out not to be so easy after all.

So John and I went out day after day, and I rolled from level flight to knife-edge flight and then back to level flight. Each time I did that simple-seeming maneuver, he would point out how I was doing it wrong. In fact, to roll an airplane from level to knife edge and then gently let it back down again, and to do it smoothly and keep the nose on a point on the horizon, is as difficult as holding a pose in ballet standing on one toe with the other knee touching an earlobe. Of the roll, John said, "That's the keys to the kingdom right there."

I practiced the quarter roll, up and back, up and back. As I progressed, John allowed me to do half a roll—up, over, stop inverted; then return to level upright flight—all without losing altitude, all with the nose on a point on the horizon. Sometimes as I'd begin to roll, John would say, "What are you looking at? You're not watching the horizon. Look out. Look as far out as you can." And I would look way out, miles and miles, into the mist. There seemed to be nothing out there, but John knew. He knew what was out there. He had made a pact with The Demon, and he was trying to get me to see it.

As I rolled in gently, slowly, blending left aileron and right rudder, I was thrown against the left side of the canopy. From knife edge to inverted, I scraped along the metal frame of the canopy rail until I was left hanging by my belt, blood pounding in my head. It's not easy to let go of instinct and relax when you feel certain that you're falling out of an airplane at 3,500 feet. All in all it was a strenuous and unnatural act. It took days.

□

Sometimes as we flew, John would remind me to breathe. "I wasn't hearing the M-One maneuver there," he'd say, which is what the Air Force calls grunting when you're pulling G's, which helps push the blood back to the brain. "Don't stop breathing or you're lost." A Zen master couldn't have said it better.

If I progressed to negative-G figures, it would become more important. "Most people can pull four G's all day," he said. "But not after prolonged exposure to negative G's. You can pull four G's and black out if you've been doing a lot of outside stuff."

Like everyone else, John eventually took me aside and gave me The Lecture. The first time, it came out in two short sentences. It was different from other versions I'd heard. He said, "Never roll on takeoff." Then he thought about that for a moment and said, "Well, never is a long time."

One day I turned my head on the takeoff roll, and he later told me how dangerous that could be. He told a story about flying formation in F104s at night in weather and having to shoot an NDB approach and tune the ADF radio by feel, counting the clicks on the knob to find the frequency and then listening to a tone to fine-tune it, all while keeping his eyes fixed on his leader's wingtip. "You don't dare look away, not even for a second, because you turn your head and that wingtip may be coming through your windshield," he said. I was just trying to take off in a silly Pitts, and it seemed as if I'd lassoed the moon.

John kept a length of clear hose in a little compartment behind his head called the turtle deck, and he used it to get the fuel nozzle past the cabane struts when refueling. I thought it strange on a $60,000 airplane, but that's aviation. "If you don't have one of these hoses," he said, "fueling this plane can be a real dick dance." The dialect John spoke was a fascinating blend of engineering and physics, a savage, brilliant poetry. We stood on the summery ramp watching the fuel pour out of the metal nozzle and down the clear poly tube, and John explained how the inverted fuel system in the Pitts worked. There was a tube that had a weight on the end, and it simply went where the fuel went. He called it the Donkey Dick.

When something didn't work out, he would say, "It didn't pass the so-what test."

We returned to the hangar after each flight, and John would talk all the way; he really liked to talk, but then that was the true fighter pilot-cum-poet in the grand old mold. As a fighter pilot might die at any moment, he had to spread his wisdom, like his seed, as far and wide as possible.

Another student of his was taking lessons at the same time. Mike was an aspiring military pilot, and as we rested between lessons on the couches in the hangar, John explained some things about combat and enemy fire. "Mike, let me break the code for you," John began. "The first Aim One, the Sidewinder, it didn't have much of an envelope. Of course, if you shoot 'em in the face, they'll never see it." He went on to describe how to evade a big missile. "Up high when it gets to Mach three and gets some air moving over those silly little wings, you get perpendicular to its flight path, wait, and then turn on it. You're pulling three G's, and it's pulling a hundred, and it stalls and tumbles end over end." Mike was thin, blue-eyed, blond, crew-cut, with a rapt expression, listening to John talk about Real Combat. John must have been like that once. He had the same look, only softened like beaten gold by experience and age.

He fell to ruminating on the Pitts. "Basically, through the evolutionary process, the engine got unfucked," he said of the Lycoming, plagued by problems when it was first introduced. He said he liked the Pitts better than the Mustang.

I said, "So did I," and he gave me a look, not knowing whether to take me seriously or not.

□

Night. Two intense flights today. Two flubbed takeoffs. I felt like a moron not only because my takeoffs were so bad but because I broke John's canopy. When we parked, he said, "Push." I pushed upward and broke the bolt that held the canopy. "You broke my fucking plane!" John shouted, and at first I thought he was joking, but he wasn't. At that moment I was glad he worked for me and not the other way around. I still owed him a bunch of money, so I figured he couldn't kill me yet.

Mike and I were waiting for John to find a new bolt. "I'd give anything to be an Air Force officer," Mike said. Then he paused for thought. "Anything except flying." He wanted, he said, "to be an Eagle driver."

John was composed when he returned. "Sorry about the demonstration," he said. It was a quiet remark that I almost missed, but John expected his students to be like fighter pilots: We never miss anything. That's the lore, anyway. I think John reluctantly recognized me as a kindred spirit of some distant-cousin sort. I had a father like him, an Air Force know-it-all who had come back from combat enlightened with the divine portent of his own survival and had taken credit for it and lived on the rest of his life as if he had been placed there to be served by the minions who would happily surround him. Or perhaps creatures like John and my father believed that they had died in combat and this was their happy hunting ground. Either way, the result was the same kind of overwhelming personality, which I found rather familiar in a smothering sort of fashion. Even his yelling at me for breaking his $60,000 airplane. It was very much like me and my father.

I told John that I was scared, and he told me about a time in the 1960s when he was learning in the F104, clipping down the final approach course doing 180 knots, when he'd been used to 120. The best glide speed was 250 knots (it's 65 in my Citabria, 90 in the Pitts), and John said he was scared to death and knew that he was in way over his head. "The United States lost five planes in the first week of the Gulf War," he said. "I remember days when we lost five planes in a single day—that's just the way it was back then."

When the F105 was a brand-new airplane back in the '60s, nothing like it had been seen, not even when the advances in new equipment were coming so fast that the records were broken every month. John was chosen as the pilot who would pick up one of the first new F105s in New York.

When he taxied out and called for his IFR clearance, the control said, "On departure, intercept the runway three two localizer, and track outbound to the compass locator. Thence to Pelee Intersection. Thence to Yugo VOR and follow the two three five radial . . ." words to that effect. It was a series of traffic-avoidance maneuvers that required John to take off and drive around in circles with the airliners. He called the controller back. "Yes, well, that's very nice, but if I do all that, I won't have enough fuel to get this aircraft out of New York."

"What do you suggest, sir?" the controller shot back at him.

John keyed his microphone button and said, "I suggest I go vertical to eighteen thousand feet and get out of your hair."

There was a long silence on the frequency as the controllers had a quick conference. No airplane could do that, so naturally there was no clearance for it. Finally someone came back on the frequency and said, "Sir, you are cleared, uh, to eighteen thousand feet . . . if you can make that within five miles from brake release."

"No problem," John said, and he pointed that fighter plane up and did it practically right over the field. John told me how much fun it was. "There I was, streaking skyward with this shiny new silver F one-oh-five on a column of flame." And it wasn't even a record by then. Now "vertical departure" is a standard clearance for fighters in congested areas. "Yeah," he said, reminiscing, "in the old days, fighter pilots would try to dive when someone was on their tail. Now these young guys simply say, 'I'm a dot.' The idea is to get out with some gas and go home rather than to stay and die." And I thought I detected in his voice just the slightest trace of nostalgia.

Today in training we did inverted turns. In order to make turns while inverted, I had to move the rudder in the direction of the turn and move the stick away from the turn. It seemed as if it would never work, but then it did, confoundingly. I hung in the seat belt, blood pounding in my brain, my eyes bulging, head throbbing, my hands heavy. The green earth was suspended above me like a tapestry filled with minutely detailed stories, if only we could read them, while my legs began to go to sleep from the belt cutting across my lap. John seemed perfectly willing to hang like that all day long if necessary. He didn't complain once, although later he told me I had been making him sick. I wasn't sure whether he meant nausea or disgust.

John had everything figured out. At lunch one day Mike and I began discussing how to determine position over the box, and without hesitation John wrote an equation on a napkin, which told us how many feet we would drift in a hammerhead with a twenty-knot cross wind.

Near the end of the week, I thought I had begun to understand why John had to be right all the time. There was no maybe in this game. There were no gray areas. It was a course you took pass-fail. For years in air shows John did loops right down on the deck. He signed his own son Matthew's Unlimited waiver, allowing him to do the same. If he wasn't right all the time, he could just as easily have signed his son's death warrant.

John's method and personal style, which many people find slightly overwhelming, has one advantage: It works. One of his students came to him and said, "I want to fly a

Pitts. Moreover, I want to win the Nationals in Sportsman category in October." She was a housewife. She came out and worked with him seven days a week. She bought her own insurance policy to cover flying John's S2A without him in the rear seat. And when she won (in October) she had fifty hours in his Pitts.

The day came up rainy and overcast. We had to do pattern work today, because we couldn't climb high enough for aerobatics, but it was something I had wanted to do. Landing the Pitts is one of its greatest challenges. I was delighted to find that there was one thing I could do well in the Pitts: I could fly the pattern to John's specifications, rolling out just over the numbers. I could hear in his voice that he was pleased, even excited, at the way I was handling the airplane. "You keep doing that, I'm going to let you touch down soon," he said.

Here is what happens with confidence, which is a drug more dangerous than cocaine: I was doing pretty well in my patterns. We'd swoop down, and just at the point of landing I'd give it the power, correct for the torque of that big engine with a touch of right rudder, and then fly away for another circuit. After one perfect approach, I felt so good that I pulled up hard and cranked it over into a wrenching left turn.

"Whoa there, fella!" John said. "Don't do *that*." Then he explained to me that the Pitts was designed with the idea of a snap roll in mind. The top set of wings is swept back to make one wing stall before the other when we add a little yaw. Making matters even more confusing, the pattern speed is the same as the snap-roll speed. If we yaw and then pull, the airplane like a well-trained puppy is going to get happy and go (as John put it) "Boss want to snap? Okay." SNAP! At Logan County Airport a pilot flying a Pitts went around after a balked landing and turned into a 90-degree bank. He pulled on the stick to yank it around just as I had, and the airplane snapped. He was about seventy-five feet off the ground, and it spun right in. It's that symmetrical airfoil. It comes unhooked very easily.

As we went around, John admonished me, "That airfoil cannot be loaded up at pattern speeds." Confidence kills.

Saturday Flight Service reported: "–X M10 ¼F" [sky partially obscured, measured ceiling 1,000, one quarter mile visibility in fog], which meant that we couldn't fly. We sat in the hangar and discussed how long we would wait before I returned to Chicago. John said, "I don't know. What's your drop-dead time?"

I left more confused than ever about what I should do. I certainly wasn't ready to buy a Pitts. I couldn't even take off in one, let alone perform or land afterward.

While training with John, I couldn't help wondering about his son, Matt. With the Great Santini for a father, I wondered if Matt Morrissey was in danger flying his airshow Stearman in the Red Baron Squadron. Or did having John as a father make him a safer pilot? I could imagine him either trying so hard that he killed himself or learning so much that he didn't. The outcome didn't seem at all predictable to me.

In fact, Matt went on to win the Sportsman category of the National Aerobatics Championships in John's S2A, and I was moved to further speculation on the requirement of complete confidence that we place upon ourselves. I wondered what it does to a person to have no doubts. I couldn't imagine that state of mind. I began to see the personality of the aviator unravel and expose its inner workings. For while having no doubts makes it possible to perform in that special way—warrior or sportsman—it makes all sorts of other things in life impossible. For example, it closes one off to the point of view of others. It cuts off intimacy and empathy, which tend to solicit from others alternatives to the single, focused point of view. Certain kinds of human interactions require giving up something of oneself in the bargain, letting go of one's point of view in order to adopt another's, if only temporarily. In other words, the ability to doubt or question is an integral part of intimacy. The inability or refusal to doubt or question oneself is an obstacle to intimacy. In fact, intimacy is a threat to people who have complete confidence. Football players were told not to have sex before a big game, not because sex drains their strength but because intimacy undermines confidence. Complete confidence is complete isolation. That's true warrior spirit.

A fighter pilot's wife observed, "I don't think that people were meant to be confident. Confidence arises out of a pathetic and desperate decision to pretend that what you think is the only thing that can be thought. Confidence is like endorphins: for emergency use only." And what are endorphins but our own natural heroin?

Art Galt was out on his tractor mowing the grass in front of the house and waving at the people passing through his driveway in cars early this morning when I returned to the airfield. When he was done, I found him in the office and asked him for a discourse on confidence.

Art thought about it and then said, "You know, Lloyd made that same mistake a few weeks before, only he was alone that time, and he didn't have full tanks. Did you see when they hit? They were almost level. It died him." Nancy Hughes lamented losing Lloyd to his airplane. Ultimately, I think she lost Lloyd to the curse of his own confidence.

EIGHT

THE CHEMISTRY OF FIRE

AMOS BUETTELL'S birthstone was the sun. It seemed that he was pursued by fire all his life, and even beyond it. It was fire that killed him, igniting Amos like a ritual offering. Everyone agrees that he was a gifted and driven pilot. He came in like a tempestuous king, born to Marc Buettell, an engineer who worked his way up from designing wire nuts to being the president of a midsized industrial company, Ideal, in Sycamore, Illinois.

Amos lied about his age to join the Marines and went off to the coast of China after World War II. When he returned he raced stock cars. He married his girlfriend, Velma, and they had a son, whom they named after Amos's father, Marc. It took a while for Amos to settle down and get the concept that there was more to life than burning gas and breaking bones turning left around a dirt oval. Amos worked as a machinist for a while, but he was too smart for that. He went to college, and his son, Marc, who was thirty-seven when I met him, remembered graduation. "Yeah, he got a degree in business administration," Marc recalled. "He called it Jewish engineering." The year was 1960. Amos was thirty-two. Marc was six.

Amos went to work for Ideal as a salesman. "And he was a good peddler," Marc said. "He was good at selling wire nuts." He took Marc along on trips when the boy wasn't in school. Marc remembered those trips fondly, as if seeing vacuum cleaner factories was a thrill to him. But in reality it was just being near Amos, having the opportunity to watch him, to sense his hugeness, to draw something from his overpowering energy and momentum, as if Marc were being allowed to reach out and take hold, not of the hand of a flesh-and-blood man of five feet eleven inches and average build, but instead of an immense black and smoking locomotive, wet with steam and slick with grease, that was moving down a mountain pass, gaining speed.

In the early 1960s, Ideal had several subsidiary divisions and was diversifying its business. Amos had been put in charge of Crown, which made specialty chemicals, lubricants, and release agents and corrosion inhibitors used by industry—all explosive, volatile, flammable stuff, the fluid precursors of fire. Crown was operating out of a one-room shop on Amsterdam Street in Woodstock when the first brick was laid for the new factory in Hebron in 1964. Marc saw a change taking shape in his father. The man who had been obsessed with stock cars and raising hell, now seemed obsessed with business. He wore a flat-top haircut and a business suit. He was driven, and that which could be thought of could be done, and that which could be done was done now, or he knew the reason why.

Amos eventually took possession of Crown Industrial Products. I would say he bought it, but he actually possessed it, the way he might have possessed a horse he caught on the open plains. *Intense* was a word I heard a lot of people use, but it didn't do justice to what Amos was. To the employees, there was something really different about the new young owner of Crown, something people sensed which made them nervous. They liked him. They just didn't know what it was they were liking.

When Amos looked at you, there was something savage about it. His eyes possessed you. He seemed to know more of you than even you knew. It was like having a domesticated lion in the office, clean-shaven, well dressed, but somehow he wasn't fooling anyone. Least of all himself. It seemed inevitable that one day something would have to give.

"I think it was Amos trying to find the true Amos all along," Marc said. "In 1970 we finally got rid of the flat-top." Then Amos started wearing blue shirts. It doesn't sound like much, but for Amos at that time it was as big a step as if he'd come to work wearing a ring in his nose. Amos had started thinking about racing cars on dirt ovals again, but somehow he seemed to have gone beyond that. Crown was a growing company. It was making money, and the money threatened to get big if Amos did everything right. But Amos was restless. A force had hold of him. He was looking around for something, something, he couldn't exactly say what.

Amos's father had started flying a Cessna 140 after the war, and he had been flying a 210 more recently. Amos was no stranger to airplanes, but he was already in his forties when he decided to learn to fly. He took some lessons in Florida, where his parents spent the winter. Back in Illinois he went to the nearest airport, Galt, and flew with Conrad Tomlinson, the old-time cigar-chomping chief flight instructor. "He was the only instructor I ever knew," Russell told me, "where they had to replace an instrument panel because he used to pound on it with his fist while he was shouting at the students. And he smoked that cigar right in the cockpit."

There were no half measures with Amos. He went

through his private, instrument, commercial, and multi-engine ratings, and he was looking around for more. One of the other instructors at Galt was George Kropf, whom Amos eventually hired to run the flight department at Crown and to be his personal mechanic, corporate pilot, and all-around aviation guru. For George, Amos was a dream come true, what every pilot hopes for: somebody with money who wants to buy expensive airplanes and make you fly them.

Amos decided to take one of his corporate aircraft around the world. Everyone told him that those airplanes—this one was a Cessna 310—were meant for dragging executives to Muncie, not for crossing the ocean, but Amos wouldn't listen. He slapped a Colemill Conversion on the airplane for speed and range, and then had more gas tanks put in than anyone considered safe. All that gasoline. Wasn't he worried about fire?

"It was a flying gas tank," Marc said.

"It was a flying bomb," others said.

"Amos had taken the three-ten to Europe," Marc said, "but he didn't tell anybody that he was simply making test runs for his round-the-world trip. When he came back and told me what he was doing, it all made sense. I knew he was planning something." Marc, a peddler like his father, was working in Iowa at the time and drove to Galt Airport to watch Amos take off for his trip around the world. Amos had bought a blue baglike jumpsuit for comfort on the long trip. Amos worked out a system whereby he would telex the Crown offices every time he landed somewhere to let Marc know how the trip was going. "And that was how I stayed in touch," Marc said. I could see that Marc had been worried, that his heart had been in the airplane with his father every lonely hour of the trip. The forsaken longing that Marc felt for Amos was no less intense than the longing lovers feel for each other when they are separated. There is nothing more desolate than a boy whose father has gone away, even when he's a man.

On the trip something happened to Amos. He didn't crash, and his gasoline bomb did not burn him up, but as he sat there through those long and solitary hours over the ocean, something changed within him. Perhaps an angel visited him. Perhaps he had a vision. He had planned his trip as an attempt to beat four world speed records for his class of airplane, and he beat all four. When he returned home, he had decided that aviation was what he wanted to do. It was the only thing in the world.

Years later, sitting in a restaurant in Wisconsin with George Kropf and Jimmy Bartz, Amos's mechanic, I asked what happened, and George smiled and said, "Amos got interested in speed and altitude. That airplane *was* a fuel tank. He set the Hawaii-to-Midway speed record in it, nonstop. He had two sets of engines for that airplane, and he went around the world once with each set."

I expressed my surprise that he had more than one set of engines.

"Oh, he'd change engines like you and I would change our pants," George said.

"But why did he do it?" I asked.

George thought for a long time and then said eventually, "I'd have to say he became obsessed."

I told him the story of *The Wind in the Willows,* and George lit up. "That's Amos!" he said. "Toad of Toad Hall. Amos used to say that he didn't have anything that didn't go fast, and it was true. If he had a snowmobile, it was the fastest one. If he had a motorcycle, it was the fastest one. Everything he had went fast." Amos drove a Ferrari and a Maserati, and more than once he and George had raced from the Crown factory in Hebron to Amos's hangar at Galt Airport. "I tried hard to beat him, but I never could. I'd arrive, and Amos would be sitting in the hangar laughing at me." His hangar is the present-day maintenance shop.

The changes in Amos had become radical. People noticed, at work, at home, at the airport. George noticed and Jimmy Bartz, noticed. For one thing, Amos shed his wife of twenty-three years. "It had been coming for a long time," Marc said.

Amos let his hair grow. The flat-top had been gone for a while, but this was different. He was turning gray, but his hair looked blond somehow. It hung well below his ears and seemed to throw off a light of its own. He wore a headband to keep his hair back and grew a full beard. Amos began to look like a Viking god. He wore blue jeans held up with a rope for a belt and Ray-Ban Aviators, a big handsome grin on his face, and sometimes he drove like that into the Galt Airport parking lot. When Amos and his girlfriend would go to dinner with Marc, the maitre d' would seat Marc and the youthful girlfriend together and put the old man on the other side. Amos and Marc would change places without a word, and heads would turn when Amos put his arm around a woman young enough to be his daughter. If he hadn't looked so much like a Viking king, Amos would have looked like a '60s hippie. At Galt, Carla remembered him as "cool-looking. He wore the wildest boots, snakeskin and things like that."

But events had begun to accelerate, and Amos was having to work to keep up. The problem was that Amos, with his birthstone of fusion, was always looking for the fire that could not be found on earth. It was as if Amos longed for a mysterious substance he'd left behind, a genetic memory of his home galaxy. Is the salmon pursued as he leaps against the white water of a mountain stream, or is he pursuing? Amos and fire had been circling each other from the beginning. Coming back from Arizona with his 402, another high-powered Cessna cabin-class twin, Amos caught fire. Nothing seemed to be wrong with the airplane, but there he was in flames. As he plunged earthward, the fire seemed to subside. He made an emergency landing in the desert. But then flames leaped out of the right engine, and Amos leaped out of the airplane. As he ran, the 402 exploded behind him.

By 1977 Amos had met Jack Reiley, who with his father had had an aircraft conversion business out in California. Before long, Jack and Amos were partners in a business in Waco, Texas, called Ram-Air, which performed modifications on light twins to make them go faster and higher, and Amos used that company to speed up his Four-series Cessnas. Many people, including Jimmy, his own mechanic, thought that a 414 was just fine the way God and Cessna made it.

Jimmy Bartz told me of one 414 on which Amos had hung two IO 720 engines with dual turbochargers, 400 horsepower each. Jimmy didn't even like to get into it.

"Why?" I asked.

"Well, one day Amos took off from Galt, and blew an engine. I don't mean he just blew it, I mean it ripped a jug right off the engine and cracked the case."

"What happened?" I asked.

"Well, it was eight cylinders with dual turbochargers on it, and a whole lot of fist behind that."

"Amos had a lot of fist," George recalled. Then he laughed. "Yeah, Jimmy didn't like to fly in that four-fourteen, did you, Jimmy?"

"Well, I'll just say that you could see my claw marks on the door where they had to drag me on board kicking and screaming for the one ride I took in it," Jimmy said, deadpan. Jimmy Bartz was a big man with tattoos on his arms and black hair and irregular teeth and features to match. Many people had described to me what a sweet guy Jimmy was, and now and then when he smiled, I could see that, but just meeting him on the street, I might give him a wide berth.

"The day Amos lunched the four-fourteen on takeoff at Galt," to put it in Jimmy's words, he flew around, put it back on the runway without further incident, got out, and said to

Jimmy, "Roll out the four-oh-two," his other corporate twin Cessna. At that time the hangar that now serves as the shop, Amos's personal hangar, housed his mechanic (Jimmy) and chief pilot (George) and all the planes he was rapidly acquiring.

George said, "Amos had two throttle positions, wide open and closed."

Jimmy said without a smile, "He had one record with that four-fourteen that I know of: how fast a dollar would fly out of his pocket."

Amos's 414 was modified for an altitude record that never materialized. But the airplane wouldn't perform as expected, and it was simply put on the line as a corporate aircraft.

People at Crown had begun to notice that Amos didn't come to work anymore. Enchanted, he abandoned his empire without preparations, as if he'd been kidnapped. "He thought he was invincible," Marc said. "Amos did not believe he would ever die, and he was the only man I know who could run a fairly large company out of his hip pocket."

Going around the world, even while setting speed and altitude records, can become a pretty dry intellectual exercise. After all, it does consist mostly of straight and level flight far above the weather. Imagine going eastbound from New York to Los Angeles for ninety-five hours with no meals, no bathrooms, and no movie. Amos needed something more, and one day in the early 1980s he mentioned to George, casually, that he thought he might like to get a Great Lakes, which was one of the best aerobatic aircraft at the time. It was an open-cockpit biplane and was used to good effect in air shows.

"For Amos," Marc told me, "to have the idea was the same as having the thing. I don't know exactly which came first, but the moment he got the idea for the Great Lakes, he must have gone out and bought one, because one day it was just there, and he was an aerobatics pilot." If events had seemed to accelerate before, Amos could not have been prepared for what was coming next.

"The Great Lakes wasn't fast enough," George said simply.

Jimmy said, "I changed the pistons for him," and as an aside, half covering his mouth, "though not according to the logs," indicating that the modification would not have been approved by the FAA. "But it didn't do anything for Amos. He said he didn't notice any difference."

"You see," George said, "first he bought the Great Lakes. It didn't go fast enough, so he bought a Pitts. Then that didn't go fast enough, so he bought another Pitts." George stopped and looked at me as if the rest were self-explanatory.

Marc showed me a photograph of Amos with his first Pitts. Amos was wearing black and had his boot up on the bumper of his black Ferrari 308, and the red Pitts was parked beside the car, and they were out in the grass somewhere. Amos looked so happy and proud, as if his dreams of speed and fire had come true. There it was. Red fire. Black ashes. Green earth. Blue sky.

"He kept that airplane for about six months," Marc said. "It was really an experiment, to see how he liked the Pitts, but it was underpowered, a simple Pitts." Then he bought *Tiger Lady*. "All Amos's airplanes," Marc explained, "were named *Lady*-something or something-*Lady*. The Great Lakes was named *Little Lady*." *Tiger Lady* was a high-performance Pitts set up for competition. It was the beginning of the end.

Marc had a sister, Amy, whom Amos had put in school in Tucson, Arizona. She had had some difficulty staying in any one school for very long, and Amos went there frequently to visit her, to check up on her and give her support. But Amos had ulterior motives in being out in Arizona so much. After he'd gone back and forth a few times with his new Pitts, he was visiting Marc one day and said, "I think I'd better be spending some more time out there, you know, just to keep an eye on Amy and see if I can keep her in school this time. And I've found this great airport there, great little strip, perfect location . . ." Galt was nice, but the weather in northern Illinois was not competition weather.

Marc told me, "I didn't see him in the midwest for another two years." Although Marc made regular trips out there to spend the weekends with his father, usually on the way back from business trips to Los Angeles or San Francisco.

It was about that time that Amos decided to get married again, and one day he called Marc and said, "You want to go to a wedding?"

"Whose?" Marc asked.

"Mine, you turkey," Amos snarled with good humor. "I want you to be best man."

With his new Pitts and his discovery of aerobatics competition, Amos took his airplane out to the Avra Valley Airport just outside Tucson and set up shop. He rebuilt a huge hangar space, outfitting it with an air-conditioned office, a garage for his car, a toilet, carpeting, stereo, on which he played Ray Stevens's "The Streak" incessantly at full volume with the hangar doors open to the breeze. He kept jugs of ice water in a refrigerator and drank it constantly, because he sweated so much during aerobatics practice. He had a neatly equipped tool room and a small shop area for repairs, and he hung a big calendar on the wall on which he marked all the contests for the entire year. Then he set up a schedule of practice. "It was a job," Marc said. "He practiced three times a day, five days a week." In the meantime Crown was left to drift like the Flying Dutchman.

Jimmy Bartz had used the same words in describing Amos's routine to me: "It was a job for him," adding, "I just can't see it, beating yourself up like that. It's like doubling yourself over and running your head into a brick wall over and over again."

"But," George reminded Jim, "he was two positions away from the U.S. Aerobatics Team when he died."

Jimmy shook his head as if it were the dumbest thing he'd ever heard of. George recalled how excited Amos would get when he was practicing. Once he was in the hangar at Galt, working on one of the airplanes when Amos returned from practice in one of the Pitts he had bought. "I had the hangar door half open, and Amos taxied in and took four or five good swipes out of the bottom of the door with his propeller. His signature's probably still there if you go take a look." It was.

For while Amos had moved his operation largely to Tucson, he had not abandoned Galt and commuted back and forth in the Pitts, which is a little bit like riding a tricycle across the Great Divide. "Amos would fly in any kind of weather," George recalled. At the time, Amos had given George the job of chasing him back and forth across the nation in the 414 or some other Cessna twin, carrying spare parts, spare girlfriends, and spare wives. "Sometimes Amos would fly through IFR weather that I wouldn't go through in the fully equipped four-fourteen. And he was in a Pitts with no instruments." On one trip, Amos flew 200 miles in solid IFR in a Pitts. "He got a hundred feet above everything he could see on the chart and just followed his compass until he broke out of the clouds." When he was at Galt between stints in Arizona, everyone knew he was there. His Pitts had so much power that the tips of its propeller went supersonic as he flew low passes over the runway, and the characteristic sound let everyone know that he was coming. They'd see him out on the ramp replacing the Lexan window, which melted between his feet from the exhaust stacks. Fire again.

Practicing aerobatics in *Tiger Lady* one hot Arizona day, the carburetor system experienced vapor lock, and Amos could not restart the engine. He tried to glide back to the airfield, but came in short and destroyed the aircraft. Marc received the call at his job in Canada. It was Amos growling on the other end of the line, "Ah, I had a little accident. I rolled *Tiger Lady* up into a ball."

Even all those years later, I could see the panic on Marc's face as he told the story. "Are you all right?" Marc asked.

"No, I'm not all right," Amos growled. "I broke my watch, and I skinned my elbows crawling out from under it."

Marc got so mad at his father that he hollered, "Don't you dare tell me you're hurt!" and he hung up. Just the thought that Amos might be hurt was horrifying to Marc.

Tiger Lady was truly crushed into a ball. It was upside down on the side of a gravel road, and the wings were shattered, splintered, and crushed down, like a toy that had been stepped on. It was difficult to imagine how Amos managed to walk away from it. *Tiger Lady* was pushed into a corner of the hangar, where it sat tilted to one side in a heap, a wooden block under one wheelless strut. Amos had another Pitts within a week, this one even more powerful than *Tiger Lady*. But it wasn't long before he had broken that one, too.

Over the few years, Amos's flying had undergone a gradual but dramatic change. George said, "He was a ham-fisted, hard-flying pilot when he started, and when he died he was a real professional. You could feel how smooth he had gotten."

But what he flew he flew hard. Amos was practicing for a contest at Oak Grove in his third Pitts; and another aerobatic pilot, Sam Burgess, was critiquing him, when a push rod to the right ailerons disengaged. A severe flutter cracked the main spar, leaving his lower right wing flopping in the breeze. Any normal pilot would have bailed out. That's why we wear parachutes. But Amos had learned something in driving those dirt tracks. It was almost a law of life for him: "Never stop driving the car," he always said. It had saved him many times in a race, when everything seemed out of control, when the situation seemed hopeless. Just by continuing to drive the car, acting as if he still had control, he had managed to save the day. Amos said it to his kids, he said it in business—never stop driving the car—and now, it seemed, it had carried over into his flying. Burgess would later say, "When I asked him why he didn't bail out, he replied, 'I thought I could get it down.' " As if he didn't have enough problems, as Amos entered the pattern, a twin-engine aircraft cut him off. Still, Amos flew the airplane to a landing, and that Pitts was pushed into the other corner of the Avra Valley hangar.

Amos had been secretly (or not so secretly) working on an airplane to replace all his other airplanes, but it wasn't ready yet. It seemed silly to buy another airplane just when *Awesome Lady* was about to roll out of the shop, ready for world competition. She was so close. Amos decided to fly the Great Lakes for a while until the experimental rocket-wet-dream-airplane-to-end-all-airplanes was done. It was based on a Pitts design, but he and an engineer from one of the big southern California airframe companies used some borrowed computer time to redesign it so that it would do things that had simply never been done before. For one thing, it was the only propeller-driven aircraft in history to be able to accelerate vertically. Well, it wasn't built yet, but that's what the computer said it would do. It would have a 720-horsepower engine. It was nearly ready for flight one day when Marc happened to be visiting Amos in Tucson on the way back from a business trip to Los Angeles.

"I had just put my tie on," Marc said, "and I walked into the kitchen. It was very early in the morning, because I had to catch a flight back to Chicago. And I saw him hang up the phone and put his hand on the counter like he'd just been told somebody died."

"What's wrong?" Marc asked. He had never seen his father so distraught.

"*Awesome Lady* burned up last night," Amos said. "The whole hangar burned. She's gone." The fire was drawing nearer. Amos could feel the flames. Now it had taken something he truly loved.

Amos was in a bind. He had no airplanes at all, for while waiting for *Awesome Lady* he had broken the Great Lakes, too. He hadn't crashed it. He had simply flown it so hard that he had cracked the wooden spar. "He was used to tougher stuff by then," Marc said. *Little Lady* was pushed back into the hangar with the two broken Pitts Specials, building what would become Amos's legacy: He left a trail of broken airplanes and broken hearts.

"He went out that afternoon and bought the Laser," Marc said.

The trend in world aerobatics competition had only recently swung away from the biplanes and toward new designs, midwing monoplanes with tremendous roll rates, less drag, and remarkable vertical penetration. The Laser was one of those designs, and the particular airplane that Amos bought had already distinguished itself in the highest levels of competition. Amos picked it up in California and flew it back to Arizona within the week.

During that time, he had not simply been punching holes in the clouds. Amos's obsessive approach to aerobatics training had paid off in placing him among the top pilots in the United States and very close to his ultimate goal of making the U.S. Aerobatics Team. Now, even without his specially designed airplane, he stood a very good chance of achieving that goal, either this year or the next.

The year was 1985. The month was February. The incident seemed so simple. Ridiculously simple. If he had jumped out of the airplane as soon as it happened, he would have survived. But it was more than that. Something was pursuing Amos, and even now Marc realizes that. As he told me the story, he often said, "You're going to think I'm crazy," but I did not. I understood that there were forces out there that neither of us could understand, and they came together on February 22, 1985, at around three forty-five in the afternoon.

Amos had a routine. He wore a big diamond ring, and before each flight he twisted it off his finger and put it in his blue jeans pocket and took off his pants and hung them over a chair. The music was playing, and the sun was sending dancing figures curling up from the concrete. Amos took one last drink of water. It was like preparing for sex. Then he put on shorts and driving gloves. He pushed the airplane out into the sun and stepped up on the wing and gingerly climbed in, stepping first on the seat, then nestling down into his parachute, which would still be cool from the shade of the hangar.

The people of Avra Valley Airport always stopped whatever they were doing to watch Amos depart, and this day was no exception. They could often see him practicing not far from the field. But he had been out practicing only a few minutes when they saw him break off his amazing unlimited routine ("He could make square corners," people used to say) and head back toward the runway.

His propeller had thrown a counterweight, a small piece of metal, just a few ounces, but it was the beginning of a catastrophic series of events. Attached to that great big engine, the vibrations set up by the out-of-balance propeller were so powerful that the motion ruptured the aluminum header tank above Amos's knees. Gasoline began spewing out into the cockpit, spraying and pooling around his rudder pedals; but Amos must have been thinking, 'Never stop driving the car.' Amos was on final, he was coming in. He had it made, if only he could keep the airplane from falling apart in his hands. His first impulse not to abandon the aircraft had taken him so low now that he couldn't jump. He opened the clamshell canopy to let some of the suffocating gas fumes out. Now he pulled the power back, thinking that it would lessen the vibrations, maybe save the airplane before the engine shook itself completely loose. Later engineers reported that he should have used full power to lessen the vibrations, but pilots are rarely blessed with that kind of wisdom in advance of misfortune. With the power at idle, the big engine backfired, igniting the gas at Amos's feet. A sheet of flame washed up over him. He was so close.

People on the ramp could see Amos holding his knees up around his chest to keep his feet away from the fire as he came down on short final inside the plexiglass canopy, like a genie inside a globe of flame.

He made the landing, but in his rush to get on the ground he was going too fast, and without the use of rudder the airplane ground-looped and flipped. As the canopy came crashing closed, it knocked his front teeth out. Now Amos was upside down, burning, screaming, and people from the coffee shop had leaped up and were running to the wreck. Despite the fire, they managed to lift a wing, and someone crawled underneath and pulled Amos from the airplane. Moments later it exploded on the runway as the landing gear melted. Amos was able to open his eyes and look at himself. He had suffered third degree burns over 85 percent of his body. He rolled his eyes back and growled, "Oh, shit. Better get me a beer. I'm gonna be late for my date."

In Chicago, Marc had several people on the phone at once, including the doctor, who put Amos's chances at one in ten, and Marc's secretary, who was trying to get him a flight out of O'Hare, which was fogged in. An hour later the airport closed, and Marc couldn't even get a corporate aircraft to take him out of Chicago. The unfathomable forces were in collusion, wind and fire and snow and fog, conspiring to tear father and son apart. They had been at it for so long now, it seemed inevitable that it would come to this frontal assault on the father with fire, the flanking motion with ice against the son.

Within fifteen minutes of the crash, the rescue helicopter had arrived. The paramedics worked on Amos for an hour and then took him to St. Mary's burn unit in Tucson. Marc said, "He was laid out on a table, smoldering, when his fifth ex-wife, Sandi, and Amy came in. They flipped when they saw how badly burned Amos was."

But Amos pointed at the doctor and said, "Don't worry.

See that guy over there in the white coat? He's gonna fix it up."

An hour later Marc talked to the doctor again, and Amos's chances had dropped to 5 percent. "I knew what he was doing," Marc said. "If it was one in ten to begin with and an hour later it was one in twenty, he was telling me that Amos wasn't going to make it."

Marc had to call his mother, Velma, to tell her. She and Amos hadn't been on speaking terms for years. "Dad's been in a crash," he said.

"Is he alive?" she asked.

Marc said, "Yeah, but he's not going to make it."

Velma asked, "Car or airplane?"

Marc said, "Airplane."

And Velma, who according to Marc would not have said shit if she had a mouthful of it, said, "Goddamned fucking airplanes." Despite the fact that they hadn't seen each other in years, Velma decided to go with Marc to Tucson to pay her last respects. It was, after all, Amos Buettell.

Amos's parents arrived at lunchtime on Saturday, and when Amos's father walked in, he took one look at his son and fainted. Someone said to Amos, "Your parents are here," and Amos became animated and tried to sit up, but he couldn't. Marc said, "He had a tube the size of an elephant's dick down his trachea."

Marc finally managed to get to Tucson at eight o'clock Saturday night, more than twenty-four hours after the crash, and although each moment that the weather had kept him away from his father had been like the Death of Ten Thousand Cuts, once he saw Amos, he couldn't stay. He had to walk out into the hall to catch his breath. "Hardened medics who had worked combat in Vietnam told me they'd never seen anything like this," Marc said. "And of course I'd never seen anything like it either."

The nurses and doctors and others assured Marc that Amos could understand him if he talked, but Marc just walked out saying, "You've got to be joking. You've got to be joking." After a time, as Marc's shock subsided, they were able to persuade him to go back in and say something to his father, and Marc stood by the bed feeling the heat now turn cold around his father's charred body.

Marc decided he had better speak to his father before it was too late. "Hi, Dad," he said. "It's Marc. I'm here, and I'll take care of things. I love you." Then he got up and left. People tried to send him back. "But it was a done deal," Marc said. Anyway, he and Amos had already discussed what to do if this happened. "You could watch the flesh just lying there," Marc told me. "But if you wanted to know what was really going on, you watched the TV monitors. He had been stable for quite a while, but then all of a sudden things started going downhill." It was well after midnight when Marc saw that Amos's own vital signs were fading and the machines were taking over the work for him. Marc had the life support equipment unplugged, and four minutes later at 2:51 A.M. on Sunday, February 24, 1985, Amos Buettell was dead. He was fifty-six years old.

The day after the crash, people were looking in the ashes trying to find that huge diamond Amos wore. Some of his friends even accused the paramedics of stealing it. But Marc went into the hangar and lifted Amos's jeans off the chair and shook them. He could hear the change jingling in the pocket. He reached in and came up with the ring.

The memorial service was held outside Amos's hangar. More than a hundred people showed up. There were sandwiches and beer, and the hangar had been thrown open, and Ray Stevens's voice tumbled out into the valley.

As the memorial service began, the people who had gathered there began to notice an immense thunderstorm gathering over the Santa Catalina Mountains. "A motherfucker of a thunderstorm," Marc said. "The evilest thing I've ever seen for weather out there, hanging at eight thousand feet just above this mountain and not moving at all. We all talked about whether it would ruin our plans, but it just stayed there the whole time."

In the middle of the service someone came over to Marc and said, "Who are those women over there?" Marc looked over.

"There was a group—and a significant group of maybe half a dozen really excellent-looking young women," Marc said, "who were gathered in a kind of cluster, and they were just completely crushed, grieving, weeping, and carrying on. And the weirdest thing was that *nobody knew who they were*." A lot of people went around asking, "Who are they? I thought you knew them."

"Well, I thought *you* knew them."

"Don't you know them?"

Nobody had the nerve to go and ask who they were, and finally they ate their sandwiches and wept and drank their beer and paid their respects and left. Marc laughed when he told that story, shaking his head, as if to say, Old Amos. What other secrets did he have? But we all want to be looked at, and those were the people who looked at Amos: the son he created and the women he attracted. When we do aerobatics, everybody looks at us.

Marc had heard a secret rumor about Amos going down to Guatemala to buy fighter planes, but he had just chalked it off to legend and myth about his father until he came across a packet of photos in his father's effects showing him in the jungle with a bunch of fighter planes. "Oh, my God, it's true!" Marc said. As I listened to Marc tell stories about his father, I could feel a kind of suicidal glee growing within me, and by the time I was finished with Amos Buettell, his almost seemed like a reasonable and actually pretty neat way to live and die. It was a few days before the spell began to wear off. I awoke one morning, thinking, Hey, wait a minute, here. I don't want to be burned over 85 percent of *my* body.

I want to be like Art Galt, an old pilot who can tell people to go to hell.

As Amos Buettell's memorial service ended, Marc brought out the box of ashes. He had had his father cremated, and now Amos's best friend, Gary Abrams, was going to fly out in a Cessna 172 (Amos's chase plane, in which someone followed him to the contests) and "scatter the ashes over the aerobatics box he'd finagled out of the FAA," as Marc put it.* Gary asked Marc if he wanted to do it, but Marc couldn't bring himself to scatter his father's ashes.

As Gary got organized to go, the wind came pouring down the mountain and hit Amos's hangar. It scattered people and chairs as if a tornado were coming. "That storm just sat there," Marc said, giving himself a chill remembering the event. "It didn't rain. It was as if something had been watching us." People ran in every direction on the desert airport, attempting to batten down the hatches, and then in the middle of it all, Gary took off with Amos's ashes and flew out over the valley, and when he came back he reported that it was "the bumpiest fucking ride I've ever taken."

"I know you're going to think I'm crazy," Marc kept saying, "but then everything calmed down, and we cleaned up and we went home." It seemed as if the forces had finally been appeased. The fire had got what it came for. But it was not quite over. Not all the scores were settled yet.

The family fell into dispute over Crown Industrial Products, and the company had to be sold to mollify everyone involved. Well, not quite everyone. There was still the spirit that had been chasing Amos. Shortly after that, Crown Industrial Products burned to the ground in a spectacular fire of solvents and chemicals and fluids—the amino acids of fire. That night the glow was seen for miles around.

After the inferno died away, I called the director of oper-

* *Amos must have had to plead with FAA officials for the waiver needed to perform aerobatics in that location.*

ations there and asked him what was going to happen. "Nothing," he said. "It's the end of an era."

I tracked down Conrad Tomlinson, Amos's old cigar-chomping, instrument-panel-pounding instructor. He was retired, and I woke him from his nap, which didn't please him any. I asked him about Amos. "Yeah, I taught him," Tomlinson said. I asked him what he thought of Amos, and he said, "He was a playboy. He had lots of money. What's he doing now?"

"He's dead," I said. "He was killed in a crash."

"Oh," Tomlinson said. "I guess I knew that, but I forgot."

NINE

UNIFORM

Bob Russell could be seen on a continuous circuit that took him from the shop to the flight desk, where UPS delivered boxes of parts, up the stairs to the office, where his desk was cluttered with books and records and dominated by a facsimile machine and a microfiche viewer, and then back down again and out to the hangars to look at an airplane, then down the taxiway between the hangars, around the parking lot, into the briefing room, where he would sit in the same spot on the torn and battered black Naugahyde couch and confabulate upon some region of aeronautical arcana to delight or infuriate or bore those gathered there for their morning coffee or afternoon Dr Pepper. Russell: a tall blue-eyed man in a torn and oil-spotted blue down vest that shed feathers as he walked around and worked and talked, as if he carried a cloud behind him on a leash. Russell had a nervous manner, a pleasant and friendly round face, buck teeth, dark hair (slightly bald on top), and projected a kind of busy peripatetic, preoccupied, determined intelligence. He was quick to smile, quick to joke, and if asked a question, was apt to take a very big breath and roll his eyes around, searching for the entry in his brain-borne Encyclopedia of Everything Known and Suspected, and then give a presentation lasting twenty minutes or more, often stopping his work (if you happened to catch him elbow-deep in the guts of an airplane) and dragging the petitioner out across the parking lot and past the front counter and up into the office to look up a pertinent Federal Aviation Regulation or to thumb through a parts catalog to find a price. Russell, it seemed, liked nothing better than to be interrupted while working. He also liked to have the right answers. He liked to have as many things pinned down as possible in this uncertain world.

Russell was the boss, the boss of the shop, and the boss of the airport. With more than a hundred airplanes on the field, either permanently or part-time, and with each annual inspection taking at least several days, when Russell added in the unscheduled maintenance (euphemism for "broken stuff"), the shop was busy continuously, usually with three, four, five, or even half a dozen planes in various stages of malfunction, disassembly, or catastrophe.

Mine was a disquieting lesson to learn. I wanted so badly to find that aviation was a precise and certain science. But every airplane always has something broken. (My system-theorist friends at Bell Labs think tanks used to express it as this axiom: "All large systems operate continuously in failure mode.") Old-time pilots often call airplanes that are perfectly maintained Hangar Queens, because they are always in the hangar looking pretty, whereas *real* airplanes are put together with baling wire and chewing gum.

Jim Liss, a commercial pilot himself and second in charge at the shop, was short and bearded and wore quilted army-green coveralls that were unzipped and rolled down to the waist, revealing his muscular upper body in a lumberjack shirt with the sleeves rolled up. Liss affected a quiet, businesslike air. He was a very orderly airplane mechanic and had a method for everything. He believed that if things were done the same way each time, according to a plan, then each time the results would be the same. But quiet as he was, Liss was always thinking, and as soon as he found the right moment, he would pounce, delivering his lines with cunning, accuracy, and impeccable timing. One winter day I came in to complain that the little spigot underneath the fuel tank in the wing was frozen on the airplane I was about to fly. I could not open the valve to take a fuel sample before flight. Liss looked up from what he was doing and said deadpan, "Use a cigarette lighter."

Liss and Russell, short and tall and different as they seemed, were actually very much alike. They were always at odds, but the conflict took place beneath the surface. Liss thought that Russell thought that he knew everything. And Russell thought that Russell knew everything, so actually they were in agreement, they just didn't know it. Liss worried sometimes that things weren't safe in the shop. "There are too many distractions," he said. "People always coming in and asking for stuff, then we stop in the middle of a job and do something else. When we come back, we say, like, 'Hey, where was I?' It's easy to let something slip."

Indeed, the shop was run more like a small town coffee shop than an emporium of engineering excellence. When I first bought half ownership of the Citabria, I liked the fact that I could walk into the shop with a problem and somebody would always walk out with me and fix it. It wasn't until much later that I began to understand that when my airplane was in there being worked on, someone else was doing the same thing. I decided that I ought to watch them perform an engine overhaul on one of the line ships and then climb in and fly away in order to test my confidence in their work.

□

I was out early one morning, preparing to practice aerobatics, when Russell stuck his head out of the office and called out to me, "We're taking the engine off *Uniform!*" I felt a twinge of *déjà vu.* I once had an assignment to write about a brain surgeon. She told me one morning, "We're going to touch the brain today." We say "Brain Surgeon" as if she were a goddess, but Russell and Liss decide matters of life and death, too, in a cluttered tin building out behind the hog house.

The great space of the shop was littered and cluttered with a lifetime of junk, like a story that paleontology would take generations to read. *Uniform,* an old orange Cessna airplane, sat in the middle of the oil-stained floor with its cowling off and oil dripping out of the quick-drain valve into a five-gallon plastic bucket. It looked like a battered and squirrel-eaten Halloween pumpkin. The prop was gone, and so were the spark plugs, which had been laid in a tray on a dolly. Someone had bothered to drape it with an old red oily cotton blanket like a surgical cart in the theater of the absurd, the blood all brown and gray.

Liss and his young assistant, Jeff, went at the airplane with wrenches, unbolting aluminum baffles and oil temperature probes, detaching the spark plug harness, while talking to the occasional pilot who came through asking for advice on a problem.

I offered to help with the engine overhaul, and Liss directed me to organize the cart on which the parts were being thrown as they came off of 37U. He wanted tools on one side, parts on the other. He had that edge of compulsiveness I would like to see in a man who was going to repair my airplane, and I knew it was frustrating for him to have to work in the chaos of Galt, but that was the job he had, and he also had a wife and two children, so that was that.

As Liss and Jeff and I worked on *Uniform,* I stuck my head inside the cockpit to get something and detected the sharp odor of vomit. I backed out quickly. "What happened in there?" I asked Liss.

"Aw, somebody rented the plane, took his friend up, and the guy threw up. It's disgusting, I know."

Lee Nusbaum came through the door dressed in warm-looking coveralls and a watch cap. He pushed some junk around on the bench in the back to make room for himself and then began working a part on the electric grinding wheel, holding the metal piece with vise grips and watching the sparks fly against his spectacles. Liss hit the carburetor with a rubber mallet. As it fell away from the engine into his hand, we were wreathed in intoxicating gasoline fumes. After Amos, my feelings about gasoline would never be the same. Everyone seemed cavalier about it. But it had taken its toll at Galt.

It was a November day in 1984 when Russell decided to drain the gasoline from a Cessna 206 that had been pulled into the shop. He wheeled a cart underneath the wing. He placed a can on the cart and a funnel in the can, and he opened the quick-drain valve. The gasoline began pouring out in an amber stream. It seemed so simple.

It had been a beautiful fall day, with the grass still green and the sun shining. All the instructors were out flying. And that gasoline flowed like a ribbon of golden silk past the plexiglass window of the Cessna's passenger-side door, and a great Canadian high pressure dome kept the moisture down. The gasoline running past the plastic window was like a comb being rubbed on a woolen sweater. The airplane was not grounded. If he had sat down with paper and pencil, Russell could not have created a better system for making static electricity. And now unseen, like a fertilized cell, a microscopic blue creature had sprung into existence, as if from out of nothing. As the gasoline flowed, the creature grew big and blue and strong. And the beauty of the golden river, the intoxicating liquor of gasoline, made the newborn creature want to leap and dance for joy.

As Russell watched, he saw something strange appear. He looked more closely at the funnel. There was a blue ring around the lip. It was a most beautiful sight, like an apparition. It was as if the finger of God had touched the funnel, and it glowed silently, quietly, without malice or fury. It was a soft glow at first, almost an inviting glow, but then something clicked in Russell's brain, and with a jolt he understood what had happened. At the same moment, he realized that the can wasn't large enough. He had meant to switch cans before the tank was empty, but now that a greater spirit had claimed possession of it, Russell was afraid to touch the funnel.

He reached for a fire extinguisher, but there was none. A minor oversight. He looked around: The hangar was full of airplanes. It was also full of wood and oil and mineral spirits, paint and plastic and all sorts of rich and intoxicating food and drink for the newborn creature sitting quietly atop the funnel, growing and sucking on the delicious treat, which poured like a soda water fountain out of a hole in the airship.

Russell picked up the phone and called Darlene, who was the office manager at the time. "Get some fire extinguishers over here, we've got a fire in the shop," he said. Then he bolted for a fire extinguisher. But his illusion—that he could control Fate out here—would not sustain him. He was caught up in the entropic world of One Zero Charlie.

When he returned with the fire extinguisher, the can had overflowed. Now the infant beast had grown big and happy, as gasoline splashed like whiskey in a bar fight, out of the airplane, over the top of the funnel, and ran down the table and onto the floor. Flames were dancing around the airplane now, leaping eight and ten feet up, leaping for joy. This was going to be a big party. There would be food enough for all. Let the music begin!

Art had joined Russell, and now they both stood, mouths open, eyes wide, watching the colors swirl into a rising cloud of sonic heated gas, rummaging in the shop for morsels and playthings.

From the office Darlene saw Art and Russell go into the shop. The door closed behind them. A moment passed. Then the door opened, and they both backed out of there quickly. They closed the door again.

Darlene was calling the fire department, and the trucks came wailing along soon enough. The fire fighters wrapped themselves in hoods and boots and breather tanks and brandished their axes and threaded their hoses. Then they opened that same little door and took a peek inside. And then they very gingerly shut the door again and backed away.

The fire chief told Art, "You don't want to go in there." That was not news to Art.

It was late afternoon. The fire department pumped the water out of Art's swimming pool and onto the roof of the shop, but it was not enough. It was as if the farmer's field had rebelled against a blasphemy of airplanes and had cracked open, revealing the angry molten center of the earth, into which it swallowed airplanes, tools, hangar, and all. The sun went down. The fire burned itself out, and the sated creatures seemed to dance back into the earth to sleep, and the roaring gassy music faded as night fell.

George Kropf had been out flying all that time, and when he returned he couldn't find the airport. The runway lights were nowhere to be seen. He called on the radio several times, but everyone was still outside. Finally Darlene heard the call on the Unicom and ran inside to pick up the microphone to inform George that the shop had burned, taking the runway lights with it. George was circling around up there with a student, running out of gas. Finally Art rounded up some people to drive out onto the runway and put on their headlights, and George was able to land safely.

In a way, the same fire that pursued Amos, had pursued him right into Galt Airport, burned down the shop, and then emptied out Amos's hangar of airplanes. The present-day shop had to be appropriated from Amos for a place to repair airplanes. But by then the fire was gone from Galt and was hunting Amos out in the Avra Valley of Arizona.

And yet the whole episode seems to have left no impression at all. Like the charred wreckage of Lloyd's Starduster peeking out from the weeds, the curled steel walls of the old shop send a message that falls upon deaf ears. Those events are regarded entirely as works of Fate, over which no one has control. And in that attitude resides the very essence of the evolution of farm and airport. And perhaps a deeper truth.

It was difficult for me when I first learned to fly and expected everything to be scientific and logical and to be ruled by laws and equations and absolutes—it was hard to accept that the culture that supported the conveyance in which I planned to place myself was essentially no more scientifically advanced than one I might find if I were to leap out of my airplane and parachute into a village of grass huts in Borneo. Galt is not exceptional. There are countless airports like Ten Charlie scattered all across the country and they are all beset by calamity. I am no longer surprised when I land somewhere in Kansas or Massachusetts or Texas or Ohio and find a place that smells and looks and feels a great deal like Galt Airport, and I always wonder if they have a secret newsletter or some other means of communicating the style and technique of the grass roots airfield.

I returned to the shop after lunch to discover that the electricity had gone out, but we continued working in the misty crooked light, which more than ever made it seem as if we were involved in some ancient endeavor of human beings and their struggle to make the material world bend and submit to outlandish dreams. I watched Liss tap a rocker pin out. He tapped with a hammer and a pointed instrument, tapped the shiny rocker pins out one by one, gently, patiently, ringing a clear and simple note, and I arranged them and their brass rockers on the cloth for him in two neat rows glistening with grease.

Jeff put a tail stand on the airplane now to keep it from tipping over when the weight of the engine was removed.

I loosened all the cylinder bolts, and Liss removed cylinders. They were caked with white combustion deposits and streaked with brown, but he said the engine was in good shape. It could have flown another 500 hours.

The lights came on again, and Liss said, "Ah, modern technology. You guys can put the fire out now."

We chained the engine to a winch on a wheeled steel stand, and Liss unbolted the mounts and handed them to me. I marked each one with an alcohol pen—U.L. for upper left, L.R. for lower right, and so on. Now with the engine finally stripped (of carburetor, starter, exhaust system, etc.) and free of all attachments to 37U (such as oil pressure gauge, throttle cable, fuel lines, etc.), we swung the scrawny-looking, dirty gray case away and lowered it to the floor, and then Liss went to the dolly to examine some of the parts, which had made up the flying machine we all knew as *Uniform.*

He picked up a spark plug and held it up to the light. He squinted through the gap. "These plugs," Liss said. "You could throw a dead cat through 'em."

I followed Russell back to the office, where he was going to arrange for the parts of the engine to be machined to new factory tolerances.

On the way we encountered a man at the front desk, a stoic farmer type who explained to anyone who would listen that his wife was on a heart machine. He kept talking to his dog as if the animal were his mistress. "I'm going to take you home and brush you out," he'd say. Or: "You sure are looking beautiful today."

By the end of the day, Russell piled the parts of *Uniform*'s engine into the back of one of the Cessna 152 trainers and flew them away to be rejuvenated. It would be a few weeks before they were ready to reassemble.

□

My friend Dr. Shinderman drove down from Wisconsin in his red 1963 Corvette, because I had promised to take him through the Sportsman sequence in the Citabria. He arrived wearing the latest acrylic polymer blue blocker sunglasses, caution-color nylon clothing—baggy pants and a baggy jacket and even baggy shoes. He looked as if he'd parachuted in with a demonstration team and a bad wind had caught him in his Day-Glo chute. In the '60s and '70s, people mistook him for Frank Zappa. Dr. Shinderman and I strapped in. Houdini could not have escaped from all the buckles and hasps and wires. As we taxied out, I explained the sequence we were going to fly—spin, Immelmann, 270 turn, and so on. I noticed that the engine seemed to be running awfully rough, and that distracted my attention from something else I was half noticing: that I was having difficulty steering the airplane.

By the time we had reached the run-up pad, the engine was so rough that I scrubbed the flight. Later, pushing the Citabria back into the hangar, I happened to grab hold of a handle near the tail. I looked down and noticed that one of my tail wheel springs was missing. That was why the airplane had been so difficult to steer. If I had taken off, I might have lost control when I returned for landing.

The next day we had the Citabria taken apart in the shop. Liss and Russell were discussing the red eighty-octane stains on the spark plugs while I gazed out the door at a sky that looked like the gray and peeling hangar paint. I watched sparrows make nests along the rafters, and I could see the chewed-up mark along the bottom of the door, where Amos Beuttell had come rumbling up in his Pitts.

After much fussing around, Russell finally took one of the magnetos off to examine the moving parts. "How often do you look inside there?" I asked.

"Oh, never, unless they break," Russell said, wielding a screwdriver merrily.

Many of the components of an airplane engine and airframe could be left uninspected for decades without violating a regulation. The magic of Russell's power was that if he said it was airworthy, then it was legal; and if it came back without crashing, then he was right. It was that little test flight in between that made me nervous.

As Russell took apart the instrument, we immediately began to see signs of its sickness, and the more little parts he removed, the more evident it became. By the time Russell had reached the inner vault, where the spark was made by the contact between a metal fish scale and a graphite button, he found that the graphite was gone. It had been vaporized through the billion 20,000-volt lightning bolts of its long lifetime.

"Well," he said, "we're looking at a mag rebuild." Then, as he handled the parts, it seemed they triggered off memories of Airframe & Power Plant school, and he began a Flaubertian discourse on magnetic flux, as a ground squirrel came out of the thawing winter field and scurried up to our open doorway and took a long look at the peculiar sight we must have presented to any creature of the natural world of northern Illinois. "Hello there, little bugger," Russell said in the middle of a sentence about field theory. Then he went on explaining that the primary coil, if it had 1,000 windings of the wire, had 1,000 volts. When the points opened, the primary magnetic field collapsed, inducing electric current in the secondary coil. The secondary coil had 20,000 windings, which resulted in 20,000 volts. Sometimes he reminded me of Homais, the apothecary in *Madame Bovary*.

Russell took off the left magneto. It looked better than the right, which was defying all of the laws of physics by the fact that it worked at all. "There is arcing on the towers, but these I think I can clean up and it'll work."

I wanted to suggest, as gently as possible, that he fix the problem and not take any unnecessary risks in an effort to save money, so I said, "Russell, fuck that shit. Replace the whole apparatus and get it right. I don't want to be hanging there upside-down thinking about this disintegrating piece of garbage running the whole show for me. Get that trash out of my airplane now."

"Well," he said, "I will if you and John want it, but I have to warn you: Some of these items can sticker-shock you." Meaning the price is high.

"Not nearly as shocking as having my engine stop," I said. The way the conversation was going, I thought I was going to have to bribe him to fix it: Okay, Russell, I'll give you an extra five hundred dollars.

I drove my battered and colorless Toyota Corolla along the runway and found the broken tail wheel spring. It now seemed so obvious that it had been about to wear through and snap off. It's one of those mysteries, such as the roll on takeoff. Sometimes pilots read checklists, note the items on them, and completely ignore the fact that they have left the gear up or failed to switch to a full fuel tank. I read the list, I touched the spring, and then I turned my mind off to the fact that it was halfway cut through as if a prisoner had been working on it with a hacksaw.

I brought the spring back to show Bob Buchik, a retired policeman who owned a Cessna 152. He had been a fixture at Galt Airport for years. He fingered the severed end and asked, "Did you land like that?"

"No," I said. "I didn't take off because the engine was running rough."

"Somebody is watching out for you," he said.

The airplane had simply been neglected. When you fly a well-maintained airplane, people don't find little pieces of it on the runway after you go by. I made up my mind to change our policy about maintenance.

Half an hour after we put the Citabria back in its hangar, there was a spectacular show: Thunderclouds at sunset opened like a great black door, and then the last light of day shone through like a celestial map, precisely stitching a rim of silver-pink light around the cottony white lower deck. In the center was a splash of cirrus like an accent, just a touch of white on the gown of the approaching night. Gradually that square door grew round and lost its shape, and night closed all about us, and lightning began to stitch up the center of the skirt with its cold fire. Rain began to fall.

The Citabria was fixed ten days later. We had more than $700 worth of new magnetos and wiring and spark plugs in it. (The tail wheel springs cost eighteen dollars—danger knows no price.) I was scheduled to return to Missouri to fly with John Morrissey again. I opened my hangar to find blue hydraulic fluid leaking all over the concrete beneath the Citabria.

While Russell worked on the problem, I stood around the briefing room nursing the hope that I might still leave. An hour later Russell found me in the briefing room eating a cinnamon roll that I'd bought out of our snack machine. He said ironically, "That's a real good breakfast to have before flying all day."

"Am I going to fly all day?" I asked.

"Yeah," he said. "Your airplane is fixed."

Everything seemed in order when I checked the Citabria. I had my luggage in the back. I had my charts, my chewing gum, my Sony Walkman with fresh batteries and a new tape of *La Traviata*. I even had two tuna sandwiches to eat along the way and a juice-pak and cookies that my daughters, Elena and Amelia, had given me. I was going to Missouri to fly the Pitts again. I was going to get happy feet.

I can't explain why I did what I did. I will never be able to explain it. The day was beautiful, and everything was ready, but I didn't leave. I taxied out. Everything seemed normal. The airplane handled well. The engine ran well. The new magnetos passed their test. Still, I did not leave. And adjacent to the runway, even the redwing blackbirds sitting on their stalks seemed to be wondering what was taking me so long.

There were no more reasons to stay. I let the brakes off, and the Citabria pulled me gently down the runway. At about forty knots the tail lifted. At about sixty the stick came back, lifting the nose, and the Citabria rolled into flight. It felt good, not unlike that moment when water skis break the surface, and then the power of the boat, suddenly released from friction, carries us away at a great rate of speed.

Still, something nagged at the back of my mind. The airplane was pointed west, almost a straight course to Missouri. But instead I turned left and remained in the pattern. I looked down at the little airfield below me, and somehow all the buildings in their random placement upon the grass, the docile-looking hangars like farm animals scattered here and there, seemed to pull me back around the pattern like a model airplane on a wire. It was such a lonely impulse that drew us back, as if a boy alone in a field down there held us tethered in the sky.

Even as my wheels touched down, I wondered what I would say when Russell or Liss or Carla asked why I had come back. At the pumps I set the brake, unstrapped, and climbed out to wonder what I was doing on this patch of earth at this hour of the day. The sun was shining, and a few scattered clouds passed overhead, and all around me the world was quiet. But something was wrong. I happened to glance down and notice oil on the ramp beneath the propeller. I knelt down and looked underneath the nose. Oil was pouring out of the engine. I stood up suddenly, as if I had touched something hot, and all at once I saw what I had done. If I had left for Missouri, my flight would have ended in a bean field somewhere twenty minutes west. My death was waiting out there for me, and I had refused to go.

We returned the airplane to the shop. Russell discovered that someone had taken off the oil cooler to remove one of the magnetos and had failed to tighten the hose again. An unspoken bond among the mechanics kept secret any blame.

Later Liss apologized. "We do our best," he said, "but we're human."

A month later, all the parts for *Uniform* had come back from the machine shop, and Russell had laid them out on two benches. They were all painted a nice new hi-temperature enamel gray. It was standard Lycoming gray, a businesslike color. It suggests a kind of Germanic seriousness. It has the appearance of a piece of metal that has been cut open by a diamond to reveal its fluid-looking, protoplasmic interior. That metallic gray is to engines what that delicious orange-pink color is to salmon: It's the meat of the matter. Now all the parts were painted that way, and Russell had taken the trouble to arrange them neatly on the cloth, and he was rolling their threaded surfaces together one by one, with the slick, satisfying feel of a perfect fit lubricated with new grease. I could tell it was pleasant work for him, the sense of something well-made going together with such ease; it seemed as if the parts had a will to join and an ability to experience a genuine joy in that union, like a kind of cool crystalline coupling.

The plane itself was an entirely different matter. The idea of attaching that beautiful power plant to 37U seemed like putting a jade necklace on a pig.

Russell's hands were now gray with molybdenum grease, gray like the machined parts, so that he appeared to be turning into the Tin Woodsman. I asked him about the gray grease, and he launched into a treatise on molybdenum disulfide, or Lubriplate MO_2 high surface tension grease. It was used to provide lubrication during the first few critical moments of engine operation after an overhaul, he said. I knew that the grease was part of the ritual, a sacred ointment, but Russell went on in his technical fashion anyway: It was that interval, those first seconds of operation, that would determine whether the power plant would survive the expected amount of time in service. "Metal on metal," Russell said with confident authority. "It's being cut like a diamond. We take this precaution so that the engine parts lap into each other. If it's done right, you can lose all your oil and keep running for fifteen minutes."

Liss sprayed the fire wall and engine mount and all the fittings with Stoddard's solvent, cleaning off the grease.

Russell mused, dreaming, in that semiconscious state induced by the pleasant task of assembly. "I still remember what it was like when I first learned to fly," he said, apropos of nothing. "Now every once in a while, conditions will be just right, and as you take off, you'll just get that feeling back again, just for a moment."

As Russell worked, he expounded on the subject of pressure carburetors. Buchik entered carrying a Styrofoam cup of coffee and looking a bit more stylish than usual in a retired-policeman sort of McHenry County fashion. He wore cowboy boots with riding heels, a blue seed cap, and pressed blue jeans. Buchik practically lived at the airport, and he always had an opinion to offer.

He said, "Lloyd had a pressure carb on that Starduster."

"It never ran right," Russell said, as if discussing the loss of the carburetor instead of the man and his son. But whereas we could not fix the man or his mistake, there was yet hope to comprehend the machine, thereby gaining power over it.

Buchik said, "You ever hear him taxiing around here? Pow! Pow! Pow!"

Russell, deep inside the work on 37U, ventured, "He didn't want to spend the money to have it overhauled."

Buchik, who had ridden with Lloyd many times, said, "When you got into the front seat, it smelled like gas."

At the end of the day, we all assembled at the flight desk and stood around with the instructors and Art and Carla and

Steve Nusbaum—everybody coming together to share a moment before going our separate ways for the night. Sometimes it seemed as if we had no life except the one we spent at Galt.

Russell and Liss and a few of the instructors gathered in the briefing room, preparing to go home, and Russell told a story about a pilot who used to be seen regularly at Galt filling his tanks with the cheap gas. "Oh, yeah," Russell said, "he screwed his Cessna one-twenty into the ground in an uncontrolled spin. That's not so unusual, people do that all the time. But this guy got it on videotape. That's pretty unusual." Everyone agreed that it was. "But there's more," Russell said. "He walked away from the crash, and when they investigated the wreckage they found thirty-eight empty beer cans inside." By now everybody was laughing. Liss had an infectious laugh, like a kid who's being tickled, and he couldn't seem to stop. Sometimes it was just like that at the end of the day, though: Giddiness came from repetition, mental exhaustion. Russell was going on. "No, no, there's more, there's more. This guy's father bought him another airplane, and he crashed that one, too. So what do you think his father did? He bought him *another* airplane, and this time the poor kid killed himself."

Brett Hansen, who had been sitting back with the tips of his fingers placed neatly together before him, smiled and shook his head. He said, "It would have been cheaper to shoot him."

Russell was philosophical. "Yeah, well, people do stupid things all over," he said.

Sometimes it seemed that our lives—the rest of our lives outside of Galt Airport—were composed of those actions that occur offscreen during the dissolves in movies. I had gone home that night, and in the morning Amelia, my youngest daughter, told me that she dreamed of flying upside down with me. "You know," she said, "like aerobatics." She was also chased by alligators in the dream, and I asked her if the flying was scary, too. She said no, it was fun. She said we flew in an open cockpit plane, and I held her hand to keep her from falling out.

Russell finished assembling the engine on a Saturday. The baffles had new red-orange rubber edges riveted all around to make a seal with the engine, and all the tubes, wires, and cables had been attached. By 10 A.M. I had taken two practice flights in the Citabria and was in the hangar watching Russell install on the floor of Uniform's cockpit a piece of carpeting that I wouldn't have given to my Labrador retriever.

"Is everything on there?" I asked.

"Yes," he said. Then he looked around. "Well, my bench is empty of parts. I've got to check."

Russell looked the airplane over carefully now, walking around it with an air of suspicion. We were going to climb into that collection of parts, which had been scattered all over the hangar, and we were going to fly away. Russell took a small red oil can and squeezed the trigger to see that it was filled. He removed the oil pressure line from the engine and injected 65 weight oil into the galleries. "This would probably save the engine in the event of an oil cavitation or a complete failure," he explained. Russell pulled the lever that opened the great shop door to the sunlight of a beautiful day.

We pushed the airplane out, each of us holding a wing strut, and Russell was doing his final check when he shouted, "Ah-ha!" There was a bolt loose. He seemed satisfied that he'd found something to correct. Like an editor looking at a cleanly typed manuscript, he knew that something had to be wrong. If he couldn't find it, it was a bad omen. We pushed the airplane back inside, and he threw the lever to close the shop door, and the giant metal skirts unfurled to the concrete floor, like a curtain closing on a stage.

When we had rolled *Uniform* out into the sun again, Russell and I climbed in, and he shouted, "Clear!" He turned the key.

The propeller turned laboriously the first time, then more rapidly the second. Everything inside sounded smooth; there were no peculiar noises to suggest that a teaspoon had fallen into the garbage disposal. The third and fourth time the propeller gained speed, and the fifth time it caught. The new engine was running. Almost immediately I could smell burning paint as the gray high-temperature enamel was warmed on the griddle of every cast steel surface, incense for the ritual offering. Russell set the idle at 1,000 RPM so that the oil would sling in globs off the cam shaft as it spun, lubricating all the parts. "You can actually feel it smoothing out as it runs." But due to the friction of the new parts against one another, he said, "you have to use a lot of throttle to hold a thousand." It was like Rip Van Winkle waking up from a hundred-year nap.

The normal procedure after the first brief period of engine operation was to open the cowling and take a close look at everything once again before flying, and so we pushed the airplane back into the shop. After pushing it in and out a few times and fixing an oil leak and a magneto problem, we were finally ready to roll.

It was three-fifteen in the afternoon when we taxied to the run-up pad, and Russell turned the nose into the wind and set the brake. He ran the engine up to 1,800 RPM. He tapped the oil gauge and squinted.

"What's the matter?" I asked.

"Ah, the oil pressure's still a little high, but it should come down when the engine warms up." A normal run-up before flight takes only a few seconds, but because this was a newly overhauled engine, we had to leave it at 1,800 RPM for five minutes. As we sat waiting, we saw Earl come taxiing down the runway with a student. Earl was an old-time tail-dragger instructor. Earl's student did a quick magneto check and took off toward Harvard and Rockford.

After five minutes, Russell performed a normal engine run-up. When he switched to the right magneto, the engine backfired grossly and fell completely silent. Our aeronautical adventure had perished in a puff of smoke, as if it had been a spell, and we were once more simply two men in a field on a chilly spring day at the forty-second parallel. The sky was moving slowly above us, as it had 10,000 years before, a ripped-up quilt of white and blue festooned with redwing blackbirds. And out there, amid the dried thistles and cornflowers, the only sound was their sovereign cries of joy in flight.

Back in the shop, Russell found that the butt splice connector he had only just installed had somehow trapped a piece of shielding: a dead mag once more, only for a different reason.

We were back on the main ramp at three-forty, waiting for aircraft to recover. It was that time of day. John Fountain was fueling the Citabria for a ride with his son, a tall redheaded man in his late thirties or early forties, while a pretty yellow Piper Cub stood by, waiting its turn for fuel. "The afternoon gas run for tomorrow morning's breakfast," Russell observed. It was Saturday afternoon, and people were making their Sunday brunch fly-in plans. "Ah, another Two-Hundred-Dollar Cheeseburger," Russell said. "That's what keeps us in business." Bob was referring to the weekend pilots who start their engines and cruise around the area for a while, stopping for a burger at some nearby airfield restaurant. By the time they've paid the insurance, hangar rent, engine overhaul, avionics repair, gas, and oil, that cheeseburger has cost $200.

The roll-out was smooth, the lift-off imperceptible, and Russell pulled *Uniform* gently away from the earth. I watched the slender, aromatic green shoots at the tips of the tallest pines go by, waving beneath us. I checked the tachometer, keeping an eye on the open fields where we might land if the engine quit again. After witnessing so many problems with the engine, I felt less than secure now that we were dangling hundreds of feet in the air, as if by whim, from that cantankerous animation of metal parts.

Russell banked left to circle the field. We were climbing. That was a good sign. "I'm going to stay in a high pattern for a few minutes at twenty-five hundred feet," Russell explained. "If anything happens, I want to be near home." He grinned. Blue eyes. A small bald spot on top of his head gave him a monastic appearance. I knew why he was grinning. The maneuver we were performing had what the Air Force pilots called a high pucker factor.

After a few circuits of the field, Russell dialed in the Kenosha instrument landing system and headed 060, remarking, "It's important to know where the airfields are between here and there. There's Westosha, Wynn Field—it's a little grass strip, but it'll do." He ticked them off. He had done this many times, flying an airplane he had just reassembled, with an engine that seemed reluctant to behave quite normally and seemed even to want to stop altogether with a loud pop and a louder silence. But as we stayed with the flight, our faith grew, and we both settled down. It is true that people can get used to almost anything. Before long, it was almost like any other flight.

The Fox River passed below us in flood. Miles of fields were flooded, as the wide swath of water lay upon the land like a rippling brown strip of bacon left to solidify in its own gray grease.

Russell reached up and rapped the glide slope antenna, which sat like a clear plastic pair of wings on the windshield above the sun visors. The glide slope, which was supposed tell us the correct descent angle to follow as we approached the field in the clouds, was not working. He made a mental note to fix it, and we broke off the approach and headed out west toward Delavan, Wisconsin, at the west end of Lake

Geneva, passing over Bong Air Base—the faded dream of the Strategic Air Command to have long-range bombers stationed all over the United States with which to attack the Soviet Union. When the guided missile became the strategic weapon of mass destruction, those grand plans evaporated, and places such as Bong were left like the ruins in Peru, mere designs, which can only be seen from the sky, etched on the earth long ago by a people we can't begin to fathom, because they were probably so much like us that they did things that were almost as strange as leveling a 15,000-foot runway and putting in twelve feet of gravel and then walking away from it and never looking back again. As we flew over it, it was as if everyone had gone to lunch and might return at any moment to begin work again. It had the feel of those scenes of Pompeii, in which a family having breakfast was covered in volcanic ash and preserved forever with the cinder of a morsel of food lifted halfway to the black mouth hole. Even long after the base had been abandoned, the government refused to return the land to the farmers who were displaced. Now it's called a wildlife refuge, which is the government's way of saying that they couldn't figure out a way to evict the birds from the trees. Some hang glider pilots were able to find enough uninterrupted length to launch their kites with a tow bungee behind a truck a few years ago, and we could see them down there, turning and turning in narrowing spirals. Russell pointed out the lateral lines across the runway, trenches dug by the government in an effort to prevent drug smugglers from landing there, so that now it was not even any use to us if our engine quit. They were finally digging up all the high-quality gravel that had been laid down. It was being trucked out to use on roads. Nature would eventually take care of the rest.

West of Bong, we passed between the AMC automobile test track and the Nestlé Chocolate company in the city of Burlington. As Russell shot the NDB (nondirectional beacon) approach at Lake Lawn, he mentioned that once our hour-long tour of the local area was completed he would take the airplane back "and tweak it." Remove another washer for the oil pressure. Squawk the radios that weren't working, such as the glide slope. Pull the cowl off and check carefully for oil leaks. Then he would put it on the line. The next person to fly it would be whoever happened to rent it. After five hours on the line, he'd change the oil. I had half expected that it would have to be blessed somehow, that some spell would have to be cast upon it before it went back on the line, but this was it. We were the test pilots, and if we survived this ride, 37U was ready for work.

On the way back to Galt, he ran the engine at full power to see if it would maintain redline. It did slightly better, and I could see his pleasure at the job he'd done. It worked right. Better than right.

A year later, *Uniform* had already flown 1,000 hours on the new engine without needing repair.

TEN

NIGHT FLIGHT

THE BRIEFER SAID the weather could not be better for my trip to Santa Fe. In the Ninety-Knot Wonder it was going to be a two-day affair. But like those who ride motorcycles, pilots of low-and-slow airplanes don't mind—they're up there because they like it.

It was barely light when I took off and situated myself for an all-day ride to the west. I cleared Rockford's radar service area and then switched off my radio and put on my Sony Walkman with a tape of country music I had prepared. I sat pounding the instrument panel in time to the beat. The sun rose behind me. It was going to be a beautiful flight.

I was never aware of the propeller pulling me through the air. It was as if I were permitted to glide along beneath the cloud deck through the whim of an invisible force which—like gravity—was certain and eternal and impossible to doubt. No more could I fear falling out of the sky than I could fear falling up off the ground and bumping against the clouds when I'm standing in my backyard.

The vast empire of mist had frightened me when I was a new and anxious pilot. Now I relished my sense of dominion over so much empty space. After a few years, we become accustomed to our world of miniatures, where the town water tower stands on tiny legs like a child's railroad model. It all looks so orderly and peaceful compared to our cluttered lives down there.

Flying low: They call it the nap of the earth, where the uninterrupted treetops seem to spread out like a carpet, so thick and green that we might land on it and step out and walk around.

On long flights, the controllers can sometimes become friends. When they'd go away for their break, I'd miss them and have to adjust to the new controller, a stranger, not an insider.

I flew into a flock of birds. Suddenly they were all around the cockpit like mysterious black streaks outside my orbiting capsule. Somehow I missed them all. They didn't want to hit me any more than I wanted to hit them.

A train passed south beneath me, more than a mile long, undulating, smooth and scaly, toward the smoking stacks of town.

A highway sliced a low hill of brown earth and tan grass—it looked like a delicious pâté, and it occurred to me that I might be getting hungry. I looked for a place to stop for lunch and found one on the chart: McPherson, Kansas.

For some time the Citabria had been draining fuel out of one tank faster than the other. Whenever I filled the tanks, the left one took twice as much gas as the right. I had been flying all morning, and the left tank was always light. The tanks are in the wings, and the aircraft is a high-wing model, so to reach the gas cap, I had to climb a ladder, and when I was flying, the tanks were overhead—one on either shoulder—

thirty-six gallons of fuel in all. So with the right tank draining fuel faster, the airplane would turn more and more to the left the farther I'd fly into each leg of the journey. I had asked Russell and Liss to fix it many times. But it was one of those knotty problems. It could be anything. I could find a mechanic who would happily take apart the wing and look around, and while the plane was grounded and the cost of investigating the problem went up and up, it would begin to seem so easy just to turn right all the time while the airplane wanted to turn left. Compared with having a roomful of surgeons open up my abdomen and look inside for a day or two, it might begin to seem like fun to have a bellyache. Furthermore, with an airplane it sometimes seemed positively unmanly to demand that the stupid thing fly straight and level. "Work out with weights," they'd say. "Make yourself strong."

So I kept flying the Citabria, and every now and then my partner and I would stop in at the shop and talk to Liss or Russell, but they'd be swamped with much more important work, and so we'd just casually say, "Hey, how about that old fuel thing, huh?" And Russell would say, "Yeah, pretty weird." Or Liss would say, "Maybe it's the vent. We ought to check to see if it's misaligned." But we all knew that we weren't going to check any vent. It was like the engine mount on the DC-10 or the strut attachment on the Decathlon, which caused Jim Batterman to pull his wing off. We weren't going to do anything at all. Not until something dramatic happened.

McPherson was my third refueling stop that morning. I was feeling confident and pleased about the trip, which I had anticipated with some trepidation, since it was to be the longest trip I'd ever made in the Citabria. I had brought sandwiches and cookies and apples, and by the time I reached Kansas, I was pretty hungry. I sat in the office reviewing my flight plan while someone (a line boy, I assumed) fueled the airplane. It was a departure from ritual for me. I always fueled the airplane myself. But I had begun to think that I might make it all the way to Santa Fe in one go, and I wanted to eat and be on my way to save time. If a red flag didn't raise itself the moment I thought of saving time, it was probably because I had allowed myself to get too hungry and wasn't thinking clearly.

All disasters are made of the same elements, the way all breads, as different as the varieties can be, are made of flour and water. The first element, especially in aircraft accidents, often involves deviating from routine procedures. But no one ingredient makes the loaf. It takes a lot of work before it's bread.

So I sat in the office eating my sandwich while someone fueled the airplane, and I studied my plan, deciding to press on until I had to stop. (Sundown would be my signal to find a place to stay for the night.) I finished my lunch and packed up and went out to the airplane, snapping chunks off a big red apple with my teeth.

Now, since my fueling routine was different, my routine for inspecting the aircraft before flight had necessarily to be different. (It was like chaos theory: Little events produce bigger results the farther down the line they progress.) Since I normally removed and replaced the fuel caps, I was not sure where to start; the caps had already been removed and replaced. I should have hauled out the ladder and removed them and replaced them again myself, but I didn't. I simply stepped up on each strut and checked to see if they seemed tight.

I drained some fuel out of each tank from the quick-drain valve beneath the wing to see if it was indeed fuel. I checked the oil. I walked around the plane to see that all the parts were still bolted together, tail wheel springs attached, tires inflated, flying wires tuned to the correct notes.

As soon as I climbed in, I smelled fuel. I noticed that I smelled fuel, and I thought about the fact that I smelled fuel—it was in my conscious mind. But I didn't do anything about it. That is generally the second element in a fermenting disaster: ignoring good information, disregarding a warning signal. I continued to taxi out to the active runway, expecting the smell to go away.

I ran the engine up to 1,800 RPM for the magneto check. Now I really smelled fuel. It was like being back in the shop when Steve was covering an airplane with fabric, using his vile chemicals. Here I go: I committed yet another major mistake, one that is characteristic of all disasters from Bhopal to Three Mile Island. It has two parts: First, I refused to believe the evidence of my senses. Second, I made up a story to explain away the evidence. I thought, Well, perhaps the line boy spilled some fuel. I thought, It's nothing. Or more probably, I stopped myself from thinking by an enigmatic process that we can never quite know, for knowing it would be the opposite of doing it. Orwell described it in his famous novel *1984*. He called it "selective stupidity." I had never smelled that much fuel in a cockpit before, especially not while running up, when one would expect the prop blast to blow all fumes away. In transcripts of interviews with technicians, which were conducted after disasters such as Bhopal, Three Mile Island, the space shuttle *Challenger*, or incidents such as the explosion that nearly stranded the crew of Apollo 13 in space—they all did the same thing: pretended that everything was normal.

I made my radio call, "Three six two five zero departing Runway one eight," as I taxied onto the active runway. I roared off heedlessly into the sky. Now all the safeties were off and the bomb was armed.

I hadn't flown far when I checked the fuel gauges, a habit developed to guard against a lost fuel cap. The left tank was remaining very full—more so than usual—while the right tank seemed to be draining rapidly. I still smelled fuel. I should have turned back and landed immediately, but I had done a great job of erasing my ability to reason, and I pressed on with a vague and unexamined hope still flickering in my breast that the matter would magically correct itself.

The problem grew worse as the left tank remained overly full while the right one emptied itself at a brisk rate. I could think of no way to explain it. Here is another common element of disasters: We don't really understand the system we are using. We think we do. We have a blurry schematic of the system in mind. But we have no deep knowledge of it. If I had been in possession of a clear mental picture of the Citabria's fuel system, I might have visualized what was happening—but I could not.

On and on I flew, until somewhere just past Hutchinson, fifteen or twenty minutes from McPherson, I was suddenly struck by the gravity of my situation. It was as if the scales fell from my eyes, and I awoke in a pool of sweat. There was a break in my dream of complacency, and I dialed up the Hutchinson tower controller to inform him urgently that I had a fuel leak and was coming in. He asked me if I wanted to land at the field directly below me, and I circled a few times, but could not find it. He immediately cleared me to his runway, holding other traffic up to let me in.

It wasn't far, but the fuel smell grew significantly stronger and the right tank significantly emptier as I plied the air slowly, so slowly, it seemed as if in a nightmare of running. I could see the field, but it was a remote and theoretical point in space as I dragged my leaden wings through the frothy air toward it. I delayed descending in case I needed the altitude to help me glide in with no power. I wasn't sure what the next step ought to be, and there was nothing in the manuals, nothing in all the training I'd had to help me. Nowhere had I heard mention of what might be done about a fuel leak.

I was almost in the pattern now, and when I banked right to make my base leg, gasoline suddenly began spraying out of the throttle quadrant at my left hand, and I was splashed with raw fuel. Instinctively, I jerked my hand away, surprised at the cold and the smell, which was now overpowering, but I continued my turn. I looked up at the fuel gauge, a float gauge in a sight glass just above my left shoulder, and as I watched in horror, the little window filled with fuel, and a torrent of gasoline spewed out of the wing root area at me. Now I was being doused with gasoline. It was all over my shirt and hair and neck and it was running down my back. I felt my skin go cold, and my hair stood up on end. I wasn't wearing a parachute, or I might have jumped, and I thought of my father with his parachute under his seat.

I keyed the microphone and told the tower, "Hutchinson Tower, two five zero has fuel in the cockpit."

"Two five zero, Roger," the controller said. "Take the first turnoff and taxi to the ramp after landing. Stay with me."

"Two five zero, negative, sir. I'm shutting down everything now, and I'll be—uh—I'll just be stopping as soon as I can. I have lots of fuel in the cockpit now."

"Two five zero, Roger, cleared to land any runway."

I said nothing as I reached for the panel. My hand was shaking so hard that I had trouble shutting off the switches. I left the magnetos to keep the engine running. Now I was on a short, steep final approach, and I was waiting for the gasoline all around me and up my sleeves and creeping down my neck to explode. I don't know why I thought so much of my father then instead of Amos, who might have held the secret I needed most. Perhaps we spend so much time trying to escape the legacy of our fathers that our very act of cowardice condemns us that much sooner to their fate.

I pointed the nose at the numbers on the runway. I felt as if I had snakes crawling all over me. I thought I was going to vomit from the smell.

It's funny the things we notice. I saw that the next airplane in line for takeoff, delayed by my little emergency, was the Starship, an experimental two-engine airplane built by the Lear company, exotic and white and futuristic-looking, and I wondered what the important people inside thought was going on out there that they should have to wait. They probably never had to wait. And I thought of W. H. Auden writing, "In Brueghel's *Icarus,* for instance: how everything turns away/ Quite leisurely from the disaster . . ."

As soon as the wheels were on the concrete, I ran the airplane off the runway into the grass and had the door open before I stopped. I leapt out and ran away, expecting it to explode behind me. When I had sprinted thirty or forty yards, I turned and looked back, still walking backward. I was soaked with fuel. I reeked. I was shaking hard. I put my hands on my knees to steady myself and catch my breath, and all at once my knees let go, and I sat on the grass as if I had meant to.

It was only then that I noticed the yellow fire trucks that had come to greet me and the firemen in their rubber suits who were climbing down with fire extinguishers and walking toward the plane with a dark look of suspicion smoldering in their eyes. They were waiting for it to explode, too. We exchanged words, but I'm not sure what they were. All I remember is that I said something to one of them, and he looked at me as if a dead man had offered him a piece of gum. Fuel was pouring out the bottom of the Citabria onto the concrete and the grass.

I looked back at that little blue airplane, so cute, with stars on its tail, and for the first time I saw its potential for becoming my enemy. I felt betrayed, but of course I had betrayed myself. My little disaster could not have been more elegant if I had sat down to plan it out on paper. The only thing I'd forgotten was my Zippo. People think of catastrophes as incidents in which the elements of chaos and disorder enter into an otherwise orderly system, but calamity requires a powerful ordering influence. We have to harness a lot of energy and give it direction in order to hurt ourselves really badly. To climb on a stool and fall is not much effort and not usually such a terrible mistake. But to climb a building requires organization and energy. It is the energy we put in that comes back out to destroy us. Without the organizing principle, the energy to harm us would be unavailable, because it would remain diffused and could not be directed back at us. No, all disasters are orderly, and as I looked back at my inconsequential and trivial blue airplane, I saw all the effort that had gone into the attempt to blow me up. Even the act of refining oil into gasoline, the invention of the airplane, contributed a great ordering principle—a narrow view of history, I admit, but the only one I could take seriously at such a moment.

I stood up and dusted myself off, and only then did I think, finally, of Amos, his knees ricked up to his chin to get his feet out of the flames. I realized that he could have been standing there just like me. Our ways divided over the matter of one happy little blue spark.

Soon the airport head of maintenance, a man in a shirt and tie (for it was an executive jet port) came out in a truck and looked over the plane with an expression on his face that let me know that he certainly wished I had landed on somebody else's field with my rag-wing weed-hopper. He stuck his head inside the open door to the cockpit and looked around. "I wouldn't have wanted to be the one to throw that master switch," he said.

"What?" I asked.

"Because that right there was your one chance to make a spark. If you were going to blow up," he said thoughtfully, "that was the way you were gonna do it."

"Great," I said, and I felt a ripple of nausea.

But he crawled into the back of the airplane and disconnected the battery cable himself while the firemen pointed fire extinguishers at him to put out the fire he was apt to start. I thought it took a lot of nerve. He had the airplane towed into a hangar for the night, and someone drove me to the Holiday Inn. They were going to call the local tube-and-fabric man from down the road to come in the morning and see if he could fix the problem. We still had no idea what it might be. Everyone thought it sounded like a fuel tank leak.

The next morning I found Gus Wiebe poking around inside my wing. My Citabria sat, tiny and frail as a grasshopper, among the hefty turboprops in the big, bright, and freshly swept corporate hangar. Gus could find no leak. He had slit two holes in the underside of the wing and had inspected the tank and its connecting fuel lines and fittings for leaks but could find no problem. "I guess we'll fly it back to our field and see if it leaks on the way."

"Who's going to fly it?" I asked, not very keen on the idea of doing it myself.

"My son, Mark," he said.

"Where's your son?" I asked.

"Right there," he said, pointing across the hangar. I looked over and saw that he pointed at a shadowy area of the hangar, where the fluorescent brightness faded beneath the wings of several large airplanes against the back wall. I squinted into the dim distance, and in another moment I perceived a movement, at first indistinct; and then I saw as it came toward us that it was a creature which I could not immediately identify. It was short and squat and it lurched from side to side and up and down, its blocky head wobbling upon a powerful body that seemed propelled not by the regular swinging of arms and legs but by some kinetic explosion of muscle power, which at each occurrence took a different tack and a new direction. I watched it proceed toward us for a moment, and then with a start I realized that it was a man and that he was badly crippled.

Mark Wiebe wore a blue jumpsuit such as a gas station attendant would wear, and he had a crooked smile and a youthful face, and he progressed toward us with a supreme effort of concentration, despite which he gave us a perfectly charming grin as he drew up close. I looked at his lame leg and at my lame airplane, and I wondered what I could say. How could I ask that man (who had just volunteered his own son to test-fly an airplane that only the day before had nearly killed me) whether or not his son was good enough to fly it? I could not. Clearly, if that boy and that father were willing to risk all for the flight, I had to be up to the bargain and be willing to risk the airplane, which was, after all, nothing but a collection of spare parts flying in close formation. It could be replaced. I was filled with admiration for Gus and Mark, whatever sort of life they'd made for themselves out here on the hostile plains, and I shook Mark's hand and said, "Take it away."

They pushed it out onto the ramp and disdained to reconnect the battery. I'm not sure if they thought it unmanly to start an airplane engine by electrical means or not, but whatever their reasoning, Gus hand-propped the plane, while Mark sat inside. Hand-propping a 150-horsepower fuel-injected engine can be tricky, and it took some doing. Finally, though, it started, and Gus and I stood on the ramp watching Mark taxi out and fly away.

Gus drove me to the field while Mark flew the plane—we could watch him following the road ahead of us—to their private grass strip and hangar and home. Gus drove an old brown diesel Mercedes. Gus's business was picking up wrecked aircraft from insurance companies and refurbishing them. He spoke of a recent acquisition, a Piper Cherokee Six, which had been scud running (flying below low clouds) in darkness at 6:30 A.M. "He hit power lines and sheared off two of his landing gear," Gus said. "He went a mile farther on before he hit the top of a hill and skidded to a stop. He was going from Harper to Fredonia, and he got about halfway there. If he hadn't hit the power line, he would have hit a bigger hill down the road a piece, and that one would have killed him sure," Gus said. "As it was, he sat in the plane for half an hour until it got light and he could see where he was." The man walked away from the crash. It was just one more instance of someone being overcome by The Impulse to fly and being unable to resist, no matter how convincing was the evidence of his senses that he ought not go.

Gus and Mark had owned their airport for seventeen years when Gus pulled the Mercedes up against the enormous rusty hangar building, where a sign said "Mercedes Parking Only." We found Mark standing beside my Citabria, looking comfortable chewing on a piece of grass in the sun. I noticed that from down here the land was just as flat and featureless as it was from the air. McHenry County's terrain seemed positively treacherous by comparison. Gus told me that the whole area used to be oil fields in the early part of the century, with old wooden derricks. Now there were salt mines beneath the area, with miles and miles of tunnels that had been left after the workers water-blasted the salt and carried it away in solution. The empty caverns were used for storage, because the temperature and humidity were always constant, and they were safe against any form of calamity, even nuclear war. The movie companies stored films down there, and the government stored secret documents. I kind of liked that, each power storing its own fantasies.

We entered the hangar, and it was like walking onto a movie set. The inside of the hangar was an elaborate and intricate and beautiful chaos of lumber and old aircraft parts such as could not have been created without the force of great effort exerted painstakingly over decades. It was not carelessness that had created that remarkable effect but a meticulous attention to detail in assembling the anarchy and tumult of a symphony. True messes, like true disasters, require great care. And this was positively baroque. I wanted to spend the rest of my life there. In fact, it reminded me of Galt Airport, and I recognized that here, way across the cornfields, was another man in cahoots with Nature, having made a pact, such as Art Galt had made, for his spot on the earth.

Hanging from every rafter were wings and tails and rudders and pieces of airplanes, so that it appeared that a great force had blown those craft to bits and they flew now in a kind of historical heaven of disembodied parts, unknown to each other, disconnected spirits that yearned to come together again like ghosts wandering in a haunted mansion. Every square foot of wall space was hung with implements and tools and rolls of fabric, sheets of aircraft plywood, and wing spars as long as telephone poles.

In the middle of the hangar was a cast-iron heating plant which looked like the black and evil symbolic creation of an artist, a potbellied stove than which there could be none larger, none dirtier, none more profane, which had burned so hot through the heavy winters, with the wind blowing in off the cut-down corn stubble and Gus feeding it smoky truck tires and greasy railroad ties, that it had turned a kind of powdery color. It was so black that it had turned white. "Everything that's burnable goes through that stove in the winter," Gus said.

While I wandered in gaping wonderment through their shop, Mark cut a gasket for my fuel cap using a razor blade and a compass, sitting at a rough wooden picnic table covered with paper plates and cups and Mercedes Benz bumpers. Gus's thinking was that, since nothing else was leaking, the problem had to be a fuel cap. Therefore a new gasket ought to work.

I spotted a Cessna Airmaster cowling, some Tiger Moth wings, a Mooney Mite, an Emeraude fuselage. There was a Tiger Moth that had crashed and was now halfway repaired, its old engine naked and silver-gray and looking like some kind of Russian plumbing fixture for making strong tea. Everywhere the building was hung with strips of torn fabric and pieces of ripped wood and metal which had no ready or evident use but were being kept, no doubt against some future contingency. At one point I went into Gus's office and saw a desk that was piled so high with papers that it rivaled Art Galt's desk.

Finally Mark had the gasket installed, and Gus put gaffer's tape over the holes he'd cut in the wing. They said the whole problem was probably a gasket, but I found it difficult to believe that all that fuel could come pouring into the cockpit on account of a bad gas cap. But then the mystery had gone back underground—which is what had made it difficult to diagnose in the first place.

I said goodbye to the Wiebes. They invited me to come back in June when the whole family would be there for a pig roast and Gus's birthday. I said I would, but I knew I'd probably never see them again.

I taxied out onto the grass and rumbled down the rutted turf runway and flew away, feeling somehow secure knowing that they had blessed my aircraft. They hadn't fixed anything, and I was aware that at any moment I might be drenched in fuel again. But deep down I didn't believe it. Even so, I filled the tanks only halfway.

I flew away from the setting sun. I cast a shadow a hundred miles long. Everybody up and down the line seemed to have heard about the incident, from the line boys where I stopped for fuel, to the controllers, to instructors at several airfields, to another Citabria owner I encountered. I was amazed to find out how efficient the grapevine was. I'd pull up to the pumps, and somebody would say, "Oh, you're the guy who had the fuel leak at Hutchinson, aren't you?" How did they all know? It's a small world, some people would say about aviation. I think that's misleading. It's more like a single organism, a fine moss covering millions of acres.

When the sun began to go down, the world below appeared to brim over with a dusky mist, like a bowl filling with gray-green froth. For a while it seemed that the end of daylight would forge a kind of impenetrable blackness out of that pastel panorama. Abruptly I became aware that landmarks had been vanishing—I couldn't be sure how long it had been going on. I grew fearful that I would be unable to see at all, or worse, that the very land itself was disappearing. But as the mist deepened and the sun faded, lights came on below me, the moon rose above, and a whole other picture emerged, one so unforeseen and contrary to reason that I could not have anticipated it, in which the world is dark but I can see nevertheless. It was not unlike one of the most ancient of human dreams, that of a grotto or cave in which, despite being underground, we can see, a dream that has existed far longer than electric lights.

I put on my lights, which cast a red glow on the instrument panel, and I flew on into the night, glad for the quiet of the radio channels and the twinkling of the lights of towns below.

Clinton's rabbit* beckoned to me in sparkling streaks of running urgency. Suddenly the insolent rashness of my position in the sky gripped me like a black tarantula crawling out of my throat, and I understood how close I had been to Amos during the past forty-eight hours. My life seemed such a tenuous thread of saliva, a spindle of drool out of the great source of great forces. I remembered Conrad writing in *Lord Jim* about the moments just before the disaster, about what had caused Jim to abandon his ship: "He was not afraid of death perhaps, but I'll tell you what, he was afraid of the emergency." I understood those words as never before.

Running low on gas over western Illinois, I decided to stop at Rockford to fill up. I had flown quite a bit farther north since leaving Kansas, and now the weather was cold once again as I taxied on the dark ramp amid the giant shadows of airliners and executive jets. The whole picture, with control tower and sodium vapor arclights and fuel trucks whipping urgently around, was so clean and mechanized and surreal that I hardly recognized it as an airfield.

I climbed out, and a fuel truck pulled up next to me, and a very fat, very pretty woman leaned out and smiled. She was so pretty, so enormous, sitting there in her tanker truck, and her teeth were all glittering in tiny white rows.

I called out over the whine of a nearby jet engine, "Can you give me some?"

An even bigger grin lit her face like morning. "You want some, honey? Sure, I can give you some!"

* *An instrument landing system (ILS) has sequenced flashing lights to lead a pilot to the runway. Pilots call that system "the rabbit" because the lights appear to run.*

□

Within a week, John Fountain experienced the fuel leak again. Liss and Russell worked over the airplane and tried this and that to fix it, but by now it was a ritual. It was shamanism. No one really knew what was wrong; no one ever would. I had become convinced that it was the spirit of fire that had pursued Amos, and that somehow we had excited it to pursue us, too.

After everyone had a crack at fixing the problem, I stepped up to test-fly the plane. John put his hand out on the wing strut between me and the airplane to stop me.

"I'll do it," he said. "I'm seventy."

I understood what he meant. He had had his time. He had flown all he wanted to fly. But he was also acknowledging what we all knew all the time: that each flight in a way was a little visit with our own death, like going to church.

I watched him take off and then I walked into the ruins of the burned-out shop, where the spirit of fire had been chas ing Amos when that old hangar got in its way. Standing in the ashes, I watched our little blue airplane bank this way and that and then disappear like a blue spark into the vapors somewhere; and I stayed there watching, as if the fire held me hostage, until John touched down again.

While Russell was trying to fix the problem, he had pulled out the gasket that Mark Wiebe had cut with razor blade and compass. Russell had sneered at it and threw it away. "That thing's no good," he'd said. And I thought, If only Russell could have seen Mark, if only he could have seen their shop, he would have had that gasket framed.

ELEVEN

KILLING PUPPIES

WHEN I WAS FLYING with Bob Murray, he suggested that if I wanted to compete, I ought to become a contest judge. It seemed to make sense. Who would know better what the judges wanted to see in our performances than the judges themselves? I attended the International Aerobatics Club judging school in Ann Arbor, Michigan.

I arrived at the motel the night before class was to begin and received a call saying that a man named Dave McKenzie would pick me up for breakfast in the morning. I was waiting for him at the appointed early hour when a big American car pulled up and a very thin, bespectacled man with albino white hair, thinning on top, wrenched himself out of the passenger side and managed to erect himself on silvery aluminum spindles. He was neatly dressed in a new gray IAC sweatshirt which displayed the pictograms for a spin, a loop, and a roll in a line across his chest.

"Are you Dave McKenzie?" I asked, taking the sweatshirt as a clue.

"Guilty!" he hollered, and heads turned. He proceeded across the parking lot with considerable difficulty, squinting up from time to time to check his progress.

We had been seated at some local hash house for no more than the length of time it takes to drink a cup of coffee, when I found myself unable to let propriety get in the way of journalism. I asked Dave what calamity had befallen him. I wondered if he was a man who had overcome a handicap by learning aerobatics or an aerobat who had received the only sports injury we have.

Dave explained in his raspy drawl that he had been flying air shows in a Great Lakes (which to the audience looks something like an open-cockpit Pitts) in July 1980 when "I did a tail-slide too low. The only thing that saved my life," he said to me as he thumbed the laminated menu, "was that the paramedics pulled me out. They were right there because it was an air show. If they hadn't, I'd be dead."

Dave said that he had taken his Swick conversion clipped-wing Taylorcraft and had pulled it completely apart. He was modifying and re-covering it in the hope that he might complete it by the end of August. After his experience with the Great Lakes, the amazing thing to me was that Dave was flying at all. And yet on he talked about his flying experiences, good and bad, fun and dangerous, and it was evident that he loved them all. He was in love with flying to the exclusion of his own physical reality; he was only alive to the extent that he flew.

The judging class took place in a cinder-block room in the basement of the airport terminal at Ann Arbor Airport. The floor was linoleum over poured concrete, and the green chalkboard made it look like a million classrooms in a million soulless schools all over the world. Chairs and cafeteria tables had been lined up facing the front.

I thought it would be impossible to make aerobatics boring, but the IAC judging school managed to do just that with its rigid codification of the wonderful things pilots do to their airplanes. By the midmorning break I found myself dozing off, and I got up to walk around the airfield to clear my head. I had noticed two pilots behind me who seemed like real Top Gun types. They were working on their free-style routines during the lectures. They were advanced competitors, and they were sniggering about something. When I returned from the break and sat down, Brian, a short young fellow with a mustache, said, "Hey, are you superstitious?"

"Yeah," I said.

"Good," he said to Jim, his tall partner. "Then this'll be good."

"Go ahead and tell him," Jim said.

Brian edged forward across the cafeteria table between us as I twisted around in my chair to face them. "The guy who sat there last year ground half his head off about two weeks after he took this course."

"Doing what?" I asked.

"Low-level aerobatics. He was sitting in that same spot. I believe that's the same chair, in fact. I'm telling you, it was not a pretty sight." He set his face in a satisfied smile and then tried to look serious once more. He and Jim looked at each other. Then Brian added, "I'm going to keep track of your progress in competitions from now on."

I returned to practice at Galt Airport with a new enthusiasm. The first day back, I ran into Gerry Molidor in the office. He arrived wearing his IAC jacket and asking, "You gonna launch right away?" I could tell we were getting near the contest season. Everyone was getting jumpy and eager.

I departed for the practice area, and while I was up, sweating hard, practicing my routine, I heard him on the frequency as he took off. Then he returned in the pattern because Kathy was there with the kids. He made a 200-mph pass right down the center line and blew away into the sky.

Soon I saw the black dot of his aircraft grow and begin wavering toward me. In less than a minute, he was upon me like a bird of prey, all of his dazzling colors filling my windshield.

He came after me. There was little I could do. He was twice as fast and far more maneuverable. I felt as if I drove a dump truck with wings. He came skating in on me and blew past again in a kaleidoscope of feathers. Then he went vertical and vanished.

Only the previous week, I had been in Gerry's basement, and he had given me The Lecture again: "It's so much fun when everything goes well, and it really spoils it when things go wrong. One little incident and it spoils it for everyone." Now I saw his colors come smearing past me again, and I could hear Gerry's high laugh in my headphones as he went by: "He-he-heeee!"

Finally I saw him pull back and move to an area just south of me, between my practice area and the field. I stopped practicing and just sat there, letting the Citabria fly itself, as he did his routine. The Eagle, spinning earthward, corkscrewing straight down, was breathtaking. Hammerheads, Cuban Eights, and Immelmanns followed one another in an endless tumbling spool of ribbon, which seemed to unwind as it fell through the sky. I just drove around in circles, watching him go. With a shock, I realized that he and I were supposed to be competing in the same category. The amazing things he was doing were simply the Sportsman routine that I'd been practicing. It was like waking to the realization that in a confused and drunken moment I had agreed to a duel with one of the Three Musketeers.

For Chapter One of the IAC, the Chicago chapter, the first serious contest of the season was held at Salem, Illinois, during the first weekend in June. Between seeing Gerry fly and training with John Morrissey, I knew I couldn't compete, but I went anyway, to work on the judging line.

This was the first year since Amos died that Galt Airport

was going to have not only serious representation there but also fliers who threatened to take the trophies home.

The day before competition, Friday, I flew the Citabria south to Salem, and everywhere I looked, spread out before me on the concrete and within the open hangars and across the grass, I saw Pitts Specials in all their splendor, green ones, yellow ones, red ones, white ones, even a purple one that looked as if it had been beaten pretty brutally over the years. The fanciest-looking plane on the field was a gleaming black Pitts S2B with orange, yellow, and red stripes running like fire to its tail. (Its owner, a Canadian airline pilot, confessed to me that he had avoided practicing his free-style routine "because it scares me. So if I don't fly it until the contest, I only have to be scared one time that way.")

We are truly in another world when we are aloft. I could see none of that—not even a hint of the contest—until my wheels had touched the ground and I had rolled over to it and become a part of it. Then if we can't see anything unless we have become a part of it, there is no objective point of view. There is only our view from within. Here is what I saw: the dazzling array of colors, the sun striking liquid finishes on the fabric wings, and the groups of men and women standing around laughing and talking or sprawled out on the grass, sitting on their parachutes, eating hot dogs and watching practice. A great black cast-iron wood-fired pit for barbecuing bratwurst and chicken had been set up in a hollow square of cafeteria tables, and two women were serving lines of people who stood waiting to eat. The black stovepipe protruding from the iron barbecue pit poured smoke up toward the north, as one of the women behind the cafeteria tables scooped ice from an Igloo cooler and poured Cokes from plastic liter bottles. Off the north end of the runway, airplane after airplane entered the box and went through its paces while the pilots on the ground squinted up and made off-color comments, while secretly marking whom they could beat and who could beat them.

Through the long summer afternoon, new pilots arrived and people wandered on the ramp, talking and eating and standing for inspection. Friday was practice day, and each pilot who signed up for practice was allowed fifteen minutes in the box. There were thirty-nine airplanes, and the schedule was booked until eight that night. As I watched, one pilot interrupted his routine and came gliding in with his engine out. I waited until some friends pushed him to the fuel pumps on the main ramp and then asked him what happened. "I ran out of gas," he said with a smile. The more competitive a pilot gets, the less gas he wants to carry. The Russian pilots, the greatest threat in world competitions, carry seventeen minutes of fuel.

Henry Haigh, Jr., son of the world champion aerobat, Henry Haigh, engaged in a friendly fight when Marty Vavra stole his hat. Henry chased Marty all over the airfield and caught him and sat on him as the pilots stood on the ramp watching and cheering them on. Henry was a great bear of a man, with youthful skin and a nearly bald head to which wisps of blond hair clung like moss on a rock. He wore a thick mustache, and his eyes were slightly hidden in the mischievous boyish folds of his fleshy face. His straw plantation hat sported a fluorescent yellow and green band. He had a big beer gut and wore shorts and sleeveless shirts. Mark Peteler observed, "Well, with Henry it's genetic, but I think Marty's weirdness is learned behavior."

One couple stood out from the start. Bob Armstrong was a hard-looking fellow with dark hair and a dark scowl that betrayed an amiable but distant nature underneath. He had a small mustache and seemed to smile only with effort, and when he wasn't flying, he sat on his parachute by the fence behind the barbecue grill and steadily rubbed on the arm of a very fair and foreign-looking woman named Michelle who had won first place in Sportsman category at the Nationals the previous year in her Pitts S2B. Armstrong didn't have such a nice airplane as hers, but he flew in Unlimited, the top category. He had an old Pitts S1C that looked as if it had been painted a fretful gray color by some inner-city gang late at night under a street lamp. The S1C was an early model of the Pitts and had only two ailerons instead of four and a flat-bottomed wing instead of the symmetrical airfoil. Most people didn't go beyond Intermediate category with the S1C. Armstrong was assaulting the citadel of aerobatics knighthood not with a Trojan horse but with a hobbyhorse. On the other hand, his modifications of the aircraft had changed its flying characteristics so much that no one was certain anymore what to call it. "I don't know why he insists on calling it a 'C,' " one of the U.S. Team members told me. "There's not much 'C' left in it after all he's done to it." Nevertheless, Armstrong's airplane seemed to be a statement of philosophy. On a ramp where so many people claimed to have the sharpest, hottest, fastest, most powerful machine, Armstrong had gone to great pains to demonstrate that whatever rank he managed to achieve, it was all pilot skill and owed nothing to the equipment.

When I met Armstrong, he was seated by the fence with Michelle, rubbing and rubbing on her shoulder, as if a genie might pop out at any moment and grant him a wish. They were talking about the food fights that were occurring every year at the Siebring contest now. "They've become a tradition," he said. "Now the people who come there for dinner after the contest ask the caterers to bring out more rolls for the food fight. They've got those good rolls that are just about the right size to throw."

It was a hot and sunny day in June, and the rippling silver waves that rose from the concrete mixed with the smell of avgas and barbecue smoke and the laughter of the pilots swaggering around in tank tops and shorts and Hawaiian shirts and T-shirts and golf shirts and straw hats. The farmland around Salem was as vast and flat and green as a snooker table, and from the main ramp there was a clear view of the runway across a stretch of burned-out prairie. Someone landed in a red Pitts Special and bounced about fifteen times trying to get the airplane to stay on the ground. Each time the wheels touched the concrete again, they made a squeaking sound, like a little animal being crushed, as the pilot tried desperately to bring the wild airplane under control. Mark Peteler watched until the airplane rolled on out of sight, still bouncing, and then he said, "He killed a whole bunch of puppies on that one, didn't he?"

Saturday morning the caterers were already making biscuits and gravy on the big black stove when we arrived. The sun was bright, the ramp was heating up, and people were applying suntan lotion and unfolding their aluminum beach chairs. I picked up some coffee and a ham sandwich, thinking it might be the last food I saw before lunch, and crossed the grass to the judging line. I found Galt's own Howard Stock, the judge to whom I'd been assigned, out on the line. Howard was big and soft-looking and had vaguely blondish-brown hair. He was like the Cheshire cat. He had an oval face and a friendly, sensitive, thoughtful look, but whenever I turned away, all I could remember were the Ray Bans. I was pleased to be assigned to him, because he was an excellent pilot and judge and was always willing to help the ignorant.

I heard someone call, "Okay, make 'em white!" and I watched as the man in charge of the panels flipped them from the orange side to the white side. The panels were large pieces of plywood painted white on one side and orange on the other. They were used to signal pilots if the box was hot (i.e., active) or not.

The day began with the Unlimited pilots, and the first maneuver was a hammerhead with a four-point roll plus another quarter roll on the way up and then a one-and-a-quarter snap roll on the descending vertical line. I was the recorder. All I had to do was listen to what Howard said and write it down. On the other side of Howard's chair, another assistant called out each maneuver so that Howard could watch without taking his eyes off the performance. It was no exaggeration to say that if he blinked he could miss something crucial. So while the assistant judge called out, "This is a pull-pull humpty bump, outside snap up, half roll down, pull out upright," Howard would watch from beneath his plantation straw hat (the fashion rage of that season), behind his clean new Ray Ban Aviators, his legs crossed under white shorts, and leaning back in his green lawn chair, fingers intertwined thoughtfully, he'd say, "Soft points. Overrotated. Dragging his right wing. Hunted for the line," and so on, mentally subtracting from the perfect score of ten and finally arriving at a number. I wrote down what he said.

Even today, after seeing many contests, I have no idea how Howard knew what he was seeing. When a Pitts takes off, it rapidly becomes a speck in the sky. The brilliant paint scheme fades, and it's simply a black thing against the pulsing blue of the heavens. As it turns its various aspects toward us, it presents an ever-changing array of optical illusions, betraying the true nature of what the pilot is doing. Is he going away from us or toward us? One moment he looks inverted, but then as he turns, it seems he has just gone inverted, so he must have been upright before. Learning to judge could take years of practice. And how much of our lives do we want to devote to sitting in a lawn chair craning our necks?

Sometimes during a figure we'd hear the engine scream and rattle until it sounded as if the air itself would shatter. Then suddenly it would go completely silent, and the craft dropped as if it had been shot. We'd hear the blackbirds cackling and the soft wind rustling the weeds and thistles. Then halfway through its plunge to earth, the aircraft would seem to explode to life again, it would howl and grind and struggle to reverse its course, and then labor skyward once again.

By lunchtime we were sunburned, and the boundary judges had come in from where they were posted to make sure no pilot strayed outside of the box's lateral limits. They complained that it was torture out there in the sun. One of them, a young aspiring aerobat who was building a Pitts in his garage, but who as yet had no pilot's license, said, "Yeah, last year I was out there judging the boundary line, and I just sat there all fucking day. And when I got up, I noticed three vultures sitting there watching me real curious like."

By the middle of the afternoon, each time I watched another outside maneuver, I could feel the blood rushing to my head and my headache grew worse. My neck hurt from looking up. I had seen just about every Pitts I had ever hoped to see in my life, and I had begun to have second thoughts about the whole endeavor.

When I first flew Gerry's Eagle, I was amazed at how fast and powerful and tight it was. But after I had been on the judging line for three hours, watching single-seat Pitts Specials fly, I looked at Gerry's ship differently. It appeared slow and lumbering and difficult to control. I realized that no matter what airplane we bought, there would always be someone rolling up to the ramp with a hotter machine. The only thing I could count on was my own skill. I had already seen Bob Armstrong poke up to the fuel pumps in his sorry-looking S1C and duck his head shyly and then climb in and go up there and blow their doors off.

I noticed that after a pilot pulled enough outside G's, oil would begin to leak through the inverted system and feed back into the engine, and sometimes the aircraft would carry a trail of white smoke from one maneuver to the next. Although the competition aircraft were equipped to make smoke, it was forbidden in competition, but I had begun to look forward to it. I found myself reluctant to admit it after working so hard on my routine, after attending judging school, and investing so much energy in the idea of competition, but the fact was, it was boring, and I found myself looking forward to the accident of smoke, because it made the displays more interesting. It was my first contest, and I loved the people and the setting, but it was like sex: I wanted to do it, but I couldn't quite get the point of watching. And I wasn't sure I wanted to do it with all these people watching me, either.

I felt my aspirations to be a contestant falling into question. Do I want to be a black dot spinning endlessly among the millions of other black dots with all the anonymity of a star in the evening sky?

There were more judges than spots for them, and when I had finished my duties, someone else took my place, and I went to sit inside an open hangar to get out of the sun and see if I had any skin left. I could hear the tenors and altos of an engine singing obbligatos to itself, the crooning wires, the thumping bass, as someone moved through Advanced. Sometimes the engine sounded like a low note on a bass trombone, played too loud on purpose for the distorted effect, and the wires, as the aircraft turned at maximum performance, sang a whistling tone, like a dive bomber in an old movie.

Another Pitts bounced in for a landing. Another one leapt into flight. I had lost track. Anyway, I didn't care anymore.

I bought a Coke and drifted out onto the ramp and found a pretty woman lying in the shade of my wing, watching her husband fly. I sat down and leaned against my tire and shaded my eyes to watch him do his routine. He was good, and I told her so. He flew an S2B. She told me, "We prayed over the contest in our room just a little while ago and asked the Lord to bless this flight."

I went to my hotel room and showered. I was sunburned. It was after seven when I returned to the field, and the airplanes were still flying. The crickets sang in the dry fields, and the heat made an undulating mirror of the runway surface even at the end of the day. The contestants flew until dark, and as the last Pitts Special taxied up to the pumps, the volunteers were breaking out the first of the beer.

Making my way through the crowd on the night-cooling ramp, I passed a group of middle-aged women, wives of pilots, and I overheard one of them say, "I use ERA. I'm getting into liking the liquid soaps."

I checked the standings for the day. Bob Armstrong's beat-up C-model came in second and third respectively, in known and free style. Henry Haigh, Jr.'s exotic and expensive Pitts came in tenth in Advanced.

Gerry was already suffering from the halo effect of having placed first in his category, and he had become somewhat animated by Budweiser and was talking about getting Howard back on line and putting together a whole Galt Airport contingent to blast into the contests, arriving in formation. He had this concept that we would be a kind of ad hoc McHenry County Air Force.

We ate dinner at cafeteria tables in the open hangar. They called it The Banquet, somewhat hyperbolically, I think. There were long tables set up on the concrete hangar floor and a cafeteria line of creamed potatoes, green beans, slaw, chicken breast in gravy, roast beef, Wonder bread, iced tea, cake, and pie. A drawing for $168 (what someone had managed to collect from people on the field in an open betting pool) went to a woman named Sandy. Someone gave Henry Haigh, Jr., a life vest as an award for being thrown into the pool more times than anyone else.

It became apparent that there was an in-group, and that the members of that group stayed together at the same hotel and called it Headquarters. There they got drunk and did silly things together and then immortalized their behavior in a newsletter. I have written about organizations from kite fliers to alcoholic jogging doctors, and they are all essentially the same. They form a tribe in which they speak a certain language and follow a certain obsession. There is always an in-group and the rest of the world is composed of outsiders.

Conrad wrote of the pepper traders of the seventeenth

century, "The bizarre obstinacy of that desire made them defy death in a thousand shapes. . . . it made them heroic; and it made them pathetic, too, in their craving for trade with the inflexible death levying its toll on young and old." Those fliers, in their quest for power and speed, often missed the essence of the quest that initially led them to fly in the first place. Like those men who burn so brightly in their quest for love that they burn through half a dozen women and become slaves to the unattainable. I think the grail lies within our hearts. But people who are convinced that it lies outside of us are apt to put their faith in a hopped-up Pitts airplane instead of in a really fine pilot to fly it. Of course, we would all like to be heroic figures, but the fact is that I'm an ordinary pilot, and if I have any special talents at all in that field, they involve recognizing enough about my own limitations to grant my children the privilege of watching me become a cantankerous old fool.

I found Gerry again and had another quiet moment with him away from the crowd. I had decided to ask what made him always give us The Lecture. The way he always said that "everything could be spoiled by one accident," I knew that he had seen it spoiled once, probably a long time ago, and I wanted to know what had happened.

He had loosened up enough to remember his glider-towing job. He had been furloughed as a young United Airlines pilot, and he and a friend of his were towing gliders for hire. His friend crashed. "He was low, trying to tow a glider out of a field where it had landed short, and he got into the trees," Gerry said. "He tried to go knife-edged to get through, and he cartwheeled and hit the instrument panel with his face." By the time Gerry got there, a man had laid the pilot out on one of the glider's wings and was trying to give him mouth-to-mouth resuscitation. "But his head was the shape of a football, and the guy kept coming up with blood and teeth, I mean, the guy was gone. I quit that day," Gerry said. "I never went back."

Later on the ramp under a misty moon I found Henry Haigh in the parking lot in his car, making it smoke sideways across the asphalt by holding the brakes and accelerator at the same time, a kind of automotive snap roll.

Sunday morning everybody was on the ramp for a briefing at 7:30, laughing and poking each other and making jokes. They had been setting up shots and chasing them with beers last night in the bar, and this morning some of them had their glasses on crooked. Marty Vavra looked over the unknown sequence in Unlimited and said, "I got the first floor figured out but after that it's touch and go."

Mark said, "I know where the box is."

Gerry said, "We'll see."

I was assigned to assist Larry Coltrin, an advanced pilot whose son also flew. I waited for Larry to appear, and when he did, I said hello, but he just walked on by as if he hadn't heard. He wore mirror sunglasses and a T-shirt that showed a cartoon dog humping someone's leg. In big bold letters it said "Safe Sex." He walked past me onto the ramp for the briefing and lay flat on his back on the asphalt while the briefer, Cliston Murray, talked over a whistling, howling makeshift PA system, which someone had rigged up out of wires and speakers. Mark, standing next to me, watched Coltrin lie down on the ramp and said, "I'll never forget being at my first contest and seeing Larry the next morning. He had on a baseball cap with a dog's face and a big tongue hanging out, and it was appropriate. He looked like shit. He just looked so hung over."

The day began with Marty. He was flying Larry's plane, a highly modified and souped-up Pitts Special. I had seen Marty in the motel hallway early that morning walking through his routine with a bag of doughnuts in one hand and a sequence card in the other. Imagining the sequence, he turned his body with the turns he read from the card. Whenever he had to go inverted, he would throw his head back to pick up the horizon, gesticulating with the doughnuts in the air before him. There wasn't much Marty could have done to make himself look more ridiculous. I suppose he could have made engine noises.

Marty started the engine and taxied out, waiting for the flag to tell him it was clear to take off. Then, as all the judges watched for the first flight of the day, Marty roared down the runway about 300 feet, his canopy blew off, and he stopped dead in the middle of the runway and cut his engine.

People ran out to see if he was on fire or some other dire thing, but no, he was just hung over and had forgotten to latch his canopy, and it had blown open when he cranked up the 300 horsepower engine. I was assisting Larry Coltrin when that happened. Larry and his son began laughing at Marty's misfortune, then suddenly Larry came to angry life. "Hey!" he shouted, leaping up. "That's my airplane!" And he ran off to see how bad the damage was. He came back carrying the plexiglass bubble in one hand and cursing his friend.

The line man started to let the next airplane go, but then Marty insisted that he could fly. The judges on the line were saying, "You ought to take a break, Marty." And: "You ought to go to the end of the line and get calmed down." One judge said, "You ought to get less fucked up."

Someone secured the canopy, and as Larry watched his beautiful airplane lift away from the earth, he elevated his middle finger in salute, muttering, "I'll bet you don't see more than a five off of my scores."

Marty flew what might have been the worst sequence of the weekend. Twice during the routine he had to stop, fly out of the box, get himself turned right way around, and then begin again—suffering many penalty points in the process. Cliston, our chief judge, turned around to address the judges after Marty was done, saying in a droll fashion, "I guess that went slow enough that you got it all."

For a while I sat at the feet of Linda Hamer, who had taught at the judging school I attended in Ann Arbor. I wanted to learn from her. Her assistant was Dave Cargill, a responsible pilot who flew in the Advanced category. I liked him. He did reasonably well, acquitted himself respectably, and didn't make a spectacle. He had a nice modified Pitts Special, and he was going to practice all summer and go to the Nationals if he could. He was a tranquil pilot.

The pilots drifted out as they had drifted in, taking off during the afternoon and evening to fly home. So ended the first contest of the season. Hot dogs and dirty latrines, hangovers and heatstroke, waiting and judging and waiting again to watch something the size of an ant buzz around in the sky.

Back at Galt the next week, I saw Howard Stock drive his little tan truck across the grass in front of my hangar, his Ray Bans glinting. I left my parachute on the seat and went to say hello.

Howard said, "Did you hear about Dave?"

"Dave Cargill?" I asked.

"Yeah. He crashed over at Kenosha on Sunday." Howard was deadpan. He was just transferring necessary information.

"What happened? Was he killed?" I felt an unpleasant chill come over me. I had just worked the judges line with Dave.

"Yeah. He went in upside down. They said an elevator bolt was missing when they looked at the wreckage."

I couldn't speak for a moment, but I know I tried to stammer something, to ask the questions that were spinning through my head. But how? But why? But I was just with him, he was there while I was lying on the grass, practically at his feet, and his ankle was dangling beside my leg, and it was beating with his pulse, lifting and dropping as if a breath moved through it. That was Dave Cargill, laughing with Linda Hamer as he called the figures, and they joked about the antics of the pilots. What about all of the animated material that was his bone and blood? And what about the spontaneous laugh, the motion that came mysteriously from within? Surely life could not be removed just like that, as if by some evil spell. Aren't we any more substantial than that?

"He was out practicing," Howard said. "Nobody really knows much. But if he lost an elevator bolt, then he probably lost control and couldn't get out." He paused and watched me for a moment, and I could see myself in his Ray-Bans, my mouth open in shock. I made an effort to close my mouth. "So, are you going up to practice, or what?" Howard asked, still deadpan.

"Yes," I said. "I was just going out."

"Be careful," he said and drove away.

TWELVE

PINK FLOYD

THE AEROBATICS SEASON was in full swing, and at Galt the fevered atmosphere of competition seemed to pervade all the operations. Almost every Sunday Gerry and Mark and Howard would declare what they called "playday," activate the box over Galt, and everyone with an aerobatics airplane would get up there and rip around upside down, gathering crowds and freaking the neighborhood cows. The two big contests of the season were approaching, Fond du Lac, Wisconsin, and the Nationals in Texas, and everyone was keyed up. It wasn't just the contestants. Everyone at the airport realized that Galt's contestant tenants could bring home trophies, put us on the map, so to speak.

In the office Carla told me, "The McHenry County Boys are really hauling in the hardware." Many regional contests were held throughout the summer, and Gerry and Mark were taking first and second place in them all. Gerry had even managed to talk Howard into flying again, and he flew to first place in the Intermediate category. ("I like Intermediate," Howard told me, "because I don't have to practice. If I flew Advanced, I'd actually have to work at it.") But Mark was becoming frantic at his inability to beat Gerry. They were first and second, but there was room in the point spread for another contestant to sneak in between them. Mark knew that Gerry was an order of magnitude better than everyone else in the Sportsman category.

Mark called me late one night. His voice was breathy and hoarse as he reported into the phone, "Gerry is flying like a madman. He flew six sequences yesterday. He was *insane*." Control had fled from our ranks. We were in the florid thrall of our mad abandon, and some of us were going to die. Each time I went up, I was aware that my wings might come off. I found myself almost waiting for it to happen, anticipating that moment as I pulled four, five, five and a half, and sometimes even six G's. I listened for the sound, waited for the feel of the bottom dropping out, and I watched outside, expecting to see one of my wings fold back like a broken bird. I wasn't going to compete—what was the point? Yet I went on nevertheless.

"I'm practicing every day," Mark said, sweating, desperate. I came to know his heavy breathing on the other end of the line, late at night. He was hoarse from yelling in the cockpit. (We all yell while we do aerobatics. I first learned while flying with the Air Force fighter pilots that yelling while pulling G's helps to push the blood back to the brain. But after a while it's like karate, where each blow just naturally seems to carry a particular cry.) Mark would wheeze at me, "I'm going to beat his ass. I'm going to get him." Meanwhile, Gerry just laughed his boyish laugh, and in his good-natured way, he blew everyone's doors off.

On a Wednesday in July, I flew the Citabria to the Experimental Aircraft Association convention in Oshkosh, Wisconsin, to meet my friend Jonas, who had built his own high-speed aerobatic airplane out of plywood, an Italian design called a Falco.

I didn't need to stop for gas, but I landed halfway there anyway at Hartford, Wisconsin, which had a special place in my heart. When I was learning to fly a tail-dragger, I took Will Giles, the boy next door, out for a ride in the middle of winter. I had just learned to fly Steve Nusbaum's orange Aeronca—my first tail-dragger experience. We had no radios, no electrical system, and almost no brakes, and although I'd been signed off to fly the thing alone, I really didn't understand the business of the tail wheel. I landed on Runway 29, and the wind was directly from the south, which is to say, directly on my left side. I was talking to Will, who was in the back seat. I was pontificating about some aeronautical matter of immense importance, and I wasn't paying enough attention to landing. When I touched down in a drift, the airplane simply started sluing around, and (doing precisely what I had been told not to do) I put on the brakes to finish it off. I should have applied full power and used the rudder to straighten it out. I had several thousand feet of concrete in which to try my landing again. But I didn't have enough experience to know that, and I simply went off the runway and into the snow. I think I must have stopped the loop there just for a second, because my wingtip didn't touch the concrete, and we simply floated and then gently settled into the lightly packed snow without breaking anything. Back in the office, the old man behind the counter said, "Don't feel bad. You're not really a tail-dragger pilot until you've ground-looped one."

So whenever I stopped at Hartford, it was something of a pilgrimage; I think I wanted to land on that runway to prove that I had it under control now. I stayed for an hour or so to watch the Russians practice aerobatics in preparation for the IAC Championship contest at Fond du Lac, and then I fueled up and flew off to Oshkosh to meet Jonas.

Simply arriving at the EAA convention is always a challenge. The FAA publishes a chart every year to explain to pilots how to get into the field. The problem is that so many airplanes arrive at the same time that the tower can't talk to them all, and so all pilots follow a published route. The tower posts forward air controllers in remote fields, where they watch with binoculars for us to come in overhead. As they spot us, they call on the radio, "Red Cessna, rock your wings if you read me." If the red Cessna rocks its wings, the controller says, "Red Cessna, thank you, follow the yellow Cub, you're number four for landing. Blue Citabria, rock your wings."

I performed my finest IAC competition wing wag, the kind we do to signal the judges that we are smoking on into the box and about to commence our performance. The controller said, "Ooo, nice job rocking the wings, that looks like fun. Follow the red Cessna, you're number five, Runway two seven, and stay north of the freeway by the blue water tower. Green Arrow, rock your wings." And so on, all the way into the enormous airport, which remained all but vacant the rest of the year but had runways large enough to accept a 747. In fact, the runway on which I landed was so wide that I touched down in formation with another airplane, one of us on each side of the runway.

People were standing on the runway, an alarming sight to say the least. But they waved us off into the grass, where we were waved on and on in turn by a seemingly endless succession of people with flags and orange vests, past a seemingly endless array of parked aircraft, while overhead, airplanes of every description flew around and around. People streamed this way and that in great herds like buffalo on the ancient plains, only they were all dressed in high-colored caps and socks and shorts and disfigured with slogans and logos. They looked like part of a charismatic Indian religion.

Most people with an abiding interest in aviation see the Oshkosh show at least once in their lives. Some people go every year. It is truly the Seventh Wonder of the Aeronautical World. There are major air shows every afternoon, featuring aerobatics in the old style, which is to say, people get killed (or come very close to getting killed) in spectacular ways. In addition, the visitor can buy anything from a compass to a whole airplane or a kit of prefabricated parts with which to build one in the garage. There are tents and hangars and buildings of all sorts filled with merchandise, T-shirts, ball caps, radios, and food (from hot dogs to steak—no tofu here), as well as workshops to help the home builder, seminars on flying safely, films, lectures, entertainment, and a huge press office. That year, there was even a booth set up to sell Stealth Condoms. "They'll never see you coming" was the motto displayed on T-shirts and a large sign mounted above the stacks of black bat-wing six-packs.

I shouldered through the crowd and happened upon Paul Poberezny, founder of this amazing spectacle, which for one week only in the middle of nowhere in eastern Wisconsin, was better attended than the crucifixion of Christ. Paul is considered a god in his context, and his followers are like the members of a cult religion. Never did the Bagwan of Rajneeshpurnam receive more largesse and adoration from his disciples. All the people who work the convention are volunteers. The people who build and rebuild the classic aircraft are volunteers. Time, money, gifts, airplanes, are all donated. People write rhapsodies about Paul and EAA, and his son was raised in the cult, its scion and prime member, and now that his father has retired, little Tommy is president of EAA, more zealous and clear-eyed and close-cropped and tightly wrapped than even the old man was. But if it's a cult, it is as mainstream as a cult can be.

Every culture has its myths. Most of them through history seem to be concerned with gods and monsters and forces beyond our ken. But the great American Myths are not about cowboys or even gangsters, they're about machines. Machines, inventions, gadgetry, toys, gimmicks—whatever you call it, it amounts to the same thing: a national obsession. There is even a psychiatric condition that is peculiarly American in which the patient believes his thoughts and actions are being secretly controlled by a machine.

It is no wonder then that the peculiarly American dream has always involved a machine—a car in every garage, a television in every room, a VCR next to every television, an Apple computer and a Nintendo game in every den, and perhaps a fax machine in Mom's study.

After World War II, the notion that everyone was going to own an airplane wasn't just the whim of a few strange individuals. It was quite a popular idea in the early 1950s, and numerous magazines wrote about airplanes as if we were all window shopping already, and it was just a matter of tooling up. Like the automobile of Henry Ford's conception, the airplanes would be lined up, honking, waiting to land at the local grass airstrip (Galt, for example). We'd go motoring off to Grandma's for the weekend, not over the river and through the woods but over the river and over the snow and over the whole damned forest, too. We'd fold our wings and park the plane in her garage. In fact, a man named Molt Taylor designed and manufactured an excellent, if oddball, craft called an Aerocar, capable of driving on the street and flying in the air. A handful of them are still flying, and they are rare collector's items.

In May 1955, *Mechanix Illustrated* began a series of articles about how to build an airplane in the basement or garage. It was a putsch that ultimately failed, but it did have a slow, almost imperceptible, effect that would be scarcely perceived for decades to come, like the nuclear tests we set off in the desert, which vanished, leaving only their invisible residue to settle over future generations.

The magazine article connected—or reconnected—two sources of great American power on one circuit. The American myth of the garage tinkerer who changes the world with his invention was connected with the ancient longing to fly.

A vital nucleus of devoted adherents was born (perhaps not coincidentally, just at about the time that Galt Airport was born). It wasn't that the article created an interest; it simply tapped into a grass roots movement that had slowly been percolating since before the Wright Brothers, and those people recognized a kindred spirit and quickly snapped up the June and July issues of the magazine to read the other installments of the article.

Of course, I say "reconnected" because the phenomenon I'm describing had happened more than once before: in the building of airplanes by the Wright Brothers, which led to a national craze in the early 1900s; in the invention of the motorcar, which led to a national craze that was still in its florid state when *Mechanix Illustrated* published "How to Build an Airplane for Less than $800—with Engine." When the Wright Brothers' motorized kite became the craze of the mechanized world, the only way to fly an airplane was to build one. A 1929 instruction book on how to fly includes a chapter with diagrams on how to build an airplane in case you don't have one. Gerry Molidor's grandfather built his Marionette monoplane in Volo, Illinois, in 1916, under the influence of just such lore.

Although to most of us the idea of building an airplane in the basement seems naive and crackpot at best, today there are 14,000 registered home-built aircraft flying, and more than 1,000 others known to be under construction. The man who started it all, the man who tapped into those deep channels of dreaming, the author of the *Mechanix Illustrated* article, was the simple boy of a poor Russian immigrant family, and possibly one of the greatest egocentric crackpot visionaries this country has ever known, Paul Poberezny. Since the country was founded by egocentric crackpot visionaries, I think that makes Paul worth closer scrutiny.

He told me, "As long as I can remember, I don't think there's been a day that has gone by that I haven't said the word *airplane*."

We were talking in his plush office at the headquarters of

the Experimental Aircraft Association in Oshkosh, Wisconsin. Paul was a big man with the same kind of big hands I had seen working on the *Stork,* the thick kind of toolmaker's fingers. Photographs of Paul in his prime show a great muscular smiling palooka in a T-shirt, standing with that kind of relaxed readiness, the posture of innate know-how, the untutored grace of the backyard mechanic, a guy who keeps things running, anyhow, with borrowed wire and honest sweat. He is the kind of man who takes what he needs to get the job done, but then he gives it all back with a smile and with interest.

By the time the war ended and the American dream of a plane in every garage had begun to take hold of the popular imagination, airplanes and airplane building had been virtually taken out of the hands of the people. The Civil Aeronautics Authority had managed to develop a complex and baffling set of laws and regulations that made airplane building the province of big business. And yet people were still flying around who had taught themselves to fly before there were such rules. Paul Poberezny was among them. His friend, Silvester "Steve" Wittman (after whom Oshkosh's municipal airport is named) had taken lessons from a legitimate instructor. His pilot's license was signed by Orville Wright. Paul's belief in the inalienable right to build and fly one's own aircraft amounted to a cult religion.

When I visited Paul, he was sixty-eight years old, ensconced at the head of his own very elaborate and lucrative 125,000-member organization. The offices were quiet and expensively appointed, with aviation memorabilia everywhere, paneled walls, indirect lighting, and views of Wittman Field and the surrounding countryside. But Paul was very much the home builder he had always been. He disdained the new headquarters building, where the others worked, preferring to have his personal office out behind the hangar where the aircraft restoration work goes on. He was personally working on building or restoring no fewer than half a dozen aircraft, including a PT-23 like the one in which he instructed in World War II.

He gave a workmanlike interview about the history of EAA. He had been interviewed so many times, he could do it in his sleep. But when we walked through the office door and out into the hangar where a Corsair, a classic Travel Air, and several other aircraft sat, as rare and precious as the original French papers of *Swann's Way*, Paul's face lit up, and he did something all fliers do when they see a special plane: He touched the material.

There aren't any signs at the EAA Air Adventure Museum that say "Do Not Touch," because you have to touch. If you've flown it, you have to touch it. There's something magic about touching. John Fountain and I had flown up to Oshkosh in the Citabria, and when John saw the Corsair, he said, "I've got about six hundred hours in this airplane," and he walked up and respectfully touched its dull gray side the way Catholics dip their fingers in holy water when they enter a church. Poberezny knows better than anyone that touching the material makes it live—that's what the fabrication of an airplane with your own hands means, to be godlike in your ability to animate the materials of the earth. Then later—often much later—by touching that same material again, you can take back some of the energy from the living wood and metal and cloth. It's that human energy, invested in those skins, that makes the airplane fly.

Paul formed his Experimental Aircraft Association with a few friends in 1953. His *Mechanix Illustrated* article came out in 1955. And by the late '50s he was lobbying Washington for the right of every American to build and fly an aircraft. Bigwigs from the CAA would come to Hales Corners, Wisconsin, EAA's original location, to visit "headquarters" and talk with the man who was trying to get an Experimental Category approved for amateur-built aircraft. You'd have thought he was lobbying for basement brain surgery. Those Washington legislators and transportation administrators would end up sitting in Paul's converted coal bin at a Formica kitchen table, scratching their heads: Who is this guy? But skeptical as they were, they saw that Paul was right about one thing: People wanted to fly that badly. Paul recognized the zeal with which people would pursue aviation; they would make heroic efforts and overcome tremendous obstacles to get off the ground. They would mortgage their houses to sweat in the basement for years just in order to put together some rag-wing flying machine in which they'd probably never go farther than fifty miles from home.

Today, EAA's annual convention and air show at Oshkosh is the world's largest convention of any kind. In seven days, it brings $75 million in revenue to Wisconsin. Some 15,000 aircraft and almost a million people from all over the world come to visit. Admittedly, most of those people do not build their own airplanes—most of them don't even fly. But they dream. Tens of thousands of people who can't fly show up in campers and spread tents over hundreds of acres around the field. People all over will tell you that America is great because of Democrats or Republicans or the NRA, but the fact is America is great because people have garages. And the whole marvelous week-long EAA festival is a tribute to the idiosyncratic lunacy of our nation of eccentric tinkerers.

Paul himself spelled out the credo of the spirit when I asked him during our interview a question about the FAA's new plan to cut up national airspace in a more restrictive manner. "Just get in your airplane and fly," he told me with a level gaze. "Nobody's going to bother you."

So why exactly didn't the revolution take place? Why didn't the dream come true? Airplanes have always been cheap and the sky has always been big.

None of us anticipated what we would find up there. In an airplane, all our worldly cues drop away, and we are plunged into a completely alien environment. Nothing is familiar. Our senses are left behind on earth, and we have to learn a whole new strategy for ensuring our own well-being. Mysterious illusions abound. As in scuba diving, we can expect vertigo and disorientation as part of our daily life in the air. The blue dome of the sky, the green bowl of the earth, and the filaments of cloud reeling out of nothingness at us or rising up like a black wall stitched across with lightning—it is a world populated by demons and landscaped out of mythology, and all of those strange apparitions confound our earthbound senses; they force us to pluck up our courage and wait—to stifle panic and simply to wait quietly—to do the next right thing, press the next right button, say the next right words on the radio, and bring ourselves safely home by the finite amount of skill that will fill the warm space between our hands.

Coming down, we feel we have flirted with the gods and taunted the devils. Surely that realm we visit is the dwelling place of other beings—not us—that is not our home. The deeper reason that airplanes did not become more popular was that most people were not willing to make the difficult adjustment. Most people, thrust into the air, eerie and extraterrestrial, were not willing to lean so heavily on the slender reed of engineering we call an airplane. Hammering away on the nose up there, cranking the crude propeller around and around, the power plant that drives our conveyance suddenly appears so much less sleek—not at all the silver bird it had seemed on the ground when we first lusted after it. Now, hanging so precariously by thread and a spark and a flame among the churning clouds, the whole idea of manned flight seems suddenly so naive and makeshift, a preposterous, ill-planned gesture, a grave and audacious mistake against the indifferent, awesome fury of the elements. It was a failure of faith, not of technology, that put the airplane where it is today.

And yet, safe upon the ground once more, there are always a few of us who find ourselves drifting into dream again: *Actually, come to think of it, that was a lot of fun.* As with drunken blackouts, we have already forgotten the miserable part where we glistened and trembled with sweat, and we remember only the bliss. Like suckers at the carnival of the emotions, we pay up and take another ride. The flame that consumed Amos and Lloyd and almost got my father, too, is the flame of internal combustion.

Airstrips such as Galt are the American Dream frozen in its incipient form, like a fetus in a bottle of formaldehyde. Here are the guys in coveralls, like cargo cults, waiting for a revolution that never happened, keeping the flame alive. We always called it the American Dream. It was never the American Plan, the American Philosophy, the American Method. No, we live in a world of dreams, so it's no wonder that flight, the very stuff of dreams, holds us in its thrall. The American Dream, like all dreams, will never come true, but we'll never wake from it, either. The Time of Heroes is over for America, but our epiphanies are still hiding out in those unlikely places, like soldiers still guarding some desolate jungle spot against the enemy long after the liberation. Our heroes now are real people, for whom airplanes are as common and utilitarian as milk cows, and yet still as mysterious and filled with wonder as if we traveled among the stars.

When I found Paul Poberezny in the convention crowd, he was oddly all alone. He stood looking lost by his red Volkswagen convertible bug, which had no doors and the name "Big Red One" painted in white on its side. The sight of Paul driving around in that vehicle had become something of a tradition at the convention. We talked for a while, watching the throngs of people sway to and fro like great fields of wheat in the breeze, blighted with some high-colored nylon fungus. Beyond them, beyond the tents and arcades, the commotion and noise, was the enormous north-south runway, above which one of the many aerial demonstrations was taking place; it was an exact replica of the famous GeeBee racer and another craft of similar lineage, short, stubby, bullet-headed airplanes with little wings that looked like birth defects.

Paul invited me to hop into the Big Red One, and we drove around. On the surface, his spirits were high, but it seemed to me as if he had practiced shaking hands vigorously and smiling broadly for so many decades that it simply came as second nature to him, as it would to an old politician, and that today it concealed a deeper melancholy. As we drove, he watched the airplanes flying low over the field, performing death-defying feats as in the old days of Arch Hoxsey, and each time one passed us overhead, he'd crane his neck to see it and then turn back to his driving, all the while never breaking the pace of his monologue. But then after the last aircraft had throttled past us in a 90-degree bank, Paul stopped the car and fell to pondering, all alone within himself. It was as if he had drifted off into his own world there for a moment and his smile drooped into a little pout, and then he seemed to shake it off and return to the present and notice that I was sitting there and the crowds were moving all about us in the streaming sun. He shifted into gear and drove on. He said, "I promised my wife I wouldn't do any more low-level last year." There was a long pause while that sank in, and I understood the promise. It's something Nancy and Lloyd Hughes might have talked about if Lloyd had lived long enough. It's something a lot of couples talk about, because it's like being on the high wire: If you perform at low altitudes for long enough, no matter who you are, no matter how good you are, gravity will get you sooner or later. "I wish I hadn't said that," Paul added. And I could just imagine Carl Wallenda saying the same thing before going back up on the wire for the last time when he was in his seventies.

I climbed out of the red Volkswagen and shook Paul's hand, and he drove away. As he receded, he waved at people out of the open top as if he were running for President.

□

I found Jonas just in time for us to sit under the wing of his airplane and watch the air show. The most remarkable thing was not the B-52 bomber or the Stealth fighter or even the Stealth Condom. It was almost the Sukhoi 26, which a Russian Team member, the diminutive Nikolai Timofeev, flew in a roll-crazy sequence that made my eyes gyrate in their sockets. At the end of the sequence Nikolai flew straight up, rolling and rolling the whole way, and when the airplane came to a stop at the apex, it literally hung on the propeller and began slowly turning the other way. The maneuver is called a Torque Roll, and not many airplanes can do it.

But even after all that, the performance that transfixed people was the glider. Where Timofeev and his Sukhoi made an amazing demonstration of raw power and outrageous balls—I felt as if I'd seen someone put a fencing foil through a tree—the aerobatic glider routine was a hypnotic and otherworldly ballet, a pure and perfect mastery of the laws of physics, gravity, and inertia. The sequence unfolded very slowly, like Tai Chi. There was no room for cheating. Every move had to be perfect; no quick roll could conceal a sloppy move. It was also absolutely silent, so there was no noise to distract us from what the pilot was doing. With the mastery of a Zen calligrapher, the glider, its long wings trailing smoke, drew figures in the sky, one after another, in a long, slowly unfurling cascade, and it was so expressive that it gave the illusion of sound, smooth and satisfying as a Mozart aria. Moreover, the tension of the act was the opposite of Nikolai's. Where the noise and smoke and speed of the Sukhoi suggested that at any moment it might explode in flames from all the sheer energy it seemed to have captured, the glider was barely suspended in the air, and every move was paid for with the precious currency of altitude. With no engine to drive it, only the pilot's delicate hands and the billowing air kept it aloft; and we all knew with the certainty of an audience in a theatrical mystery that in the end he would come face to face with the hard green earth as his adversary.

When he was almost finished, he passed low over the field and the pyrotechnic smoke pots on his wing tips were beginning to burn out. They threw off orange sparks and spurts of smoke in irregular gouts, and he pulled three heart-stopping loops, the last of which was so low that his wheels disappeared from view behind a berm at the side of the runway. Immediately he touched down and the spell was broken and people applauded their relief.

Returning from Oshkosh, I stopped again at Hartford and was lucky enough to catch Patty Wagstaff in practice. She was up when I arrived, and I landed beneath her. On the ramp I found a British International Aerobatics judge speaking into a microphone, recording his comments for her, while her husband Bob taped her performance with a video camera. Her young mechanic stood by watching. Patty is a knight of the modern world. She looks as if she ought to be cast as Joan of Arc in a movie. Bob was a big man with a gray beard, shaggy hair, and a tendency to wear khaki or corduroy. He was soft-spoken and quietly intelligent, with piercing green eyes that seemed to betray some other element of his nature that was not so openly expressed. While Patty flew the Extra 260 monoplane, Bob drove their white van, which contained the video equipment and clothes and their basic living supplies.

After her routine, she landed and then immediately retired to the van with Bob and the British judge to review the tape and try to identify ways to improve her performance.

I looked up and saw Randy Gagne taking off in a pinkish-purple SU26, "Pink Floyd" painted on the side. Randy, with a single black glove on his right hand, looked somewhat sinister, like a Russian KGB hit man, but he was neither. He was an American instructor and competitor from the Pompano Air Center in Florida which had brought some members of the Russian team to compete at Fond du Lac. Pompano Air Center was distributor of Sukhoi aircraft for the United States, and so this was, in a real sense, a promotional tour for selling the SU26 and the new two-place Sukhoi trainer, the SU29.

Almost the moment he left the ground, Randy snap-rolled. There are exceptions to the roll-on-takeoff rule, and one of them was Randy. A significant gathering of the others were standing on the ramp within fifty feet of me.

Randy turned crosswind and downwind. He couldn't have been more than 300 feet up, and he rolled left, right, left, right, about ten times in rapid succession, snapping and rolling and snapping again. I could see by how easy it looked that he was just warming up, getting the feel of the airplane.

I looked up just in time to see Randy uncork that 360 horsepower engine and screw the purple airplane into the blue sky. I had never seen anything like it. Involuntarily, I laughed out loud with delight at the astonishing figures he was making. When John Morrissey became coach of the U.S. Aerobatics Team, he told me about going to Russia to spend three weeks trying to figure out how they always humiliated us at the Nestor Cup competitions. When I asked him how he liked flying the Sukhoi, he said, "Well, I've been crawling in people's windows at night stealing money to try to buy one."

A man named Wes, who was acting as the box monitor, watched and said, "That doesn't feel good." He was referring to the outside maneuver he saw Randy performing. "It hurts. And when you pull for a while and all the blood goes to your ass, then when you push all those negative G's, it feels like something's going to come squirting out of your ears."

A few minutes later Randy broke off his routine and landed. When he got out, he was complaining that a big piece of something had hit his foot. "It didn't fall out of my pocket, either," he said.

One of the crew members asked, "Did you take the vibrator with you last night?"

When the mechanics looked into the problem, they found

that a big piece of the airplane had actually detached itself under the force of Randy's flying and had fallen on his foot. Lucky it didn't hit him in the face. Even a dime could do serious damage when it's going 180 miles an hour.

Patty finished her critique session in the van and stepped out and crossed the ramp to sit on a bench talking to a couple of the other pilots about what she looked for in a man. "An aura in the eyes. Bright eyes," she said, and I thought of her husband's piercing green eyes. "A spark of intelligence, nice complexion," she mused. "It's real important to me. Presence. Power of presence." She was searching for a way to describe the quality she knew in her mind but the words she had at her disposal were not completely satisfying to her as she played them on her tongue and lips. "Not power of macho, self-confidence. Not uniforms and badges. Personal presence."

Behind her Rick Massegee, who would also make the U.S. Team that fall, stood on the wing of his black Sukhoi talking, while a mechanic bled his brakes. There were now three broken Sukhois. That's how it was in aerobatics: Only a fine line separated the two vastly different conditions of winning a competition and no flight at all. One minute everything was working. The next minute everyone was grounded. What Gerry had said—that the act of putting the airplane together started the process of its disintegration—was particularly true of the airplanes flown in Unlimited category, such as the Sukhois and Extras and all the competitive monoplanes. Flying anything in Unlimited will break it. It's why Amos had to buy so many airplanes. Once, when I was talking with Mark Peteler about how far he planned to go in competition, he said, "Let's face it. If you want to fly Sportsman, you can do it for the rest of your life and not get hurt. But if you're going to be in Unlimited, or even Advanced, you have to have your plane in perfect condition at all times, and if there's the least hint of anything wrong, you have to have two hundred thousand dollars ready to plunk down and buy a new plane the next afternoon, or you're going to get killed. It's that simple." One of the reasons the U.S. had trouble winning the Nestor Cup was that the system of IAC competitions did not select only the best pilots. But it often selected the ones who could afford to play.

Patty was going on about men. "Guys in bars who look like they want to fight versus guys who don't need to." She thought about that for a moment and then added with a conclusive and satisfied smile, "But they'd win anyway." All the while she was watching Tom Meyer, a young man with a blond pony tail and a Decathlon who was flying in the Intermediate category and sleeping in a tent at night on the grass out beyond the fuel pumps.

Patty told me that she had started aerobatics ten years earlier flying a 150 Decathlon. She had moved up to a 180 Super Decathlon, then four Pitts specials in a row, and now the big monoplanes.

I asked Patty about the elastic bandage she wore on her elbow. She said she had tendinitis from working the stick, like tennis elbow. I asked her if she did exercises for aerobatics and she said she believed that aerobic exercise was bad for aerobatics. Patty said, "It makes your arteries soft or something." She sat there on the wooden bench, her knee ricked up, her legs bare in the sun, her face turned toward the sky. She looked like an artist's model, thin and graceful and classic. She was so alive and the substance of her was so palpable and solid, I could almost feel the metabolic warmth of her, like the engine of the sun, shining down on everything. The thought was inconceivable that she could be anything other than just as alive as she was now. Then I learned that she had taken over Amos Buettell's hangar at Avra Valley Airport, and I didn't want to watch anymore.

Steve and I flew down in the Aeronca to visit Don Ericson one day. I landed on the private strip, which was not much wider than our wingspan, and Don met us and drove us to his house. He had a workroom set up in his country home, with a stream running through the backyard just down the road from St. Charles, Illinois. I sat at the workbench, with aluminum shavings scattered on the floor among sheafs of computer paper with aeronautical calculations and drawings, and I listened to Steve and Don talk about the *Stork*. One complete wing was hanging before them at eye level, rigged with spar and ribs and drag wires crisscrossing its interior to give it rigidity against the stress of plunging through the air. They talked like this:

"You see, when you pull this handle up, the flaps extend twenty degrees. If you pull it to the next notch, they go thirty degrees, but the leading edge slots also come out, and that's where you get your really big advantage in low-speed operation. This whole front portion of the wing drops down and locks into place."

Dominating one wall of Don's shop was a great machine for bending sheet metal. Scraps and corkscrews of aluminum were scattered everywhere, glittering in the sunlight that fell through the windows all around, but there was a deeper order to his shop beneath the superficial clutter. Each of his tools was hung on a board, and each had its own outline with shapes like Louisiana and Delaware. Through the picture windows I could see sheep grazing in the grass, and I saw how Don might have daydreamed in a peaceful place such as this, wondering when his heart was going to stop (for he had failed his medical because of heart problems). Sitting, as I was, watching the sheep drifting like clouds over the green fields, he must have begun to see the possibilities. The *Stork* was light enough to be picked up and carried by two people. Its wings folded back, so that it could be put on a trailer and stored in a garage. It could take off on fifty feet of level grass. Don intended to build a strip right there in the meadow behind the workshop. Its efficient Hirth engine could burn auto gas, so it was inexpensive to operate. Rated at twenty-five horsepower, the engine fit legally into the ultralight definition. But Don had found that by tuning the exhaust he could boost the output to thirty-five horsepower. It was a glorious pursuit, an unending ribbon of extravagant, preposterous dreams leading down a road littered with money, and whether one was picking it up or scattering it out like seed, it was all the same road and what mattered was the joy of traveling it. The wings had been built and rigged and torn apart and rebuilt and tried on like a pair of slacks and removed yet again, but so far the *Stork* was little more than a sculpture of steel tubes in the back of a barn. And Don was still grounded for lack of a medical certificate, although eternally filled with purpose, drive, enthusiasm, and hope. The airplane had not yet flown—it might never fly—but all of his plans seemed to be made manifest in the very destiny of welded tubing, just as certainly as the deluge was made inevitable when Noah sawed and set the first sap-scented beams of the Ark.

Almost a year after my first visit, I returned to Don's house. The *Stork* had been given a white-painted skin of Dacron stretched so tight that when I snapped my finger on it, it made a musical note like a timpani. It shone with mirrored coats of paint—remarkable that this gleaming object of snowlike purity had risen from the muck and grease of the old shop at One Zero Charlie and Don's cluttered workshop in St. Charles. "It's essentially finished," Don told me in a confidential tone. "We're trying to keep it kind of hush-hush."

"Why not fly it now?" I asked.

"We're still tuning the exhaust," he said. There were a few details left to be handled, but he was planning to fly it out of the 900-foot airstrip at Steve's farmhouse as soon as the exhaust was done. "Quietly," he said. "Without fanfare."

"Are you sure it will fly?" I asked.

"Oh, it'll fly, all right," he said without hesitation. "The question is, how well."

But the wings, beautiful as they were, finished as they were, still hung from the ceiling in his workshop. And the fuselage was parked in Don's garage. The engine and a pilot's seat were installed, and I climbed in to see how it would feel. I put on the harness, and Don and Steve stood nearby as we discussed the position of the flap handle and whether a pilot of my average size could reach it comfortably. I sat there "flying" the *Stork* for a few minutes, looking at the bolt attachments and the beautifully welded joints and all the silver cables snaking this way and that. Before long I found myself looking out the window at the sheep grazing across the little stream that ran past Don's house. And the sheep had begun to look a little bit like clouds out there, and I caught myself thinking, Hey, I could build something like this . . .

Since the beginning, people have turned out in great numbers for aviation events, but the sine qua non has always been death. Most of us cannot remember how our ideas of powered flight were formed, but there are still a few fossils walking around who can talk, and this is how they tell it: certain peculiar individuals came out, and with a kind of grim exuberance and a gleeful determination, they killed themselves before huge crowds. That's how we came to understand powered flight.

The Wright Brothers' most famous flight took place on December 17, 1903, at Kill Devil Hill in North Carolina. Most accounts of aviation history build upon that with more and more details of how those simple repairmen tinkered their airplane design together out of old bicycle parts, but not only is that an inaccurate portrait of the Wright Brothers, it has little to do with what actually shaped our view of flying. In fact, from the outset the Wrights were horrified at the public view of flight.

Orville and Wilbur worked largely in secret. They worked not with a wrench so much as with paper and pencil and a wind tunnel, calculating the fundamental aeronautical equations we still use today and testing their theories on models just as Northrop and Lockheed do today. The "pioneers" of aviation who went before them leaped off cliffs in desperate attempts to get aloft, but the Wright Brothers were positively unorthodox in their insistence on surviving their experiments. It may be that the truth about their clandestine and celibate lives was too embarrassing for the public record of the time, and that may be why we know so little about them. We may never know.

Glenn Curtiss was no better, a gloomy, aloof, and unglamorous figure who preferred hiding away in his garage to talking with people. No, those "giants" of aviation weren't giants at all; only lunatics had been willing to attempt flight before the existence of airplanes, and only some sort of disturbed crackpot could invent a flying machine. By the time the general public knew anything about aviation, the shaping of its culture was out of the control of the Wrights and Curtisses.

The events that shaped our views of aviation and continue to color them to this day came a few years later. The Wright Brothers flew in 1903, but they didn't announce it to the world until 1908, when others were already doing it. What shaped our view of aviation was the public spectacle of the air show.

By 1910 the first International Air Meet had come and gone at Dominguez Field in Los Angeles, leaving in its wake a handful of dazed and dazzled would-be airmen, such as Arch Hoxsey, who, like Toad of Toad Hall, was instantly enthralled with the very idea of aviation and was ready to throw over everything to achieve its ecstasies. In fact, he quit his job as an auto mechanic and took up flying. The historian Don Dwiggins wrote in his series *Adventures in Flight:*

> He did things with a Wright Flyer that the Dayton brothers didn't believe possible. And the public loved him—grinning, waving, chewing gum and laughing at death in the later style of Lincoln Beachey, whose career would begin where Hoxsey's left off.

Hoxsey was neither the first nor the most skilled of the "early birds" who filled the skies over America with homebuilt contraptions after Kitty Hawk. But he had something special, something that made the audiences love him and fear for his life when he flashed low overhead, balanced on the lower wing of his powered boxkite, peering down through pince-nez glasses and waving a gloved hand at his proud mother, Minnie Hoxsey, who tried hard not to let her fear show.

But in that single year, Arch Hoxsey was to witness a scarcely believable transformation in his public. They urged him on to greater and more daring feats, knowing that one day he might make a mistake and be killed. And Hoxsey gave them what they wanted—thrills and more thrills—and finally his life.

What Arch Hoxsey did that drew so many people was to handle the airplane with exuberance. He wasn't doing aerobatics yet. True aerobatics would only begin after 1913, when French pilot Adolphe Peguod learned to fly upside down in Louis Blériot's Modex XI, which the latter had used in the historic crossing of the English Channel. But in 1910 Hoxsey was verging on what flight instructors, pushing the boundary of understatement, call "unusual attitudes," that is, making the airplane do things that are not necessary for "normal flight." One of his maneuvers was called the Dive of Death, and people all across the east and midwest—Detroit, Pittsburgh, New York—turned out in remarkable numbers to see him.

The Wright Brothers supplied the airplanes Hoxsey flew—indeed, Hoxsey was flying them to promote their utility in war and commerce. (From the beginning, the Wrights had intended their machines for use in war.) Nevertheless, Wilbur scolded Hoxsey for the way he flew, saying, "I am very much in earnest when I say that I want no stunts or spectacular frills . . . under no circumstances make more than one flight each day. Anything beyond plain flying will be chalked up as a fault and not as a credit." Never has an airman had a clearer challenge to upset the sponsor. And few pilots could resist. The test pilot of the first 707 surprised Boeing brass when, before a crowd of airline executives, prospective customers, he decided to pull a barrel roll in the big silver jet. It felt so good, he did two of them. When he landed, his boss requested that he not do it again.

Hoxsey and his wingman, Ralph Johnstone, a classmate from the Wright flying school in Alabama, were billed together on the circuit as "The Heavenly Twins." In the autumn of that first year of their air-show careers, while flying together in two Wright Flyers, Ralph stalled, spun, and became caught in the flying wires of his craft where he could no longer reach the controls (of course there were no seat belts). He crashed before a crowd of spectators, who rushed the wreckage and tore it apart for souvenirs. Thus was the relationship between the audience and the air-show pilot born, and our public view of flying was galvanized in one grisly episode.

The day after Christmas, Hoxsey was back at Dominquez Field, attempting to recapture the altitude record that Johnstone had earlier set and then lost to the French. The crowd that watched Hoxsey numbered more than 40,000, making the second International Air Meet the largest spectator event in California history. After successfully setting the new record at 11,474 feet, defending the honor of his country and his dead classmate, Hoxsey set his ship into a Dive of Death, pulling out at the last possible moment. It was while the cheering spectators were still carrying him around on their shoulders, while the band was playing in his honor, that the head of the Fédération Aéronautique Internationale announced that the barograph had been fitted with the wrong graph paper, and that the results were therefore unofficial. The French retained the altitude record.

Twice more Hoxsey attempted in succeeding days to recapture the altitude record for America, and unofficially he did so. But each time some technical difficulty allowed the

French to retain the old record. On December 31, 1910, Hoxsey climbed his Wright Flyer into a Santa Ana wind over the seashore. Just before his take off, his mechanic, Al Hazard, had warned him not to do it. A telegram had just arrived reporting that fellow pilot John Moisant had died earlier that morning while flying in Louisiana. But Hoxsey, joking that he would live forever, went ahead with his last attempt.

He was nowhere near the previous heights he had achieved when the wind and mechanical problems forced him back. He began his signature return to earth: the Dive of Death, powering down from almost 7,000 feet at a steep angle. As he descended, his ship inexplicably executed a half roll, spun out of control, and then crashed in a cascade of splinters right in front of the crowd. There was almost a pitched battle as mounted police and spectators fought for the pieces of the broken airplane. Al Hazard held them back, using the pointed end of a cracked wing strut for a lance. Hoxsey's altitude record has never been made official.

The legacy of pilots such as Hoxsey and Johnstone is our attitude toward flying: It's inherently dangerous, and you have to be at least slightly crazy to do it. They both had their first flying lesson in May 1910. They were both dead by the end of the year.

Gerry won at Fond du Lac. He took first place in Sportsman category and won a trophy called the Pitts Cup, for the most points earned in his category. It was late in the season, and all the top fliers were hopped up about the competition. Gerry and Mark were beside themselves with it, in a frenzy of activity. They couldn't stop flying, they were flying in their sleep, and every day they rushed out to the field, and even if it was too foggy to go, they'd just stand there in the hangars rubbing their airplanes with a cloth.

One morning just before Nationals, we were standing out on the ramp at Galt Airport when Art appeared in his best dark blue suit to tell of a fellow who jumped out of an airplane at Rockford for a show of some sort and landed in front of his wife and kids with both main and emergency chutes tangled in the same knot. As we talked, I saw Carla come to the window and look down on us from the second floor of the muddy old building on which the orange wind sock waved in the breeze. She stood for a moment, taking in the scene, then stepped back and dissolved in a pattern of bright reflections.

Gerry recalled the fellow who had his wife videotape him while he parachuted onto the top of the St. Louis arch. The man actually made the landing, but his planning hadn't gone much beyond that. For example, he hadn't anticipated the problems involved in getting down. The arch was slippery, shiny steel. "He slid all the way down, while she filmed it," Gerry said with a thin smile. Things had not changed so very much after all since Arch Hoxsey.

Mark, Gerry, and I were going out to fool around in the practice area. I wanted to do my routine a few times. But Gerry and Mark were burned out on practice; they wanted to dogfight, and they asked if I wanted to tag along and mix it up a little bit. Their airplanes were much faster and more maneuverable than mine, but it didn't matter. We could work around each other, Gerry said.

Gerry had his son, Gerry, Jr., with him and was taking the child along for the ride. Gerry, Jr., had his parachute on and was in the front seat of the Eagle waiting. I had taken on fuel and strapped into my parachute and then snapped into two seat belts, cinched them as tight as they would go, and then squirmed around under the pressure of all that equipment to situate myself. I imagined it was what it would feel like to be strapped into the electric chair.

As I taxied out, I saw Gerry's multicolored Eagle and Mark's fire-engine-red Pitts moving along the runway ahead of me. There wasn't going to be room for all three of us on the run-up pad, and as we reached the end of the runway, I looked for a place to pull off to let them roll past me for takeoff, reasoning that I'd go last and try to catch up with them out there.

I heard Gerry key his microphone and address me. I had known Gerry for long enough to recognize that devilish streak in him, and there was something in his tone of voice that should have tipped me off, but I couldn't imagine at that moment what he might have up his sleeve. "Laurence, if you're ready to go, why don't you just take off and we'll catch up with you?"

I was thinking, This is like one of those jokes the other students play on you when you're in grade school, like they tie your shoelaces together. Only we were grown-ups, and these were high-performance airplanes. I sensed that something was coming, but I couldn't imagine it—tin cans tied to my tail? What?

I touched my PTT (push to talk) switch and said, "Okay, Gerry. Galt Traffic, Citabria three six two five zero departing Runway two seven, Galt." Then I put the throttle to the fire wall and was off the ground in a few hundred feet. I held the nose down to accelerate to maneuvering speed so that I could tear on out of the pattern once I cleared the trees. There were no more transmissions from the field below me, and I figured that Gerry and Mark were fooling around, tweaking out their tricky engines. I announced on the radio that I was "departing the pattern to the north," and without hesitation I flung the airplane into a hard right turn, 90-degree bank, wing-over, and hauled the nose around, pulling three G's.

At that moment a vision I am not likely to forget filled my windscreen. The first thing I noticed was not the spectacular paint scheme over which Gerry had labored for so many months. It was Gerry, Jr., eight years old. I could see his cute smooth face and his big bright eyes—they were very big at that moment—looking at me from a distance of only a few feet. The world seemed to go silent, and all the motion of our remarkable machines slowed to a series of old snapshots, as if we paged through an album remembering a time years ago when Gerry decided to play a trick on me and overtook me in the pattern, scooting around to the right side without announcing his presence, just as I made a hard three-G turn directly into him—with his eight-year-old son on board. I can't imagine what Gerry, Jr., thought was happening. My airplane was not maneuverable enough for me to change my mind. I was in a 90-degree bank, and I was pulling, and it all happened so quickly. One moment Gerry, Jr., was looking me in the eye, looking as if he'd seen an astounding vision, an epiphany of light in a blue airplane with stars on it, and a man looking straight at him with a startled expression on his face—and I felt as if I were seeing myself as a child, hung there for a wide-eyed moment, receiving this marvelous gift, a glimpse of something terrible and wonderful. Then Gerry's Eagle was rolling upside down in a crossing maneuver, and he slid over the top of me, inverted, and skated away into the sky, upside down, as I went on to the north. And I thought again of W. H. Auden, "the expensive delicate ship, which must have seen something amazing, a boy falling out of the sky, had somewhere to get to and sailed calmly on."

Not a word was said. We came within a second of meeting up there, all three of us, all of us too young, with Mark Peteler behind, just lifting off in a perfect position to sit helplessly watching. Then Gerry was gone, and I was climbing away toward the practice area, and Mark blew past me with a roar that I heard (my hearing had finally returned), and I heard Gerry cackle on the radio, saying, "He-he-he-hey, Laurence, did you see me?"

"Affirm," I said. And that was all. We didn't discuss it further in the air, because we knew we'd done something harrowing and proscribed. We had violated the code of The Lecture, and we'd done it with Gerry's little boy on board, and the What-If Factor of the experience was all just too ghastly and daunting to contemplate.

I remembered seeing Kathy Molidor on the ramp, coming out while Gerry was polishing his engine, bringing him two hot dogs wrapped in aluminum foil, which he took from her and ate almost without putting a semicolon in his sentence. Kathy who stood on the ramp and held hands with the children while their little white fuzzball dog, Pittsie, ran around barking and Gerry flew by at 200 miles per hour. Then there were my children at home, trusting me to do this deranged thing safely. I had asked Elena, my ten-year-old daughter, if she wanted to go with me in the Citabria, and she said, "No. No way. No aerobatics airplanes for me." I asked her if it frightened her that I did aerobatics, if she was worried, and she answered, "No, as long as you don't do aerobatics with me in the airplane, I'm not worried." And now we had almost betrayed that trust.

We motored out to the practice area. Mark went vertical and vanished in the sun. I rolled inverted and was flying along upside down, just getting the feel of the controls, warming up, when his red airplane appeared again on my right side and blew past me as if I'd been standing still.

I did some snap rolls, left and right, and watched as Mark and Gerry mixed it up half a mile or so in the distance. I saw Mark come after him from behind, then Gerry simply did what he had done to avoid me, he pulled up, rolled inverted, and kept on going around Mark. He would wait, flying along upside down, and then at the propitious moment dive in a Split-S type of maneuver, coming in fast behind Mark for the kill. It was quite spectacular to see. I couldn't possibly have kept up with them, and so I hung back in my area and practiced my figures, running through various parts of the sequence that needed work, and wondering why I did it at all.

We were about ready to RTB, as the fliers like to say, return to base, and we came in one after the other, drawing a crowd to the ramp merely by our calamitous arrival. We pulled up to the fuel pumps together, and people stood at a shy distance, but we knew they were watching us as we climbed out and hung together in a little group, the four of us, talking about what we'd done.

"That was a pretty interesting maneuver," I told Gerry.

He laughed and laughed. "You all right, Gerry?" he asked his son. The boy nodded his head. "Well," Gerry said, turning to me, "I saw your ailerons go to full deflection all of a sudden as I was passing you, so I knew something was up." I understood what he was saying: The Citabria's roll response is sluggish. If I had been flying a Pitts, I'd have hit him. He would never have seen the ailerons move.

I allowed that it was a good thing I was flying with the guy who took first place at Fond du Lac, because a lesser pilot probably wouldn't have gotten out of the way.

"A better pilot wouldn't have gotten *in* the way," Mark said.

"That's right," Gerry said, and I couldn't help thinking again about The Lecture, about how we should do it safely, how one slip could ruin everything, how we ought not to fool around on takeoff or low level, how we weren't air-show pilots, and where would it all end? We were all thinking the same thing: What goes through a pilot's mind in the crucial moments before he makes that fatal mistake? We ought to know. We'd only just been through one of those moments. And yet there we were, playing fighter pilot for the crowd standing around shooting down our watches with the dogfighting maneuvers of our hands and *everybody was watching* us. It was wonderful.

Gerry took second place in Sportsman category at the Nationals in Denton, Texas. Mark and Howard wound up the season with a significant collection of trophies, too, and one day they pushed their airplanes out of the hangars and lined them up, and they brought out all their trophies and plaques and lined them up on the asphalt, and the three guys put on their Ray-Bans and ball caps and IAC jackets and knelt on one knee, genuflecting like knights on the oily asphalt, and had someone shoot a photo, which they framed and gave to Carla to put on the wall in the briefing room. It seemed somewhat premature to me, being immortalized on that wall. But then no one had specifically said that you had to be dead to get up there.

Patty Wagstaff was the first woman ever to win the big prize at the Nationals, first place in Unlimited category, which of course put her on the U.S. Team, where she'd been several years running. She would go on to achieve second place in the World Cup in France. Another pilot who made the team for international competition was Joe Frasca, a young, handsome, and very accomplished pilot from a well-known family of aviators. On his way back from the nationals, he was approaching an airport in Arkansas for fuel when his monoplane experienced a structural failure. Miraculously, Joe was able to get out safely. He jettisoned his canopy, remembered to take off his seat belt and his headset, and then climbed out and jumped. He even remembered to pull the rip cord on his parachute. And the parachute worked, too. It opened big and full with a resounding pop, just as it was designed to do. The one thing Joe forgot was to fasten his leg straps, and when the parachute opened, he slipped right out and fell to his death.

THIRTEEN

THE TWO-HUNDRED-DOLLAR CHEESEBURGER

JIM LISS always had a scheme, something to get him out of the shop and into the air. One day I struck up a conversation with him about buying an airplane as an investment. Prices were always going up. It was better than a bank account. He said the four-seat Cessna 182 was still the best bet. They were much in demand and brought a handsome price in Europe. "But I've got a much better deal for you," he said. "Did I tell you about hauling bodies?"

"No, I don't think so," I said, expecting one of his jokes.

He proceeded to tell me about visiting a funeral home and discovering that they charge $1.25 per mile to haul dead bodies. That was forty cents better than he could get for hauling the live ones. "You know, people die just about anywhere. They're on vacation or they're somewhere where they're not going to be buried, and they die. Well, the family has to get them home somehow. Now the majors [the airlines] have a pretty good deal on hauling dead bodies, but if you're someplace that's not on the route, then you have to get the funeral home to drive them, and that costs a buck and a quarter a mile. The guy there told me he wouldn't drive them at all if I'd fly them. I'd be doing it right now, only a coffin won't fit in my two-ten. I measured it every which way, and it just won't fit. You know, you can't tip them."

I didn't know, but I asked why.

"They'll leak," he said.

"Leak?"

"You know, they're all full of embalming fluid," Liss said.

"So what about, you know, turbulence?" I asked.

"Oh, no problem. The coffin's sealed, and they'll just bounce around a little in there, I guess. It's all padded and everything." Liss thought about the conversation we were having, and its bizarre nature was not lost on him. He was a master of bizarre jokes. "I asked the guy," he said with a straight face, "if we couldn't just put them in baggies and sit them up in the seats, you know, strap them in, because that way we could take six at once, but he said, no fuckin' way. The law says you've got to have 'em in a coffin or at least a cardboard box, so we need a larger airplane with a cargo door."

"I get it," I said. "So you want me to buy a Cherokee Six."

"That's it," he said. "Three hundred horsepower. Big cargo door. We could start right away."

"Jim, this is extremely weird, you know that, don't you?"

"It's a need. The market is there," he assured me.

"I'd worry about turbulence," I said again.

"Nah, the guy showed me. He grabbed this one stiff by the nostrils, like this." Liss stuck two fingers up his nose to demonstrate. "And pulled him up and showed me. They're stuffed with cotton and wax up the nose, down the throat, and up the ass. They want 'em ready to display when they get there, so you can't mess 'em up."

I marveled at the lengths to which we would go in order to

fly. Truly, it seems, flying has no real economic or practical purpose, at least not the way we do it. In the end, we unconsciously make up our minds that we are determined to fly or be damned, and then we invent elaborate mythologies to explain that impulse to those who might not share it. All Liss really wanted was to fly; he'd be happy if someone gave him a nickel that he could take home and show his wife.

My favorite example of that phenomenon was Dr. Boone Brackett, my instrument flight instructor. Now here was a man who earned untold amounts of money practicing surgery. His empire was vast. His successes were known far and wide. Yet what did he crave more than anything? More than professional standing, more than money, and sometimes seemingly more than life itself? Flight. So much did he crave it that in his mid-fifties, Dr. Brackett went to law school so that he could join a law firm. But his true motive was flight, for the law firm had promised that if he passed the bar, he would be allowed to fly his airplane around the country taking depositions in medical malpractice and personal injury cases.

Dr. Brackett had accumulated 2,500 hours and an Airline Transport Pilot rating in barely three years. When I asked him how he'd done it, he said, "I flew at night. It's really nice. There's nobody up there, and you get great service from ATC."

"But when did you sleep?" I asked.

"I didn't," he said.

As I flew with him more and more, I came to realize that he meant it quite literally. Since he was in surgery during the days, we flew at night. It wasn't unusual for him to call me at seven in the evening, as he was finishing up the last patient, and say, "Mr. Gonzales, this is Lone Star Airlines calling. Get the Warrior ready. File for Lafayette, Indiana, and meet me on the ramp at nine."

We trained at Midway Airport, the busiest airport he could find, and by the time we copied our clearance, our

Piper Warrior taxiing like a pilot bird among the whalelike 737s and DC-9s, I would be falling asleep at the wheel, and Dr. Brackett would be bubbling over with enthusiasm and excitement. The view of Chicago never failed us. As we lifted off, it was like ripping the lid off an immense pit of electric snakes. And Brackett never became jaded by it. "God, this is great!" he would say. "Look at this. Don't you just love it?"

We can't look out the window during instrument practice, which is why there have to be two pilots on board. So I would put on my hood if the weather was clear—a device that looked like the bill of a comically large baseball cap—limiting my view to the instruments. I'd settle in on the gauges, and Dr. Brackett would keep up a running commentary on my flying. He was a good teacher with an even manner. He made me a practical, competent, confident instrument pilot. But now and then I saw his human side show through the heroic armor he wore of surgeon and warrior and lawyer and aviator.

As an instrument student, the concept of flying 130 miles per hour through the air merely by glancing at a scattering of needles on the dashboard seemed the most extravagant sort of sorcery. One night we were plying the darkness and plundering clouds on our way toward Lafayette in the warm glow of the amber panel lights in the cockpit, when I noticed a lapse in Dr. Brackett's monolog. I thought nothing particular of it and flew on, speaking now and then to an air traffic controller.

"Zero five Hotel, now direct Boiler when able," came the static voice of the midnight-shift controller.

"Direct Boiler for zero five Hotel," I answered, tuning the VOR receiver to 115.1 and turning onto a southeasterly course, while noting the time, eleven-fifteen, and mentally going through the checklist Dr. Brackett had taught me: Turn, Time, Twist, Throttle, Talk, Track. We were to recite that mnemonic checklist out of memory each time we passed a station: Turn onto the new course; note the Time;

Twist the omni dial to the new course; Throttle down if we were to descend at that point; Talk if we had been instructed to report reaching that point by ATC; Track, i.e., make sure we stayed on the newly selected course. It was to keep us from forgetting something as we navigated from one radio facility to the next in the low obloquy of engine noise and the hypnotic gas of clouds. I settled the aircraft on the new course and said, "Twenty minutes to Lafayette, do you want me to fly the full approach?"

Dr. Brackett and I were connected through the headsets we wore. I was concentrating on my flying so much that at first I didn't recognize that he hadn't answered me. Then I repeated the question: "Dr. Brackett? Full approach or vectors for the ILS, sir?" Pause. "Dr. Brackett?" I turned up the volume on the intercom. "Dr. Brackett?"

I pulled off my hood. He was slumped back in his seat, his mouth open, snoring away at a ferocious rate. I wanted to get a camera and photograph it: the only known photograph of Boone Brackett asleep. I could sell it to his surgical residents. I could blackmail him. The possibilities were endless. But then I thought, What the hell. If we were in clouds, we wouldn't be able to see anyway. It was nearly midnight. We were on radar.

I put my hood back down and flew on into the night, talking to ATC, gliding down the ILS to Lafayette. The wheels squeaked onto the concrete with a slight bump and Dr. Brackett stirred and changed position. As I was taxiing to the ramp for fuel, he awoke and looked around. After a moment, he said, "Good job," stretching, yawning. "Nicely done."

"Thanks," I said.

"What's the next leg?" he asked.

"Bloomington, I think," I said. "Lemme check the charts over here at the ramp."

"Okay," he said, opening the door. "I'll see if we can get somebody out here to pump fuel for us at this hour."

I parked, and Dr. Brackett stepped down and crossed the

ramp toward the terminal building. It was a clear and windless cold winter night, and the place looked deserted. All the airliners had gone to bed, and there was no sign of humanity. I checked our charts, planned the next leg of our journey, prepared the approach plates I'd need, and climbed down. Just as my feet touched the concrete, Dr. Brackett came jogging back over with a strange grin on his round, bearded face. He looked like images of Pan I had seen in mythology books. He was missing only the horns.

"I think if we give the line boy another few minutes, he'll finish up and give us some fuel," he said mischievously.

"What's he doing?" I asked.

"Screwing his girlfriend on a row of seats in the terminal building," he said.

A few minutes later we pretended to arrive again. We walked through the office door, where we found a sullen teenage boy who shuffled out to fuel our aircraft. The pretty girl in the flowered cotton dress sat on a chair to one side, assiduously picking at her fingernails and sipping a Coke while a late-night rock and roll station played "Suite Judy Blue Eyes." Dr. Brackett and I tried to pay attention to our charts while reviewing the next leg of our journey, but he couldn't suppress a secret smile. "God, I love aviation," he growled.

We all had a scheme. We were never content to leave well enough alone. Like Don Ericson and his *Stork*, we had to reinvent the wheel, no matter how many times we saw it roll. There seemed to be no limit to the number of people willing to turn large fortunes into small fortunes just by tinkering with airplanes. Amos was only one example.

In fact, it was because of a scheme of Steve Nusbaum's that ultralights appeared at Galt for a time in the 1980s, at a time when ultralights threatened to take over aviation and win the heart of America in that special profligate and dissipated way that Americans have of giving their hearts away en masse at the drop of a hat, as if some sort of depraved and twisted vein of chivalry ran through the population, ever untapped, just waiting to burst forth at the slightest provocation—the invention of the motorcar, the speedboat, the television, the microwave oven, the CD, or videotape recorder. Every single time, we were virgins anew, teenagers, swooning in disordered passion at the sight of the first homely face that smiled at us, until we underwent a dark and mysterious change, awakening as the scales fell from our eyes, and we recoiled in horror: How could we have been so in love with *that thing?*

It was in that atmosphere of pounding blood and fresh passion that Steve and Carla brought Art Galt their idea for an Ultralight Air Park. It would have a new kind of training: simple tail-dragger training, none of that complicated FAA regulation stuff, no talking on the radio or solving trigonometric functions.

Steve and Carla put a sign out, and scarcely had they thrown open their doors when they were knocked down by the hordes of would-be pilots clamoring for the experience of a lifetime.

"Business," he said, "was fantastic." By the beginning of 1985, Steve had auctioned off all that remained of his seawall business (his prior occupation) and had sold five J3 Kittens, the latest and most popular ultralight, for which Steve had been lucky enough to acquire a dealership.

It was around that time that pilots began to see very peculiar things at Galt. For example, someone might be roaring down the runway at a hundred knots or so, too late to stop, when a thing as fragile and slow as a dragonfly would suddenly be poised in the windshield, as big as a billboard; and plastered against the sky would be the face of a pilot wearing goggles and gloves and maybe even a flying scarf, and showing his defiant dentures. Then just as quickly, the apparition would be gone.

But as the ultralight craze spread across the country, it

became apparent that people were killing themselves in droves, either at the mercy of faulty equipment or for lack of proper training or simply because people under the spell of The Impulse are a danger to themselves and others. Word began to get around.

During the full sales year of 1985, Steve sold twenty-five new J3 Kittens, an ultralight scale model of the famous Piper J3 Cub. All over McHenry County there were happy prospective aviators waiting for Steve to deliver their brand-new Kittens so that they could start building them in their pole barns and be flying them by spring out of the newly mowed ultralight strip at Galt Airport. Three of those new Kittens were delivered before the North Carolina company went bankrupt. It seems that a non-pilot, someone with no flying experience, killed himself in one of their craft, and his estate overwhelmed the manufacturer with an immense product liability suit.

C&S Ultralights lost its insurance about that time. Suddenly Steve and Carla were unable to train and unable to sell. The ultralight craze had peaked and was winding down. The nation was not going to be taken over by ultralight aircraft. No one cared anymore.

No one, that is, until Don Ericson came along with his scheme, and like Tom Sawyer, cajoled Steve into building it with him. For it seems that even if the nation isn't going to be overwhelmed by airplanes of any kind, not ever, not as a whole, there will nevertheless always be that occult group of dedicated sextons in the garages of America, working, working by candlelight, by the midnight beat of the paint-spattered transistor radio, keeping the dream alive.

I flew over Steve's farm one summer afternoon, circling the old barn and house, but the landing strip he'd hacked out of the cornfields looked too short, so I put the Citabria down at Galt and drove the four miles back. Steve had just finished converting a barn into a workshop, and it was fairly spectacular. Hidden behind a paintless facade was a hangar that looked big enough and bright enough for him to build a rocket that would take him to the moon. The ceiling was neatly finished with silver insulation and hung with dozens of fluorescent tubes. The walls were outfitted with racks for hanging the tubing out of which fuselage and wings would be made. Tables with jigs on them were laid out. Tools were neatly arranged. Somehow out of the chaos of Galt, Steve had emerged with this . . . *idea,* and it was completely different from anything I had seen so far: It was an idea of order. It was so utterly contrary even to the farmhouse and outbuildings surrounding it that I had to go outside and come back in to convince myself of where I was. Something had happened. Steve would finish Don's *Stork* and begin his own two-place *Stork.* If he succeeded, he would manufacture more and more of them as the demand dictated.

Steve and Chance and I were unloading the stainless steel tubing for the two-place prototype, when Don Ericson arrived in his Cherokee truck, towing the wingless *Stork* on a trailer. The *Stork* was finished except for the final assembly and a few details, such as the exact fit of the wings to the fuselage, the plexiglass windows being trimmed just so, the reduction drive for the engine. Don stepped down from the truck wearing a snap-brim cap and scuffed penny loafers and slate-blue pants, his spectacles dangling on the end of his nose. He had to drive back to St. Charles to get the wings, but he couldn't have been more excited if the plane had been about to fly that day.

I stuck my head into the cockpit of the *Stork* and saw the newly sewn canvas baggage sling in the back. Everything was just so. It had all the class of a brand new buggy.

"It smells like a 1930s airplane, doesn't it?" Don asked. And then he went around touching it here and there like a mother preening her baby bird, saying, "I really love it. I wouldn't trade it for any airplane they have."

I said something about finally being able to fly once again, referring to the fact that he had lost his medical, and he dismissed it with a wave of his hand. "Oh, I could probably get my medical back now." I understood what he was saying: It wasn't the point anymore.

There is a Zen koan about a boy who seeks out the greatest master swordsman in the land and begs to be taught swordsmanship. The master agrees to teach him, but he puts the boy in the garden and makes him do the weeding. Everytime the boy is not looking, the master sneaks up and hits him with a stick. That goes on for years. Finally one day the master is sneaking up behind the poor boy, who is weeding the field as usual. But when the master swings, the boy ducks, and the master misses. Triumphant, the boy leaps up and throws down his hoe. "*Now* will you teach me swordsmanship?" he demands.

"*Now* you don't *need* swordsmanship," the master says.

Don didn't need his medical anymore. "I have a good heart now," he told me. And I knew what he meant.

I wintered in Wonder Lake. I continued to practice aerobatics when the weather permitted, with no attempt to resolve the seeming contradiction of my decision not to compete. It was the logic of quitting surgery to fly around in circles. It was the logic of flying dead people around in order to justify flying at all. And it was like going up in the clouds to shoot approaches on a day when it wasn't necessary to go up at all. It was an old familiar companion, and I had become resigned to it.

One morning I arose at dawn to find that Wonder Lake had thawed. A few ice floes remained, with Canada geese standing on them. The sun was just up and lit the far shore, striking the houses there and making them leap away from the woods, which were still dark in their winter nudity and tinted faintly yellow by the willows.

I showered and I went to dress and paused as I chose my socks. I was going to wear an old pair for knocking around in the hangar and working around my airplane, but then I stopped myself and selected my favorite pair. I understood that it would do me little good to have them in the drawer. I wondered what Lloyd Hughes chose to wear on his last day.

When I arrived at the field, the sky was a thousand miles of clear, and the wind was up. I hadn't conceived of doing anything but flying and practicing, and the narrowness of my view put me in a strange state of mind. I didn't consider *not* going, although I saw the wind blowing thirty-five knots, which was a bit large for my meager skills and my modest airplane. I blasted off and found calm air in the upper altitudes. I racked the poor protesting Citabria through the new Sportsman sequence. I powered the plane around and upside down and stayed pretty well over the farmers' fields that I had designated in my mind as my imaginary box. The new sequence included a snap roll, which in the Citabria was not the easiest figure in the world. (I had called John Morrissey for advice on it, and he said, "Well, it's like a U-turn on the freeway; you can probably get through it, but it's not a great idea.") Even so, I was executing a snap of some sort and feeling pretty confident in my ability to fly the routine and not embarrass myself. I could get through it.

I finished practice drenched in sweat and trembling with the exertion. I'm not sure how I decided when to end a practice session. I think when I panted so frantically that my gum would fly out of my mouth and stick to the microphone, then I'd decide it was time to stop.

I probably should have taken a few minutes to relax before landing in that wind, but I had really forgotten about it by then. Having forgotten my resolve *not* to compete, I think I was composing my acceptance speech for some world-class aerobatics award, as my wheels touched down on the runway in a drift.

I knew right away that something was wrong as I awoke. I had neglected to close the throttle all the way, too, and the stick was not fully back in my gut for a proper three-point landing. Everything was wrong in other words, and I was just coming back to the real world with the afflictions of physics, trigonometry, and angular momentum flanking me with demands.

Within seconds, the landing gear was chewing up the grass, and my craft was wallowing toward the midfield run-up pad, hard by a line of parked airplanes. If a plane had been waiting there, I would have collided with it.

Now I was completely in the grass, inches from the parked aircraft, it seemed. The whole drama took no more than a few seconds. I came fully awake and jammed the throttle forward. The blast of wind from the propeller restored lateral control. I held the nose down firmly and steered my way over bumps and jolts back to the runway. The 150-horsepower engine had me airborne again in a hurry. Moments later I climbed away, shaken and shamed by my foolishness.

I pulled up my favorite pair of socks and flew around to recompose my rattled nerves. I toured the area of Twin Lakes and Lake Geneva, looking down as the homes slipped past beneath me. There goes Doc Shinderman's house and Marc Buettell's. There's Nancy Hughes's place. Dave Cargill crashed right over there. And out that way was the Pitts from the photograph on the wall. All the others passed in procession beneath me, and I felt a calm and rational sense take over once more. When I was thoroughly in control of myself, I considered it carefully, and then I landed the Citabria without a squeak from the tires.

In the front office Bob Russell was standing at the flight desk, and he looked up from something he was writing when I came in. It was a steady, searching look without his usual bantering, good-humored deviltry. "Little trouble with your cross-wind landings today?" he asked.

The lake thawed and spring came again, and fires burned in the front yards of Wonder Lake. The wind came up hard one day when I was going out with John Fountain to practice flying the back seat of the Citabria, because I couldn't see out the front that way. I wanted to become accustomed to having no forward visibility so that I could fly the Pitts. (Yes, there was still the paradox of the Pitts facing me.)

John and I went up to Lake Lawn. The wind was twenty knots and gusty out of the north. When we got up there, we found a Galt convention. Bill Tate had a student in 95L and Jay Pettigrove had a student in *Uniform,* and the three of us went around and around, taking off and landing and taking off and landing, and sometimes talking to each other along the way. Since I couldn't see anything as I landed and the day was windy and bumpy, it was interesting enough to keep me happy.

On the way back John wanted to try some rolls, but I reminded him that we were carrying a lot of loose things in the airplane. There was nothing more disconcerting than rolling an airplane upside down and finding the amazing collection of stuff that fell to the ceiling. Once I went out to practice, and a set of steel channel locks came zinging past my ear and crashed into the ceiling as I rolled. I gingerly picked it up off the roof of the airplane and held it while I rolled the airplane upright again. It wasn't unusual in our Citabria to find ball-point pens rocketing around during inverted flight. If it wasn't that, it was just a lot of dead yellow jackets.

I could tell that John was disappointed that he wasn't going to go upside down. He pulled some 2- and 3-G turns, just horsing around; and then he did some Lazy-Eights and listened to the weather from Janesville on the way home. We were just doing pilot kinds of things to make ourselves feel like pilots.

With our thirty-knot tail wind, we were probably hitting 150 knots on the way back to Galt. The wind was blowing fierce out of the north when John landed directly crosswind, and he laid it on so smoothly that I couldn't even tell when the wheels touched. All you have to do to get landings like that is to repeat the procedure five times a week for a few decades.

We pushed the airplane into the hangar together—John held the strut, I held the tail—and he wrote down our time in the log, and we put our things away in the gray plywood storage box and locked it with a padlock. The big metal doors rumbled and rattled as I pulled them along their rails. The wind whistled down the long length of the hangar, in among all the airplanes parked there in the relative darkness, the gravel floor, the bits and pieces of people's obsessions hanging on hooks, and here and there a car under a tarp, which someone had stored for the winter. John snapped the Citabria door closed and locked it with the little silver key. He brushed his hands together. His hands were soft and leathery like fine old gloves now; and as he dusted them lightly, he looked at his palms, which were mapped out with a million lines like the topography of the land over which he'd flown, and he stopped for a minute there in the half-darkened hangar, and I thought for a second he was going to cry, just thinking back over all the hours and miles he'd flown, going nowhere, but maybe the wind had just blown a cinder into his eye. I had the door almost closed, and the wind was rattling it like stage thunder, and it seemed to rouse John from his reverie; and he brushed his hands one last time on his pants, stuck the jangling ring of keys into his pocket, and stepped out into the sunlight.

ACKNOWLEDGMENT

I COULDN'T have written this book—or even conceived of it—without the help of many people. But my greatest debt is to the people of Galt Airport, with whom I fly, who let me into their lives and took the time to tell me their stories. I hope they receive this in the spirit in which it was written: affection, admiration, respect. Special thanks to Jan and Don and Marc and Noa. Thanks also to Miller Williams.

9 781416 576419